Hunting Market Anomalies

Machine Learning Techniques for Contrarian Trading

Victor Trex

Published by NobleTrex Press

For permissions and other inquiries, write to:
P.O. Box 3132, Framingham, MA 01701, USA

Contents

Introduction

Financial markets are often described as efficient aggregators of information, yet they routinely exhibit short-lived dislocations that reverse once attention, liquidity, and risk capital re-equilibrate. This book is about those dislocations-market anomalies with a contrarian character-and about the disciplined use of machine learning to discover, validate, and deploy them responsibly. Our central thesis is modest and practical: while pockets of mean-reversion do exist, they are scarce, small, and fragile; only a workflow engineered for integrity can convert them into robust, risk-adjusted evidence rather than alluring mirages.

We call that workflow Honest Alpha. Honesty here is methodological, not moralizing. It means point-in-time data that reflect the world as it was, not as we now know it; experimental designs that respect temporal dependence; and evaluation practices that temper optimism with appropriate statistical penalties. It also means acknowledging frictions-commissions, spreads, impact, borrow constraints-that dominate short-horizon outcomes. The pages that follow aim to move readers from curiosity to capability, equipping them with the concepts and tooling needed to pursue contrarian ideas without self-deception.

The opening chapter, Foundations of Financial Markets & Anomalies, builds the vocabulary and mechanics required to talk precisely about reversals. We formalize return definitions across asset classes, review microstructure where many contrarian pressures are born, and quantify trading frictions that can turn elegant signals into untradable ghosts. We situate anomalies in the tension between efficiency, behavioral bias, and limits to arbitrage, motivating why mean-reversion may persist yet be costly to capture.

Because most false discoveries begin with bad data rather than bad models, Data & Research Infrastructure for Honest Alpha sets the backbone. We discuss point-in-time sourcing, symbology, and storage; cleaning and corporate action adjustments; and the defenses against survivorship, look-ahead, and selection bias. Particular care is given to labeling schemes and sampling clocks, since what one chooses to predict and when one measures it are defining choices in contrarian research.

Statistical & Time-Series Foundations provides the mathematical substrate. We examine distributional features of returns, including fat tails and dependence, and we revisit inference under small samples and autocorrelation. Multiple testing is addressed head-on, with procedures that control false discoveries in data-mined settings. We treat stationarity diagnostics and the canonical models of mean-reversion-ARIMA, GARCH, cointegration, and Ornstein-Uhlenbeck dynamics-as tools to understand, not to enshrine, market behavior.

With reliable data and statistical hygiene in place, the Machine Learning Pipeline for Contrarian Signals presents a leakage-aware workflow. We define targets and losses suited to low-signal regimes, detail regularization that trades variance for bias constructively, and design time-aware cross-validation-walk-forward and purged K-fold-that respects label overlap. We discuss hyperparameter search under nested validation and survey model families from sparse linear baselines through gradient-boosted trees to neural sequence models, emphasizing the value of simple, transparent benchmarks.

Feature Engineering & Alpha Design translates economic intuition into computable predictors. We develop price-based features that capture overreaction, microstructure features derived from order-flow and depth, event-driven and seasonal effects, and pairwise spread constructions rooted in cointegration. Throughout, we stress alignment between hypothesized mechanisms and measurable signals, avoiding feature alchemy that cannot survive costs and slippage.

Backtesting, Evaluation & Robustness formalizes how research becomes evidence. We construct point-in-time simulations that replay information flow from signals to fills, incorporate transaction cost and impact models, and measure performance with attention to path risk and attribution. We implement defenses against multiple testing-deflated Sharpe, probability of backtest overfitting, and superior predictive ability tests-to quantify uncertainty rather than hand-wave it away. We close with research hygiene, reproducibility, and explainability practices that build institutional trust.

Portfolio Construction, Execution & Adaptive Deployment completes the arc from signals to live portfolios. We connect scoring to sizing under risk and drawdown constraints, discuss factor-neutralization and hedge design, and align execution tactics with microstructure to minimize implicit costs. Recognizing that regimes change, we introduce detection methods and adaptive retraining, together with live monitoring, compliance safeguards, and model-risk governance that anchor the endeavor in real-world stewardship.

This textbook is written for graduate students in financial engineering and data science, for quantitative researchers and practitioners, and for the curious empiricist who values clarity over mystique. A working knowledge of probability, statistics, and time-series analysis will be helpful; familiarity with programming and databases will accelerate adoption. The text is deliberately practical and modular: each chapter stands alone yet contributes to a coherent pipeline, from idea to impact.

Finally, a caution and an invitation. Contrarian trading is not a hunt for certainty but for edges that are small, conditional, and perishable. The goal is not to fit the past exquisitely, but to build systems that learn with humility, fail gracefully, and improve with evidence. If this book helps you ask sharper questions, design cleaner experiments, and deploy with greater responsibility, then it will have served its purpose. The anomalies are out there-honest methods make them visible.

Chapter 1

Foundations of Financial Markets & Anomalies

Prices do not wander randomly in a vacuum-they emerge from a noisy, constrained, and deeply human trading mechanism. This chapter peels back the surface of 'the market' to show how instruments are defined, how orders actually become trades, and how real-world frictions and recurring behavioral mistakes conspire to create pockets of predictable mean reversion. By the end, you'll see market anomalies not as curiosities in an academic paper, but as structural by-products of how modern markets truly function-and why carefully designed contrarian strategies can keep finding edges where theory predicts none should exist.

1.1 Asset Classes and Return Definitions

Contrarian trading is, at its core, about how prices and returns behave over time. Before we can search for reversals or build machine learning models to detect them, we need a precise language for what is traded and how its performance is measured. This section introduces the major asset classes that will appear throughout the book, explains how their payoffs are structured, and then develops the return definitions we will use to compare reversals across time, markets, and currencies.

What We Trade: Core Asset Classes

In practice, a machine learning contrarian strategy may touch many instruments: stocks, futures, options, currencies, exchange-traded funds (ETFs), and more. All of these can be grouped into a small set of core asset classes. For each, we want to understand three things:

- *What payoff does the asset deliver?* (cash flows, final settlement, optionality)
- *When is the payoff delivered?* (one-off at maturity vs. continuous income)
- *How is the position typically margined and traded?*

These features determine how we should define returns and how to interpret reversals.

Equities

Definition and payoff. An equity instrument (common stock, ETF, or equity index future) represents ownership or exposure to the residual value of a firm or basket of firms. For a single stock, the investor:

- receives *dividends* (cash distributions per share) at the discretion of the company;
- benefits if the *price* of the share rises;
- suffers losses if the price falls or the firm deteriorates.

For an equity index (e.g., S&P 500) or ETF, the payoff aggregates across many underlying stocks, usually following a transparent weighting rule (market value weight, equal weight, factor tilt, and so on).

Participants and horizons. Equities attract a wide spectrum of investors: intraday high-frequency traders, multi-day to multi-month quantitative funds, and long-horizon asset managers. This heterogeneity matters for contrarian trading: short-term reversals often reflect inventory imbalances and microstructure noise, while medium-term reversals may reflect overreaction to fundamental news or flows.

Fixed Income

Definition and payoff. Fixed income instruments—bonds, notes, bills—promise a schedule of cash flows:

- periodic *coupon payments* (e.g., annual or semi-annual interest);
- return of *principal* at maturity;
- in some cases, embedded options (callable, putable, convertible).

For a default-free zero-coupon bond, the payoff is simplest: pay a price P_t today, receive a single payment (the face value) at time T.

Price vs. yield. In practice, bonds are often quoted in terms of *yield* rather than price. However, for trading and anomaly detection we almost always work with *price returns*, sometimes adjusted for carry and roll-down (concepts developed later in the book). Yield changes and price changes are tightly related but not identical; a small yield move for a long-duration bond can correspond to a large price move.

Foreign Exchange (FX)

Definition and payoff. An FX spot trade is simply an exchange of one currency for another at an agreed rate $S_t^{A/B}$ (units of currency B per unit of currency A). Holding a currency pair is equivalent to:

- being long one cash money-market instrument (earning its interest rate),
- and short another (paying its interest rate).

A *currency forward* or *FX swap* builds in the interest rate differential between currencies as *carry*. FX returns therefore combine exchange rate changes and interest rate differences.

Commodities

Definition and payoff. Commodities include energy (oil, gas), metals, and agricultural products. Most institutional exposure occurs through *derivatives* (futures, options) rather than physical storage.

For a commodity futures contract:

- the holder agrees today on a price F_t for delivery at future date T;
- gains or losses are realized daily through *marking to market*, rather than only at T;
- the position is margined, not fully funded up front.

The economic return on a commodity future has several components (spot price move, roll yield, collateral yield). For short-horizon contrarian trading, the dominant term is usually the mark-to-market price change.

Derivatives (Options, Swaps, and Beyond)

Definition and payoff. Derivatives are contracts whose value depends on an underlying asset or index. A call option on a stock, for example, has payoff at maturity

$$\max(S_T - K, 0),$$

where S_T is the stock price at time T and K is the strike price. Swaps exchange cash flow streams (e.g., fixed vs. floating interest rates).

For our purposes, derivatives introduce two complications:

- Their returns can be extremely nonlinear in the underlying.
- They are often traded on margin with *daily* cash flows (variation margin).

Short-term reversals in derivative prices may reflect changes in implied volatility, skew, and other risk-neutral parameters. When we study anomalies in derivatives markets, we must be careful to define the return on the full position (including margin and financing), not just the percentage change in quoted premium.

How Payoff Structure Influences Return Measurement

The structure of an asset's payoff determines what we should count as "return" in our data.

- For *equities*, total return must include both price changes and dividends.
- For *bonds*, total return must include coupon payments and any reinvestment, and account for the time value between coupon dates.
- For *FX*, total return includes spot moves and interest differentials (carry).
- For *commodities and futures*, return is primarily the daily mark-to-market of the futures price, plus any collateral yield on margin.
- For *options*, payoff is a nonlinear function of the underlying, and the capital at risk is the option premium or margin; we must define returns relative to that economic exposure.

When we later compare reversal strategies across asset classes, we will normalize everything to consistent, properly adjusted total returns, typically expressed as a percentage per period or annualized measure.

Simple vs. Log Returns

To detect reversals, we work with returns rather than raw prices, because returns are additive over a portfolio and comparable across instruments. There are two main return conventions: *simple* (arithmetic) returns and *logarithmic* returns.

Simple Returns

The *simple return* from time t to $t+1$ on an asset with price P_t and P_{t+1} and cash flow (e.g., dividend, coupon) CF_{t+1} paid at $t+1$ is

$$R_{t+1}^{simple} = \frac{P_{t+1} + CF_{t+1} - P_t}{P_t}.$$

If there is no cash flow, this reduces to the familiar percentage change:

$$R_{t+1}^{simple} = \frac{P_{t+1} - P_t}{P_t}.$$

Simple returns are intuitive ("the price rose by 2%") and mesh directly with portfolio weights: the return of a portfolio is the weighted sum of constituent simple returns, as long as the weights are fixed over the period.

Log Returns

The *log return* (also called continuously compounded return) is defined as

$$R_{t+1}^{log} = \ln\left(\frac{P_{t+1} + CF_{t+1}}{P_t}\right).$$

When there is no cash flow, this becomes

$$R_{t+1}^{log} = \ln\left(\frac{P_{t+1}}{P_t}\right).$$

Log returns have two key advantages:

- *Time additivity:* Over multiple periods, log returns add exactly. If $P_0 \to P_1 \to \cdots \to P_T$, then

$$\ln\left(\frac{P_T}{P_0}\right) = \sum_{t=0}^{T-1} \ln\left(\frac{P_{t+1}}{P_t}\right).$$

- *Symmetry:* A $+10\%$ simple return and a -10% simple return are not symmetric (you end up slightly below where you started), but the corresponding log returns reflect the compounding correctly in an additive way.

For *small* returns (say, daily returns of a few basis points to a few percent), simple and log returns are numerically very close:

$$R^{log} \approx R^{simple} - \frac{(R^{simple})^2}{2}.$$

In many high-frequency applications, analysts use whichever is more convenient. For longer horizons or larger moves, the difference becomes non-negligible, which can alter estimated reversal magnitudes.

Arithmetic vs. Geometric Compounding

When we summarize returns over many periods, we must distinguish between *arithmetic* and *geometric* averages.

Arithmetic Average Return

The arithmetic average of T simple returns $R_1, \ldots, R_T$ is

$$\bar{R}^{arith} = \frac{1}{T}\sum_{t=1}^{T} R_t.$$

This quantity is useful for forecasting one-period returns and for some statistical procedures. However, it does not equal the long-run growth rate of capital.

Geometric Average Return

The geometric average (or long-run compound return) is

$$\bar{R}^{geom} = \left(\prod_{t=1}^{T}(1+R_t)\right)^{1/T} - 1.$$

This is the per-period return that, if earned every period, would generate the same final wealth as the actual sequence of returns.

Because negative returns hurt more than equally sized positive returns help (due to compounding), we typically have

$$\bar{R}^{geom} \leq \bar{R}^{arith},$$

with equality only if returns are constant. For volatile strategies—and many contrarian strategies are volatile—the gap can be substantial.

For log returns, the average log return

$$\bar{R}^{log} = \frac{1}{T}\sum_{t=1}^{T} R_t^{log}$$

is exactly the long-run continuously compounded growth rate and is closely related to $\bar{R}^{geom}$.

Total, Excess, Gross, and Net Returns

So far we have treated return as a single object, but in empirical work we need to be explicit about what is included.

Price vs. Total Return

- A *price return* series uses only changes in traded price P_t.
- A *total return* series adds in income (dividends, coupons) and reinvests it.

Formally, if income CF_{t+1} is reinvested at the same asset return, then the total return index I_t evolves as

$$I_{t+1} = I_t \left(1 + \frac{P_{t+1} + CF_{t+1} - P_t}{P_t}\right).$$

Many classic equity reversal anomalies were originally reported using price returns only. When re-estimated on total returns (particularly in markets with high dividend yields), some of those anomalies weaken or change shape. For cross-country comparisons, failing to include income can bias which markets appear to exhibit stronger reversals.

Excess Returns Over a Benchmark

Most contrarian strategies are *long–short*: they buy past losers and sell past winners (or vice versa). Their performance is naturally expressed in terms of *excess return* over a benchmark.

If R_{t+1} is the strategy's total simple return and R_{t+1}^{bench} is the return on a benchmark (e.g., risk-free rate, market index), then the excess return is

$$R_{t+1}^{excess} = R_{t+1} - R_{t+1}^{bench}.$$

Using excess returns:

- removes the effect of market-wide moves (for equity strategies),
- isolates the contribution of the contrarian signal,
- aligns empirical work with asset pricing theory, which typically models expected *excess* returns.

Throughout this book, when we say that a reversal strategy "earns 50 bps per month," we almost always refer to an *excess* return over cash or a broad index, unless explicitly stated otherwise.

Gross vs. Net Returns

Finally, we distinguish between:

- *Gross returns:* before any trading costs, fees, or frictions.
- *Net returns:* after deducting explicit and implicit costs (commissions, bid–ask spreads, market impact, financing, stock borrow costs, and management fees).

Many anomalies look attractive on a gross basis but shrink or disappear when realistic costs are included. Later chapters on trading frictions and implementation will formalize these adjustments. For now, it is enough to emphasize that *a profitable gross reversal pattern is only a necessary, not sufficient, condition for a tradable anomaly.*

Currency and Cross-Market Comparability

Contrarian strategies often span multiple markets and currencies: a global equity strategy, a cross-asset macro strategy, or a multi-currency bond strategy. To compare returns and reversals across markets, we must handle currency consistently.

Local vs. Base Currency Returns

Suppose an asset traded in currency C has local simple return R_{t+1}^{local}. Let E_t be the exchange rate (units of base currency per unit of C). The return in base currency is

$$1 + R_{t+1}^{base} = \left(1 + R_{t+1}^{local}\right)\left(1 + R_{t+1}^{FX}\right),$$

where

$$R_{t+1}^{FX} = \frac{E_{t+1} - E_t}{E_t}$$

is the simple return on the exchange rate.

Intuitively, your base-currency wealth grows if either:

- the local asset price rises (positive R_{t+1}^{local}), or
- the foreign currency appreciates relative to your base currency (positive R_{t+1}^{FX}).

When we talk about cross-country reversal strength (e.g., larger reversals in emerging vs. developed markets), those inferences can look very different in local vs. base currency terms. It is therefore essential to state explicitly which convention is used.

Hedged vs. Unhedged Returns

An investor can also hedge currency risk, for example by using FX forwards. The *hedged* return isolates the underlying asset performance plus the interest rate differential embedded in the hedge, while removing most spot FX risk.

For a global contrarian equity portfolio, deciding whether to study hedged or unhedged returns is not a cosmetic choice: currency volatility can dominate short-horizon equity reversals in some periods. Later chapters will show how to control for this in backtests.

Why Return Definitions Matter for Reversal Detection

At this point, it may be tempting to view these distinctions as largely accounting details. In fact, they materially affect the detection and economic interpretation of contrarian signals.

Scaling and Sampling Frequency

A contrarian signal often depends on returns over a specific look-back window (e.g., previous one day, previous one week, previous one month). The choice of:

- simple vs. log returns,
- arithmetic vs. geometric aggregation,
- daily vs. weekly vs. monthly sampling,

can change both the magnitude and even the sign of measured reversals.

For example, consider a daily strategy that buys the worst performers from the previous day. If returns are very small, simple and log returns yield nearly identical rankings. But in stressed markets, where daily moves are large, using log vs. simple returns can reorder the extreme losers and winners, altering the composition of the contrarian portfolio and its backtested profitability.

Income and Carry Adjustments

Ignoring dividends, coupons, or carry can create apparent reversals that are actually just the mechanical unwind of expected income. For instance:

- A high-dividend stock may appear to "rebound" after going ex-dividend if you look only at price; including the dividend shows no true anomaly.
- A high-yielding currency may systematically depreciate to offset its interest advantage; looking only at spot FX moves might suggest a reversal or momentum pattern that disappears when carry is included.

A rigorous contrarian study must define returns in a way that fully reflects all economically relevant cash flows. Otherwise, machine learning models may lock onto artefacts of the chosen convention rather than genuine mispricings.

Cross-Asset and Cross-Country Comparisons

Finally, when we compare reversal strength across asset classes or regions, using inconsistent return definitions can lead to spurious conclusions. Examples include:

- comparing equity *total* returns in one country with equity *price* returns in another;
- mixing local-currency and base-currency returns in the same analysis;

- treating futures returns (which are implicitly levered by margin) on the same footing as unlevered cash asset returns.

To avoid these pitfalls, the remainder of the book will:

- specify precisely which return convention is used in each empirical exercise;
- strive to use total, excess, net-of-cost returns wherever feasible;
- pay close attention to sampling frequency and compounding when defining reversal signals.

With this foundation, we can proceed to the mechanics of how trades occur—market microstructure—and see how the plumbing of modern electronic markets naturally gives rise to the short-term dislocations that contrarian strategies seek to harvest.

1.2 Market Microstructure Essentials

In the previous section we treated asset prices and returns as if they were generated by a smooth, abstract process. For detecting price reversals, this high-level view is not enough. At very short horizons (seconds, minutes, even hours), prices are shaped less by fundamentals and more by the mechanics of how orders are submitted, matched, and executed.

This section opens that black box. We will:

- describe how different order types interact in a modern electronic limit-order book;
- show how these interactions determine short-horizon price movements;
- explain why these mechanics naturally create transient dislocations that contrarian strategies can exploit.

Throughout, you should think of every trade in your dataset as the visible outcome of a complex queueing process in the underlying order book.

From Intent to Execution: Order Types

An order is simply an instruction to trade a specific quantity of an asset under specified conditions. The most important order types for our purposes are:

- **Market orders:** "Trade now, at the best available price."
- **Limit orders:** "Trade, but only if I can get at least this good a price."
- **Stop and stop-limit orders:** "Start trading once the price has crossed a trigger level."

These basic types appear with many venue-specific variations, but the economic logic is universal.

Market Orders: Demanding Immediate Liquidity

A market order specifies only direction (buy or sell) and quantity. It does not specify a price. The trader is saying: *"Execution certainty matters more to me than the exact price."*

- A *buy* market order will trade against resting sell (ask) limit orders, starting from the *best ask* (lowest price).
- A *sell* market order will trade against resting buy (bid) limit orders, starting from the *best bid* (highest price).

Because they "hit" existing quotes, market orders are called *aggressive*. They consume liquidity and often move the last-traded price.

Limit Orders: Supplying Liquidity

A limit order specifies direction, quantity, and a limit price:

- A buy limit order with price p_{limit} says: "Buy up to this quantity at any price $\leq p_{limit}$."

- A sell limit order with price p_{limit} says: "Sell up to this quantity at any price $\geq p_{limit}$."

If the limit order is better than current quotes (for example, a buy limit order above the best bid), it may execute immediately, fully or partially. Any unexecuted quantity becomes a *resting order* in the limit-order book, waiting for future market orders or opposing limit orders to match against it.

By posting limit orders, traders *provide* liquidity and earn the bid–ask spread as compensation, but they risk non-execution or adverse selection (trading mostly when informed traders know prices are about to move).

Stop and Stop-Limit Orders

A stop order adds a trigger condition:

- A *sell stop* is typically placed below the current price to limit losses: "If the price falls to P^*, sell immediately."
- A *buy stop* is typically placed above the current price to enter on strength or cover a short: "If the price rises to P^*, buy immediately."

A pure stop order becomes a market order once the trigger price is hit. A stop-limit order becomes a limit order once triggered. Clusters of stop orders near key price levels can generate sharp, self-reinforcing price moves when those levels are breached, which are often followed by partial reversals once the stop-driven flow is exhausted.

The Limit-Order Book: Where Orders Wait

Most modern electronic markets are organized around a *continuous double auction* with a central limit-order book (LOB). The LOB is a real-time ledger of all active (resting) limit orders:

- on the *bid* side: buy limit orders at various prices;

- on the *ask* side: sell limit orders at various prices.

For each price level, the book aggregates available quantity and maintains a time-priority queue of individual orders.

Bid–Ask Spread, Depth, and Queue Priority

At any moment:

- the *best bid* b_t is the highest buy price in the book;
- the *best ask* a_t is the lowest sell price in the book;
- the *bid–ask spread* is $a_t - b_t$ (often expressed in ticks or basis points);
- *depth* at a price is the total quantity available at that price level.

Limit orders at the best bid and best ask form the *top of book*. Orders deeper in the book (worse prices) form additional layers of liquidity.

Within each price level, orders are prioritized by arrival time (first-in, first-out). A trader posting a buy limit order at the best bid joins the back of the bid queue; her order will only execute after earlier orders at that price are filled.

How Orders Become Trades

Trades occur when an incoming order *crosses* the spread:

- A buy market order or a buy limit order with price $\geq a_t$ executes against the best ask (and deeper asks if large enough).
- A sell market order or a sell limit order with price $\leq b_t$ executes against the best bid (and deeper bids if large enough).

Each match between a buyer and seller creates a *trade print* with:

- a trade price (the price level in the book that was hit),

- a trade size (matched quantity),
- a direction (buyer- or seller-initiated, from the perspective of the aggressor).

The last-traded price jumps to the price of the most recent execution. This is the price you see in standard price time series, but it reflects only the marginal trade, not the full state of the book.

Walking the Book and Short-Horizon Price Impact

Now we connect order flow to price dynamics. Consider a sequence of aggressive buy orders hitting the book.

- A small buy market order that is fully absorbed at the best ask executes without moving the quote; the last-traded price equals the best ask.
- A larger buy order may *consume* all quantity at the best ask and start trading at the next ask level up, causing the best ask (and often the mid-price) to move up.
- A very large order can "walk the book," trading through multiple ask levels and shifting the entire visible supply curve.

The same logic applies symmetrically for sell orders. This mechanical linkage between order size, book depth, and price changes is called *price impact.*

Instantaneous and Transient Impact

It is useful to distinguish:

- *Instantaneous impact:* The immediate price move caused by a given order or short burst of orders.
- *Transient vs. permanent impact:* How much of that move remains after liquidity providers react and new orders arrive.

Suppose a large buy program executes over a few seconds:

- Initially, the program walks the ask side of the book, pushing prices up sharply.
- As prices rise, new sell limit orders arrive at higher prices (traders "lean against" the buying pressure).
- Once the buy program finishes, there may be a temporary excess of sell-side liquidity and fewer motivated buyers at the new higher levels.
- The mid-price drifts back part of the way—a *short-term reversal*—until a new equilibrium between supply and demand is reached.

For contrarian trading at high frequency, we are often trying to detect situations where the initial impact has *overshot* any change in fundamental value, and where there is reason to expect at least a partial reversion as liquidity replenishes.

A Schematic View of the Limit-Order Book

Right after defining core order types and before we dive deeper into dynamics, it is helpful to have a concrete visual model of the book. Figure shows a stylized limit-order book with:

- a horizontal price ladder;
- bid and ask volume bars at each level;
- arrows indicating a burst of aggressive buy orders walking up the ask side;
- arrows indicating the subsequent partial reversal as new sell orders appear and the mid-price drifts back.

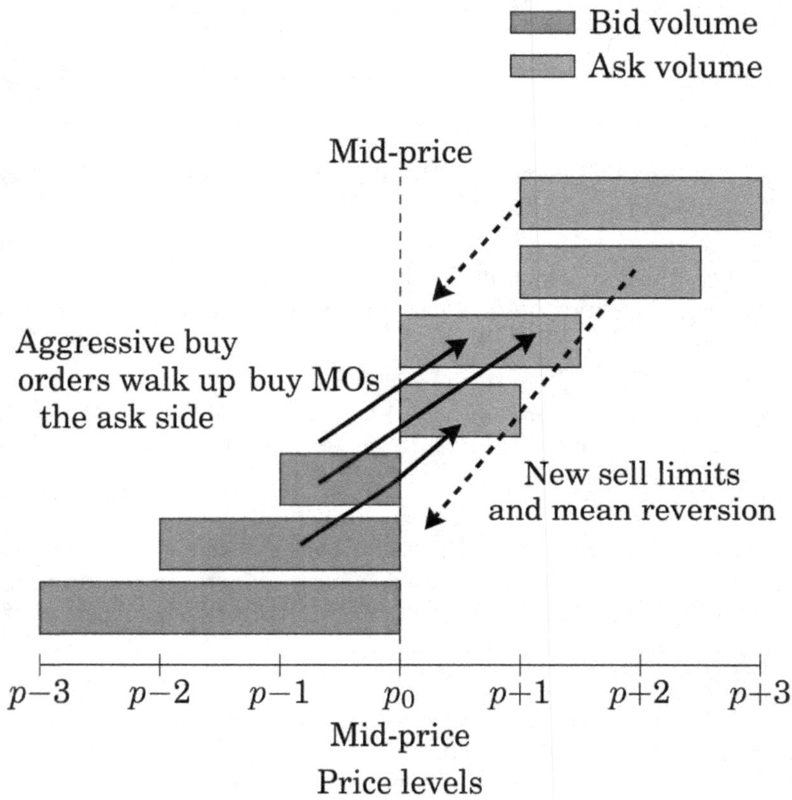

How Limit-Order Book Dynamics Shape Short-Horizon Prices

Having defined the book, we now connect its dynamics to the short-horizon returns that contrarian strategies seek to forecast.

Order Imbalance and Short-Term Pressure

At any instant, the market faces a stream of incoming orders. Over a short interval (say, one minute), we can summarize this stream by:

- the total *aggressive buy volume* (market and marketable limit orders buying),
- the total *aggressive sell volume*,
- the evolution of *posted depth* at and near the best bid and ask.

If aggressive buy volume greatly exceeds aggressive sell volume, and if ask-side depth is thin, the mid-price will tend to rise as buys walk up the book. Conversely, a wave of aggressive selling through a thin bid will push prices down.

This *order imbalance* is a key proximate driver of high-frequency returns. For a contrarian trader, extreme transient imbalances—where the book is momentarily one-sided—often herald a subsequent partial reversion once the flow normalizes.

Quote Dynamics and Mid-Price

The *mid-price* is defined as

$$m_t = \frac{b_t + a_t}{2},$$

halfway between the best bid and best ask. Many high-frequency models focus on mid-price changes rather than last-traded price, because:

- the mid-price smooths out some of the noise due to inside-spread trades;
- it directly reflects the best available prices to both buyers and sellers.

Limit-order book events move the mid-price when either:

- aggressive orders remove all depth at the best bid or ask (the quote "jumps" to the next level), or
- cancellations or new limit orders improve or worsen the best bid/ask.

Short-horizon returns are thus aggregations of discrete quote jumps, not a continuous diffusion. This discreteness and the strategic behavior of liquidity providers give rise to patterns—such as over-shooting and bounce-back—that contrarian strategies can exploit.

Mechanics That Create Transient Dislocations

We now highlight several microstructure mechanisms that frequently generate short-lived price dislocations.

Inventory and Risk Management by Liquidity Providers

Market makers and other liquidity providers hold inventories of the assets they quote. When they absorb a wave of buying pressure, their net long inventory grows. To control risk, they may:

- widen their quotes (increase the spread);
- skew quotes upward (raise both bid and ask) to encourage selling interest;
- reduce posted depth on the bid side.

These reactions can initially *accentuate* the move (higher quotes after buy pressure), but once inventories are rebalanced and volatility subsides, quotes can drift back, producing a mean-reverting pattern in prices.

From the perspective of a contrarian strategy, a key question is whether a recent price move reflects:

- genuine new information about fundamentals (likely to persist), or
- temporary inventory and risk management adjustments by liquidity providers (more likely to revert).

Microstructure variables like quoted depth, spread changes, and order imbalance help distinguish these cases.

Latency, Fragmentation, and Short-Lived Mispricings

Modern markets are fragmented across multiple venues, often with slightly different order books for the same instrument. Communication across venues is fast but not instantaneous. As a result:

- a large trade on one venue can momentarily move its mid-price away from the consolidated best price;
- stale quotes on slow venues can be picked off by faster traders;
- cross-venue price discrepancies can open up for milliseconds to seconds.

These micro-arbitrage opportunities are typically harvested by the fastest algorithmic traders. For our purposes, the important point is that the *initial* adjustment to a shock may be uneven and noisy across venues, often followed by a swift re-synchronization that looks like a short-horizon reversal in coarser data.

Intraday Liquidity Cycles

Liquidity is not constant through the trading day. Typical patterns include:

- **Open:** High volume, wide spreads, and shallow depth as information is incorporated.
- **Midday:** Lower volume, narrower spreads, deeper books.
- **Close:** Rising volume, often wider spreads as intraday positions are closed.

Because the limit-order book is thinner and more fragile at the open and close, the same size order can cause larger price impact in those windows, and reversals can be more pronounced once liquidity normalizes. Many documented intraday reversal anomalies are, at root, reflections of these liquidity cycles.

Stop Orders and Cascade Effects

When prices approach widely watched levels (prior highs/lows, round numbers, moving averages), traders often have clustered stop orders. If the level is breached:

- triggered stops become aggressive orders (market or limit), amplifying the move;
- the book can be rapidly "swept" in one direction;
- once the cluster is cleared, order flow can dry up.

If the underlying information content of the move was modest (e.g., a small piece of news or mere technical level), this stop-induced cascade can be followed by a partial reversion as other traders step in to take the opposite side at improved prices.

From Microstructure to Contrarian Signals

Finally, we tie these mechanics back to the design of contrarian trading strategies.

Microstructure-Based Reversal Intuition

At very short horizons, many contrarian signals can be reinterpreted as:

> *"Betting that the transient component of recent price impact will mean-revert once liquidity providers and slower participants adjust."*

Examples include:

- buying after an unusually large aggressive sell imbalance into a temporarily thin bid, expecting mid-price recovery as depth replenishes;

- selling after a sharp one-sided buy program in a low-liquidity period, expecting partial give-back once volume normalizes;
- fading price spikes coinciding with obvious stop-trigger levels, when book data show rapid but short-lived quote depletion.

Such strategies are fundamentally about microstructure, not long-horizon valuation.

Data Requirements and Practical Constraints

To harness these effects systematically, we need:

- high-frequency data: order book snapshots, trade prints, and possibly message-level data;
- careful timestamp alignment across venues and feeds;
- robust handling of cancellations, partial fills, and hidden liquidity.

Machine learning models trained on coarse daily data will miss much of this structure. Conversely, models trained on microsecond-level data must confront extreme noise and data volume. Subsequent chapters will discuss how to choose a level of granularity that preserves the key microstructure-driven reversals while remaining tractable.

Separating Microstructure Noise from Fundamental Moves

A recurring theme in this book is the distinction between:

- *microstructure noise*: very short-lived price moves primarily driven by order book mechanics;
- *informational moves*: price changes reflecting new information about fundamentals or risk.

Contrarian strategies profit by leaning against the former while avoiding betting against the latter. Understanding the limit-order book is therefore not just a technical curiosity; it is essential for:

- specifying lookback windows and holding periods appropriate for microstructure-driven reversals;
- designing features (order imbalance, spread, depth, trade signs) that proxy for transient pressure;
- setting execution rules that avoid turning a predictive edge into losses through impact and slippage.

1.3 Trading Frictions and Constraints

In the previous sections we treated returns as if they were clean functions of price and income, and we saw how short-horizon prices emerge from the mechanics of the limit-order book. To turn a contrarian signal into an implementable strategy, however, we must pass through one more filter: *the market's tollbooth.*

Every time you trade, you pay explicit and implicit costs and face structural constraints. These frictions compress paper anomalies into smaller, sometimes vanishing, net profits. In this section we:

- define and quantify the main components of trading cost;
- show how these costs scale with trading intensity (turnover);
- describe funding and shorting constraints that can mute contrarian profits;
- connect these elements back to realistic, implementable contrarian P&L.

A Taxonomy of Trading Costs

We start with a simple taxonomy. When you execute a round-trip trade (enter and then exit a position), your total cost per unit of notional can be decomposed into:

- **Explicit costs:** directly observable charges.
- broker commissions,
- exchange and clearing fees,
- taxes and levies (where applicable).
- **Implicit costs:** embedded in execution prices and risk.
- bid–ask spread,
- slippage vs. a reference price,
- transient and permanent market impact,
- opportunity cost (partial fills, missed trades).

A disciplined research process makes these components explicit in the backtest, rather than treating them as an afterthought. We will begin with the three most important building blocks for contrarian strategies: commissions, spread, and impact.

Commission and Fee Costs

Per-Share and Ad Valorem Commissions

Most brokers charge either:

- a *per-share* or *per-contract* commission (e.g., $0.001 per share), or
- an *ad valorem* commission as a percentage of traded notional (e.g., 0.5 bps per side).

If you trade quantity Q at price P, and your per-unit commission is c_{unit}, then:

$$\text{Commission cost} = Q \cdot c_{unit}.$$

If your commission is c_{bps} basis points (bps) of notional per side, then per side:

$$\text{Commission cost (bps)} = c_{bps},$$

and the round-trip cost in bps is $2c_{bps}$.

In liquid developed markets with institutional accounts, commissions can be very small per trade. Still, for high-turnover contrarian strategies that trade frequently, even a few basis points per round-trip accumulate quickly.

Exchange, Clearing, and Regulatory Fees

On top of broker commissions, exchanges and clearinghouses often charge fees per share, contract, or notional traded. Regulatory fees (e.g., levies to fund oversight) may also apply. For modeling purposes you can either:

- fold these into an "all-in" commission estimate per side, or
- model them as a separate fixed-per-share or bps component.

The key is that your backtest should be calibrated to the *true* total explicit cost of your likely execution venue and broker arrangement, not to an optimistic or outdated schedule.

Bid–Ask Spread and Slippage

The Cost of Crossing the Spread

In the microstructure section, we defined the best bid b_t and best ask a_t, and the spread $s_t = a_t - b_t$. If you submit a small buy *market* order when the spread is s_t, you will typically:

- pay the best ask a_t,
- while the "mid-price" is $m_t = (a_t + b_t)/2$.

Relative to the mid-price, your execution incurs an *immediate* cost of $+\frac{s_t}{2}$. When you later sell by crossing the spread again (now paying $-\frac{s'_{t'}}{2}$ relative to the mid at exit), your round-trip spread cost is approximately one full spread, or:

$$\text{Round-trip spread cost} \approx \frac{s_t}{2m_t} + \frac{s'_{t'}}{2m_{t'}} \approx \text{one spread in \% terms.}$$

For many contrarian strategies that must react quickly, it is difficult to avoid paying the spread, especially on entry when the signal appears. This makes the spread a central parameter in feasibility analysis.

Slippage vs. Benchmark Prices

Traders often judge execution quality relative to a benchmark, such as:

- the mid-price at signal time,
- the volume-weighted average price (VWAP) over a period,
- the closing price for end-of-day strategies.

Slippage is the difference between the actual execution price and the benchmark. It can arise from:

- crossing the spread,
- market impact pushing the price against you during execution,
- delays between signal time and order arrival.

In backtests, neglecting the spread and slippage is equivalent to assuming perfect execution at the mid-price or close—an assumption that systematically overstates contrarian P&L.

Market Impact

Conceptual Decomposition

When you submit a non-trivial order into a limit-order book, you change the state of the book and often the price. Market impact is the component of price movement *caused by your own trading*. We can conceptually decompose it into:

- **Transient impact:** the initial price move as your order consumes liquidity and others update quotes, which partially reverses after you finish.
- **Permanent impact:** any lasting shift in the price level once the market has fully digested the information inferred from your trade.

From the perspective of execution cost, you care primarily about the total price concession paid across the life of the order relative to the initial benchmark.

A Simple Impact Model

A common modeling approach assumes that expected impact grows with the "size" of your order relative to typical volume. Let:

- Q be the total quantity you wish to trade,
- ADV be the average daily volume in the asset,
- $\phi = Q/\text{ADV}$ be your participation rate.

A stylized impact model might posit that the average price concession (in bps) scales like:

$$\text{Impact} \approx k \cdot \phi^{\alpha},$$

where k and α are empirical constants (e.g., k on the order of tens of bps for full-day trades, and α between 0.5 and 1). Even if the exact form varies by asset and venue, two qualitative points are robust:

- impact *increases* with order size as a fraction of volume;
- the relationship is *convex*: doubling size typically more than doubles cost.

High-turnover contrarian strategies can easily push into regions of significant impact, especially in less liquid names.

How Costs Scale with Turnover

Turnover links signal frequency to cost. Define:

- portfolio notional at time t, N_t;
- traded notional over the period $[t, t+1]$, $V_{t,t+1}$.

The period turnover is:

$$\text{Turnover}_{t,t+1} = \frac{V_{t,t+1}}{N_t}.$$

If your average round-trip cost (commissions + spread + impact) is C_{rt} bps, and you fully turn over the portfolio T_{rt} times per year, your expected annual cost burden is roughly:

$$\text{Annual cost (bps)} \approx C_{rt} \times T_{rt}.$$

A strategy that trades once per month with $C_{rt} = 10$ bps has an annual drag of about 120 bps. A high-frequency strategy that effectively turns the book over daily with $C_{rt} = 5$ bps faces a cost drag of more than 1,000 bps per year.

Illustrative Cost Decomposition Across Turnover Levels

Before getting into numerical examples, it is helpful to visualize how the composition of cost changes as turnover increases. Figure shows a stylized bar chart for three turnover regimes:

- *Low turnover:* infrequent trading, costs dominated by commissions.
- *Medium turnover:* more frequent rebalancing, spread costs grow in importance.
- *High turnover:* aggressive trading, market impact becomes the dominant component.

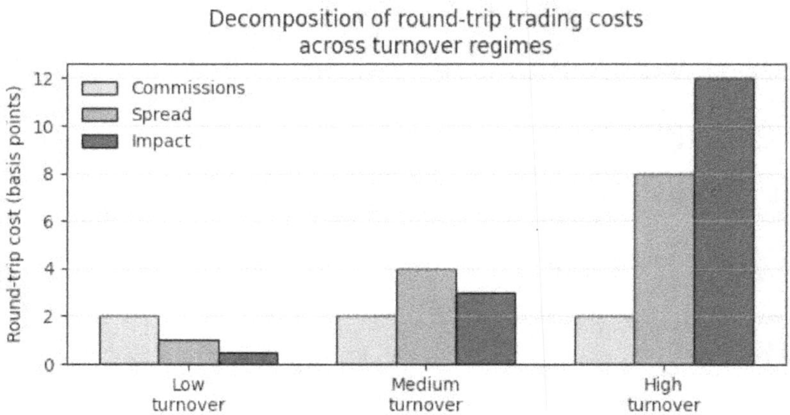

Stylized decomposition of round-trip trading costs into commissions, spread, and impact across different turnover regimes. Numbers are illustrative basis points per round-trip, highlighting how impact becomes dominant at high trading intensity.

The exact magnitudes will differ by asset class and venue, but the qualitative pattern is stable: as you trade more often and more aggressively, the share of cost coming from spread and impact grows nonlinearly.

Funding Costs and Leverage

Contrarian strategies are often implemented with leverage, especially when individual anomalies have modest raw Sharpe ratios. Leverage introduces *funding costs*, which act as another drag on returns.

Cash Borrowing and Margin Rates

Suppose you finance a leveraged long position by borrowing cash at an annualized funding rate r_{fund}. If your gross (pre-funding) expected return is μ_{gross} and your leverage is L (so you hold L dollars of assets per dollar of equity), then your equity-level expected return is:

$$\mu_{equity} \approx L \cdot \mu_{gross} - (L - 1) \cdot r_{fund} - \text{other costs.}$$

Funding costs are particularly important for:

- futures-based strategies, where the "all-in" return already embeds interest rates and margin funding;
- leveraged ETFs or swap-based implementations that pass through financing charges;
- hedge fund-style structures that borrow at spreads above cash rates.

When interest rates rise, previously attractive low-risk anomalies can become unattractive once funding is properly accounted for.

Rehypothecation, Haircuts, and Collateral

In prime brokerage relationships, positions posted as collateral may be subject to *haircuts*: you can only borrow a fraction of their market value. This limits effective leverage and can force deleveraging in stress periods. Forced deleveraging can itself exacerbate reversals, but for the strategy designer it is a constraint that may cause theoretical P&L to be unattainable in practice.

Shorting Constraints and Stock Loan Costs

Many contrarian strategies bet on relative value: long recent losers, short recent winners. The short leg introduces its own set of frictions.

Locate Requirements and Hard-to-Borrow Securities

To short a stock, you typically must:

- obtain a *locate* from your prime broker, confirming the securities can be borrowed;
- pay a stock loan fee (a borrow rate) for the privilege of shorting.

Some securities—small caps, heavily shorted names, or special situations—are *hard-to-borrow*, with borrow rates that can exceed tens of percent per year. If your contrarian signal often selects such names on the short side, gross backtested profits can be entirely eaten by borrow costs.

Rebates and Short Rebate Rates

In some markets, cash proceeds from short sales earn a *rebate* at a rate below the risk-free rate. The effective cost of shorting is the difference between the risk-free rate and the rebate rate, plus any incremental fees. These economics can change over time, meaning that backtests calibrated on one regime may overstate returns in another if shorting conditions tighten.

Short Sale Restrictions

Regulatory constraints, such as:

- uptick rules or price tests,
- bans on shorting certain sectors or instruments during stress,
- limits on naked short selling,

can periodically make it impossible to implement the short leg of a contrarian strategy, just when the signal appears most profitable. Robust strategy design must consider how performance looks if shorting becomes temporarily constrained or prohibitively expensive.

From Paper Anomalies to Net P&L

We now connect the cost components back to observed anomalies.

Per-Trade and Per-Unit Cost Formulas

For a given trade in asset i over period $[t, t+1]$, we can write the expected round-trip cost in basis points as:

$$C_{i,t}^{rt} = C_{i,t}^{comm} + C_{i,t}^{spread} + C_{i,t}^{impact} + C_{i,t}^{funding} + C_{i,t}^{borrow}.$$

If your strategy trades fraction $\tau_{i,t}$ of the portfolio in asset i during that period, and the portfolio's pre-cost return is R_{t+1}^{gross}, then the expected net return is approximately:

$$R_{t+1}^{net} \approx R_{t+1}^{gross} - \sum_i \tau_{i,t} \cdot C_{i,t}^{rt}.$$

Even if R_{t+1}^{gross} looks attractive in backtests without costs, the dollar-weighted turnover $\tau_{i,t}$ and the distribution of $C_{i,t}^{rt}$ across names can reduce or reverse the edge.

Reordering Strategy Attractiveness

An important practical consequence is that realistic costs can *reorder* which strategies appear most attractive:

- A high-frequency intraday contrarian strategy with a 30 bps daily gross edge but effective round-trip costs of 25 bps may be economically inferior to a slower, weekly contrarian strategy with a 10 bps weekly edge and 2 bps of cost.
- A cross-sectional equity reversal strategy that relies heavily on micro caps might show the highest gross Sharpe ratio, yet a variant restricted to mid- and large-cap names may deliver higher net Sharpe once impact and borrow costs are accounted for.

Thus, cost-aware modeling is not just a matter of subtracting a flat haircut. It shapes which anomalies are worth pursuing and how aggressively they can be traded.

Implications for Machine Learning-Based Contrarian Strategies

Finally, we highlight the implications for the machine learning focus of this book.

Cost-Aware Labeling and Targets

If the label you try to predict is a *gross* return, but your performance will be judged on *net* returns, your model may happily learn signals that are profitable before cost but systematically unprofitable after cost. Better approaches include:

- defining prediction targets as *net-of-spread* or net-of-commission returns;

- incorporating a per-asset estimate of marginal cost into the label (e.g., predicting $R^{gross}_{t+1} - \hat{C}^{rt}_{t}$);
- feeding cost proxies (spread, depth, liquidity measures, borrow rates) into the model so that it can avoid trades where gross edges are unlikely to overcome costs.

Cost-Constrained Portfolio Construction

Even with a good predictive model, portfolio construction determines how cost-intensive the resulting strategy will be. Techniques such as:

- adding a turnover penalty or explicit cost term in the optimization objective;
- imposing maximum position changes per period;
- favoring higher-liquidity names when multiple candidates have similar signals;

can dramatically reduce cost drag with modest impact on gross alpha.

Backtesting Discipline

Finally, any empirical claim about a contrarian anomaly must be evaluated through a strict, cost-aware backtesting lens:

- use realistic, time-varying estimates of spreads, commissions, and impact;
- model shorting costs and funding explicitly if the strategy relies on leverage or shorts;
- stress-test results under adverse cost scenarios (wider spreads, higher borrow fees).

Only anomalies that survive this gauntlet deserve serious attention. The next section, on market efficiency, behavioral biases, and anomalies, will step back from the mechanics and frictions to ask: *why* do some of these cost-aware contrarian signals persist at all, and how do they fit into the broader theory of efficient markets and limits to arbitrage?

1.4 Market Efficiency, Behavioral Biases & Anomalies

So far, we have worked from the ground up: we defined assets and returns, opened the hood on the limit-order book, and quantified the costs and constraints that stand between a theoretical edge and realized P&L. We now step back and ask a more conceptual question:

> *If markets are supposed to be efficient, why do contrarian opportunities appear to exist at all?*

This section frames classical market efficiency theory against the empirical evidence of persistent anomalies, with a particular focus on mean reversion. We will:

- review the Efficient Market Hypothesis (EMH) and what it predicts about return predictability;
- define what we mean by a *market anomaly* in data;
- survey key contrarian-related patterns (short-term reversals, medium-term overreaction, and other mean-reverting phenomena);
- explain these patterns through behavioral biases and institutional constraints that limit arbitrage.

The goal is not to "disprove" efficiency, but to understand the pockets where it is *predictably incomplete*.

The Efficient Market Hypothesis

The Efficient Market Hypothesis is a set of ideas about how prices should behave when markets work "well." The starting intuition is simple: if many rational, competitive investors use all available information to maximize expected return for a given risk, then *obvious* profit opportunities should be quickly exploited and disappear.

Forms of Efficiency

It is useful to distinguish three classical forms of EMH, which differ in what counts as "available information":

- **Weak-form efficiency:** Prices fully reflect all information contained in *past prices and volumes*. Under this view, you cannot systematically earn excess returns by using only historical returns or simple technical rules.

- **Semi-strong-form efficiency:** Prices fully reflect all *publicly available* information (including fundamentals, news, and past prices). Here, neither technical analysis nor fundamental analysis based on public data should produce persistent abnormal profits.

- **Strong-form efficiency:** Prices fully reflect *all* information, public and private. Even insiders cannot systematically earn abnormal returns.

For our purposes, weak-form efficiency is the crucial benchmark: most contrarian strategies use past returns, volume, and other trading data as inputs. If markets are truly weak-form efficient, then any apparent predictability based on these variables must be either compensation for risk, a statistical artefact, or a temporary blip that disappears once discovered.

What Efficiency Does *Not* Say

A common misunderstanding is that EMH claims prices are always "correct" in some absolute sense or that they never move irrationally. In fact, EMH is a *joint* hypothesis about:

- how information is processed and incorporated into prices, and

- what the correct asset pricing model is (e.g., CAPM, multi-factor model).

If you find a predictable pattern in returns, you have shown that *either* prices are not fully efficient *or* your model of risk and expected return is incomplete (or both). In practice, most anomalies—including contrarian effects—are interpreted as a mix of mispricing, risk premia, and data issues.

What Is a Market Anomaly?

In empirical asset pricing, a *market anomaly* is a pattern in returns that appears inconsistent with a standard benchmark of efficiency and risk.

More concretely, a pattern is typically labeled an anomaly if:

- it implies *predictable* excess returns (e.g., based on past returns, accounting ratios, flows);
- the predictability persists across time periods, markets, or samples;
- it cannot be easily explained away by known risk factors, transaction costs, or data errors.

Crucially, an anomaly is always defined relative to a *model.* A simple moving-average rule that seems to beat a naïve i.i.d. return model may not be an anomaly once you account for time-varying volatility, risk premia, or liquidity conditions.

In this book, our primary interest is in anomalies that exhibit some form of *mean reversion*: prices or returns that move away from a reference level and then tend to move back.

Contrarian-Related Anomalies

Contrarian strategies try to buy what has recently underperformed and sell what has recently outperformed, betting that prices will partially revert. Several well-documented empirical patterns fall into this family.

Short-Term Reversals

Short-term reversal refers to the tendency of assets that underperformed recently (over one day to one month) to outperform in the near future, and vice versa. In cross-sectional form:

- at each rebalancing date, rank assets by their very recent returns;
- form a portfolio that is long recent losers and short recent winners;
- hold for a short horizon (days to weeks).

Many markets show a modest but statistically detectable positive average return to such strategies before costs. At very high frequency (seconds to minutes), microstructure-induced reversals (e.g., bid–ask bounce, order book replenishment) are even more pervasive.

From an EMH perspective, pure short-term return-based predictability in excess of risks and costs violates weak-form efficiency. From a more nuanced perspective, short-term reversals may be:

- compensation for providing liquidity and absorbing order flow imbalances;
- artefacts of how trades are recorded (bid–ask bounce, non-synchronous trading);
- by-products of behavioral overreaction to noise, quickly corrected.

Medium-Term Overreaction and Reversal

At somewhat longer horizons (several months), another pattern emerges: assets with extreme past performance sometimes exhibit *overreaction*. A stylized pattern is:

- over 6–12 months, strong outperformers continue to outperform (momentum);

- beyond that horizon, the strongest prior winners tend to underperform, and the strongest losers tend to outperform (long-horizon reversal).

This "momentum then reversal" pattern can be interpreted as:

- initial underreaction to news (prices move in the same direction as past returns as information diffuses);
- followed by overshooting and eventual correction (prices revert as expectations are revised).

Contrarian strategies that exploit medium-term overreaction typically:

- identify extreme prior winners/losers over a medium lookback (e.g., 12–36 months);
- take the opposite position (short winners, long losers);
- hold over an extended horizon (years).

These strategies are more exposed to fundamental risk and less to pure microstructure noise than ultra-short-horizon reversals.

Event-Related Reversals

Specific corporate or macro events can also trigger predictable reversals. Examples include:

- **Earnings and news surprises:** prices often underreact to earnings news, leading to post-earnings announcement drift in the same direction as the surprise, followed by correction when overly optimistic or pessimistic expectations are tempered.
- **Liquidity shocks:** forced sales (e.g., from margin calls, redemptions, or index rebalancing) can push prices away from fundamentals; when pressure abates, prices revert.

- **Market-wide crises:** in stress episodes, correlations spike and illiquid assets may overshoot on the downside; measured contrarian portfolios that buy into such dislocations may earn elevated returns as prices normalize.

Here, reversals are often tied to identifiable temporary pressures rather than anonymous noise in returns.

Behavioral Explanations for Mean Reversion

One line of explanation for anomalies focuses on *behavioral biases*: systematic ways in which humans deviate from the ideal of rational, Bayesian updating. Several well-studied biases can naturally give rise to overreaction or underreaction, and thus to contrarian opportunities.

Overreaction and Representativeness

The *representativeness heuristic* is the tendency to judge the probability of an outcome by how much it resembles a stereotype, rather than by base rates. In financial markets, this can lead investors to:

- overweight recent earnings or price trends;
- extrapolate short-term patterns too far into the future;
- neglect mean reversion in fundamentals.

When good news arrives, investors may over-infer a permanent change in prospects and bid prices up beyond what is justified. The reverse occurs for bad news. Over time, as more information accumulates and the exaggerated expectations are corrected, prices revert.

Underreaction, Anchoring, and Conservatism

On the other side, *anchoring* and *conservatism* refer to the tendency to stick too closely to prior beliefs and adjust insufficiently to new information. Investors anchored on past averages may:

- update slowly when fundamentals genuinely change;
- underreact to early signals, leading to gradual price drift in the direction of news;
- later overshoot when the weight of evidence becomes undeniable.

This multi-stage adjustment process can produce both momentum and subsequent reversal: underreaction in the early phase, overreaction in the later phase.

Herding and Feedback Trading

Herding occurs when traders mimic each other's actions rather than relying solely on their own information. Reasons include:

- inferring information from others' trades ("they must know something");
- career concerns ("better to fail conventionally than to succeed unconventionally");
- behavioral comfort in following the crowd.

Herding can amplify price moves beyond what fundamentals warrant, especially when combined with feedback traders who buy because prices are rising (or sell because prices are falling). Once the herd runs out of fresh capital or sentiment shifts, flows reverse and prices mean-revert.

Disposition Effect and Limited Loss Realization

The *disposition effect* is the tendency for investors to:

- sell winners too early to "lock in gains";
- hold losers too long to avoid realizing losses.

This behavior can dampen the supply of shares from recent losers (fewer willing sellers at low prices) and increase supply from recent winners (more selling pressure at high prices). Such flow asymmetries can create predictable post-performance drift and eventual reversals as portfolios are rebalanced or external shocks force loss realization.

Limits to Arbitrage: Why Mispricing Persists

Even if some investors behave irrationally, shouldn't rational arbitrageurs quickly step in, exploit mispricing, and restore efficiency? The key idea of *limits to arbitrage* is that in the real world, this corrective force is constrained by risk, costs, and institutional frictions—exactly the microstructure and trading frictions we discussed earlier.

Fundamental Risk and Noise Trader Risk

An arbitrageur betting against mispricing (e.g., shorting an overpriced stock) faces:

- **Fundamental risk:** the possibility that adverse news about the firm justifies the current price or moves it even further in the "wrong" direction.
- **Noise trader risk:** the risk that mispricing becomes worse in the short run because of continued irrational trading, triggering mark-to-market losses.

Because arbitrageurs have limited capital and face margin requirements, they may be unable or unwilling to hold positions long enough to ride out interim losses. This risk limits the size and aggressiveness of arbitrage trades, allowing some mispricing to persist.

Funding, Margin, and Shorting Constraints

The frictions from the previous section play a central role here:

- *Funding costs* reduce the net return to leveraged arbitrage, especially in low-rate environments where gross spreads are narrow.

- *Margin requirements* can force premature unwinding of contrarian positions during drawdowns, even if the long-run thesis remains sound.
- *Shorting constraints*—high borrow costs or an inability to locate shares—limit the ability to correct overpricing on the short side.

These forces are particularly severe precisely when mispricings are often largest, such as during crises and liquidity panics. This asymmetry helps explain why contrarian returns often appear pro-cyclical and risky.

Career and Organizational Risks

Professional money managers are agents for principals (clients, boards, investment committees). Their incentives are not identical to those of a risk-neutral, long-horizon arbitrageur. Key organizational frictions include:

- **Career risk:** deviating from benchmarks or peers and underperforming in the short term can lead to redemptions or job loss.
- **Benchmark constraints:** managers may be required to stay close to a benchmark index, limiting their ability to take strong contrarian positions.
- **Risk limits:** internal VaR or drawdown limits may mechanically cap exposures precisely when mispricings are most extreme.

As a result, even managers who *see* a contrarian opportunity may be unable to exploit it at scale. Their demand for "arbitrage" is itself state-dependent and cyclically constrained.

Reconciling Efficiency and Anomalies

With these ingredients in hand, we can frame a more nuanced view of markets, one that is especially helpful for designing machine learning-based contrarian strategies.

Residual Inefficiency After Rational Pricing

Think of the market price at any time as the sum of three components:

$$\text{Price} = \text{Fundamental value} + \text{Risk premium adjustments} + \text{Residual noise / mispricing}.$$

Classical EMH and standard asset pricing models aim to account for the first two terms: how information about cash flows and risk is transformed into fair expected returns. The empirical anomalies we study live largely in the third term: *residual* deviations caused by behavioral biases, institutional frictions, and microstructure noise.

Contrarian trading, in this view, is about:

> *Systematically identifying and harvesting those residual deviations that are large enough, persistent enough, and cheap enough to trade after costs and constraints.*

Risk vs. Mispricing: A Practical Stance

For any specific anomaly, it is often hard to cleanly separate risk premia from mispricing. For example, short-term reversals may partly reflect compensation for providing liquidity in stressed times (a risk premium) and partly the unwinding of behavioral overreaction (mispricing).

For practical strategy design, what matters most is:

- whether the pattern is robust across samples, definitions, and realistic cost assumptions;
- whether it can be captured within your funding, risk, and organizational constraints;
- how it behaves across market regimes (calm vs. crisis, low vs. high volatility).

Machine learning can help model these regime dependencies and interactions, but the conceptual lens remains: we are not trying to "defeat" markets in general; we are trying to exploit specific, limited failures of full efficiency that are stable enough to be learned.

Implications for the Rest of the Book

This section provides the conceptual backdrop for everything that follows:

- **Modeling targets:** When we train models to predict reversals, we are implicitly modeling the residual component of price dynamics after accounting for broad risk and trend effects.
- **Feature design:** Many useful features (order flow, volatility, valuation ratios, flows) proxy for behavioral or institutional pressures that give rise to anomalies.
- **Evaluation:** Our backtesting and statistical procedures must distinguish true residual predictability from mere overfitting to noise, especially in the presence of multiple testing.

In the next chapters, we will formalize these ideas with the statistical and machine learning tools required to identify genuine contrarian signals, avoid false discoveries, and design trading strategies that respect the frictions and constraints we have just discussed.

Chapter 2

Data & Research Infrastructure for Honest Alpha

Most quant blow-ups don't start with bad models-they start with bad data. This chapter shows you how to build a research pipeline where every price, feature, and label respects the information that was truly available at the time, so any anomaly you "discover" has a fighting chance of surviving contact with live markets.

2.1 Point-in-Time Data Sourcing & Storage

Most "smart" backtests are accidentally dishonest, not because the researcher is trying to cheat, but because the data pipeline quietly lets information leak backward in time. In the previous chapter we built intuition for how anomalies and contrarian effects are defined in returns. In this section we turn to the plumbing that makes those definitions trustworthy: point-in-time data and storage.

The goal is simple to state but demanding to implement:

> At any historical timestamp t, your model must see *only* the information that a real trader could have known at t, and in the form it was known then.

To reach that goal we need three ingredients:

1. A precise definition of what "point-in-time" means in practice.
2. An understanding of how different data vendors and feeds behave.
3. A storage design that enforces point-in-time constraints by construction.

What "Point-in-Time" Really Means

It is tempting to think of a dataset as a fixed table: each row is a security on a date, and each column is a feature (price, earnings, size, etc.). That mental model is convenient for statistics but wrong for trading.

In reality, every field in your table has a *life history*. A single earnings-per-share number, for example, might:

- be computed internally by the firm on day 0,
- be filed with the regulator on day 5,
- be picked up by vendor A on day 6 and by vendor B on day 7,
- be corrected in a restatement three months later.

If your backtest on January 10, 2018 uses an EPS value that was only corrected in March 2018, you are inadvertently letting the future leak into the past. The backtest becomes a trivia contest where the model is allowed to know future corrections.

To avoid this, every data point you use should be associated with at least two times:

- **Event time** (t^{event}): when the underlying economic or market event actually happened. For a trade, this is the exchange timestamp. For an earnings announcement, this is the official announcement time.
- **Availability time** (t^{avail}): when that information became available to your trading engine or research system. This includes reporting lags, vendor ingestion delays, and your own overnight batch processes.

A feature is point-in-time correct at trading decision time t if it respects:

$$t^{avail} \leq t.$$

Anything with $t^{avail} > t$ is a look-ahead error, even if it refers to an event with $t^{event} \leq t$.

This leads to three practical rules:

1. **Never rely solely on "as-of date" fields.** Many datasets include an "effective date" or "period end". This is usually t^{event}, not t^{avail}.
2. **Prefer feed histories over static snapshots.** A static fundamental table updated monthly usually contains the latest, possibly restated values. A feed history records what the vendor knew and when.
3. **Join on availability, not just on calendar date.** When joining prices with fundamentals, ensure that for a decision at t you join only fields whose availability time is earlier than or equal to t.

Once you see the world this way, "point-in-time" stops being an abstract ideal and becomes a set of timestamp and versioning constraints you can encode directly into your database and code.

Anatomy of Market Data Sources

Different vendor types handle timing, corrections, and symbology in different ways. Understanding these behaviors is a prerequisite to building a point-in-time store.

Exchange and Consolidated Feeds

At the lowest level are *exchange feeds* and *consolidated feeds*:

- **Exchange feeds** publish every quote, trade, and auction event for a given venue (e.g., NYSE, NASDAQ). Timestamps are typically the exchange's own clock.
- **Consolidated feeds** aggregate across venues, building a unified view of the national best bid and offer (NBBO), trade prints, and depth.

These feeds are closest to the economic truth of what traded when. Their advantages:

- Fine-grained timestamps (microseconds or milliseconds).
- Explicit cancel/correct messages that show when a bad print was removed or fixed.
- Very clear separation between event time and any downstream processing time you impose.

However, they have costs:

- Very high volume (billions of messages per day).
- Complex structure (order book events, condition codes).
- Limited historical depth unless you archive them yourself.

For contrarian strategies at intraday horizons, these feeds are often indispensable. For daily or weekly horizon work, you can down-sample them into bars while preserving point-in-time behavior.

End-of-Day (EOD) Price Vendors

Many quants start with end-of-day price vendors that publish:

- Open, high, low, close, and volume (OHLCV) per symbol per day.
- Corporate action factors (splits, dividends).
- Possibly returns already adjusted for those actions.

Key characteristics:

- **Latency.** EOD data often arrives hours after the close, or the next morning. For a daily strategy that trades on the next day's open, this is acceptable. For same-day trading, it is not.
- **Revision policy.** Vendors may correct past days' data when errors or late corporate actions are discovered. Unless you keep every revision, your research view drifts toward a "cleaned" future-aware history.
- **Symbology.** Vendors maintain their own symbol identifiers. Over time, tickers change, firms merge, and new identifiers are created.

Using EOD data in a point-in-time way means you must either:

1. Capture and store vendor files *as they were* each day (including subsequent corrections as new versions), or
2. Use a vendor that explicitly provides point-in-time or "as-reported" histories, with availability timestamps and versioning.

Fundamental and Reference Data Providers

Fundamental datasets (income statements, balance sheets, analyst estimates, ratings) and reference data (industry classifications, share counts, corporate actions) are the most common source of look-ahead bias.

Typical pitfalls:

- **Period end vs. report date.** A fiscal quarter may end on March 31, but results are filed on April 25 and the vendor might not publish them until April 26.
- **Restatements.** Companies restate prior periods; some vendors overwrite historical values. Without versioning, your March 31 feature vector includes information that only existed after the restatement.
- **Coverage creep.** Vendors expand coverage over time. Backfilling coverage histories without availability dates can make illiquid or foreign names appear to have been available earlier than they were.

For anomaly research, you want:

- Announcement or filing dates (event times).
- Vendor publication dates (availability times).
- Version identifiers for restatements and corrections.

With these in place, you can simulate a realistic investor who only learns about earnings, downgrades, or share repurchases when the world actually learns about them.

Alternative Data Providers

Alternative data (web traffic, credit card panels, satellite imagery, supply-chain data) is inherently messy from a timing perspective:

- Signals may be delivered in batches with substantial lags.
- Vendors may recalculate historical series as they improve cleaning methods.
- Symbology mapping (from merchants, locations, products) to securities is often probabilistic and evolving.

For such data, insist on:

- Explicit delivery timestamps for each file or record.
- Version tags when historical data is recomputed.
- Transparent mapping tables between the vendor's entities and your security identifiers, also versioned over time.

Without this, it is nearly impossible to use alternative data honestly in backtests.

Symbology and Corporate Hierarchies

A surprisingly large fraction of silent errors in research pipelines come from mishandling symbology—the way securities are identified and tracked through time.

Ticker Symbols vs. Persistent IDs

Ticker symbols are human-friendly but churn constantly:

- Companies change tickers for branding reasons.
- Mergers and spin-offs reassign or recycle tickers.
- Different venues may use different tickers for the same underlying security.

By contrast, persistent identifiers such as PERMNO (in CRSP), FIGI, or vendor-specific permanent IDs are designed to remain stable across such events. Best practice is:

- **Internally key everything by a persistent ID.** Treat tickers as attributes that vary over time.
- **Maintain a historical symbology table.** For each persistent ID, store the full timeline of tickers, listing venues, and status (active, delisted).

This ensures that when a ticker changes, your model still recognizes the firm as the same entity.

Corporate Hierarchies

For some anomalies (e.g., value, profitability, cross-sectional contrarian effects within industries), you care about firm-level attributes, not just security-level ones. A single corporate family might issue:

- Multiple share classes (e.g., with and without votes).
- Bonds, preferred stock, and other instruments.
- Cross-listed shares on foreign exchanges.

A robust research store will explicitly model:

- **Issuer or company entities.**
- **Security entities** linked to issuers.
- **Listings** (security on exchange) linked to securities.

Each of these layers has its own timeline: firms merge or spin off subsidiaries, securities are issued or retired, listings are created or delisted. Modeling them separately makes it easier to define your investable universe correctly and avoid, for example, double-counting a firm that has two tickers at once.

A Layered, Point-in-Time Storage Architecture

Now we can combine these ideas into a storage design that enforces point-in-time behavior. The core concept is to separate concerns into layers and attach rich timestamps and versioning metadata at the boundaries.

Layers: Raw, Staging, Research-Ready

A minimal but effective architecture uses three main layers:

Raw Ingest Layer

- **What it stores:** Vendor files or feed messages exactly as delivered (compressed if needed).
- **Key fields:** Vendor name, feed type, ingestion timestamp, original filename or sequence number, plus the raw content.
- **Purpose:** Immutable audit trail. If a vendor revises data, you see old and new; if you change your cleaning logic, you can rerun it on the original bits.

Staging / Normalization Layer

- **What it stores:** Parsed records with standardized fields: security identifiers mapped to your internal ID, numeric fields converted to consistent units, and separate columns for event time and vendor publication time.
- **Key fields:**
  - Internal security ID and entity relationships.
  - Event timestamp t^{event}.
  - Vendor publication or load timestamp t^{vendor}.
  - Version identifiers when the same logical record is revised.
- **Purpose:** A clean but still vendor-faithful record of what you knew and when, across sources.

Research-Ready (Point-in-Time) Layer

- **What it stores:** Time-series tables optimized for backtesting: bars, factor values, labels, and universe membership each on their own timeline.
- **Key constraints:**
  - Every row includes a decision time t and the underlying event and availability times of its inputs.
  - Construction logic enforces $t^{avail} \leq t$ for all features.
  - Versioning of calculation logic and inputs so you can reproduce past experiments.

- **Purpose:** Fast, safe access for model training and evaluation without reimplementing point-in-time filters in every experiment.

Right after introducing these layers, it is helpful to visualize the overall flow.

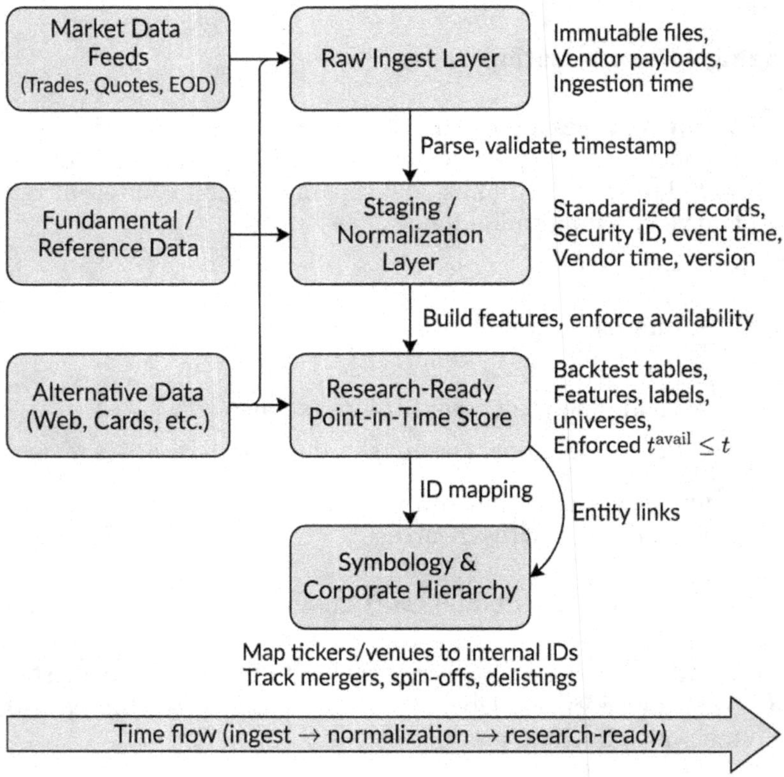

This diagram encodes two important design principles:

1. **Data flows forward only.** The raw layer is append-only; staging and research-ready tables are derived from earlier layers, never the other way around.

2. **Timestamps and IDs get richer as you move right.** You never lose information about when and from where a field arrived; you only add structure and constraints.

Timestamp Design: Event, Vendor, and Load Times

To implement point-in-time joins, your staging and research-ready tables should distinguish at least three concepts:

- t^{event}: when the market or fundamental event happened.
- t^{vendor}: when the vendor first published or modified the record.
- t^{load}: when your system ingested or recalculated it.

Often you cannot observe all three perfectly—for example, some fundamental vendors do not expose their internal arrival time. But you should store everything you can observe, and design APIs for research that always filter by an availability constraint such as:

$$t^{avail} = \max\{t^{vendor}, t^{load}\}.$$

From a modeling perspective, when you ask for features at decision time t, the data access layer should automatically apply:

$$t^{avail} \leq t - \Delta,$$

where Δ is a safety margin capturing network, processing, or trading latency. This ensures that even if your vendor is late or clocks are slightly misaligned, you are not inadvertently seeing into the future.

Versioned Snapshots for Reproducibility

Point-in-time correctness is not only about preventing look-ahead; it is also about being able to say, years later, "this is exactly the dataset I used for that experiment."

To achieve this, your research-ready layer should support versioned snapshots:

- **Data versioning.** Tables carry a data version tag (e.g., a date or hash) indicating which upstream raw and staging files they were derived from.
- **Code versioning.** The transformation logic (SQL, Python) used to build features is also versioned (e.g., Git commit hash).
- **Experiment manifests.** Each backtest or model training run records the data and code versions it used, along with configuration (universes, horizons, hyperparameters).

Technically this can be implemented with:

- Partitioned tables keyed by snapshot date.
- A separate "manifest" table that maps snapshot identifiers to raw/staging inputs.
- Automated build scripts that rebuild snapshots incrementally as new data arrives.

From a conceptual point of view, you are freezing a *view of the past*, not just a set of arbitrary files.

Enforcing Point-in-Time Constraints in Practice

With the architecture in place, the last step is to transform "good intentions" into code-level guarantees.

Database Schemas That Encode Time

Design your schemas so that it is harder to write biased queries than unbiased ones.

For example, for a fundamental table:

```
fundamentals_pt (
    security_id BIGINT,
    period_end_date DATE,
    event_time TIMESTAMP, -- announcement / filing
    avail_time TIMESTAMP, -- when usable for trading
```

```
    version_id BIGINT,
    revenue DOUBLE PRECISION,
    earnings DOUBLE PRECISION,
    ...
    PRIMARY KEY (security_id, event_time, version_id)
)
```

A typical feature extraction query then looks like:

```
SELECT *
FROM fundamentals_pt
WHERE security_id = :sid
  AND avail_time <= :decision_time;
```

Notice that the schema forces you to be explicit about availability. A table that only has period_end_date silently invites mistakes; a table with avail_time and a documented convention does not.

Time-Aware Joins in Feature Pipelines

When you join multiple point-in-time tables (e.g., prices, fundamentals, and alternative data), you want to respect each table's availability constraints. A robust pattern is:

1. Generate a *decision calendar*: for each security, list decision timestamps t (e.g., daily at 15:55 or intraday at bar close).
2. For each data source, join using:
   - A match on the security identifier.
   - A condition avail_time $\leq t - \Delta$.
   - A "last observation carried forward" rule on event_time or similar, to select the latest available record as of t.
3. Materialize the resulting feature table in the research-ready layer, tagged by snapshot version.

By centralizing this pattern in a small number of reusable functions or stored procedures, you reduce the risk that an ad hoc research notebook will quietly bypass the availability filter.

Guardrails for Researchers

Finally, put a few guardrails around your research environment:

- **Read-only access to point-in-time tables.** Researchers should not modify research-ready tables directly; changes should flow from controlled ETL processes.
- **Discourage direct vendor pulls.** It is tempting to hit vendor APIs from a notebook "just for exploration". This bypasses your point-in-time filters. Prefer pulling from the research-ready store; if a new dataset is needed, integrate it properly first.
- **Automated tests.** For each dataset, maintain small unit tests that simulate specific edge cases (e.g., a late earnings report) and verify that features at given decision times do or do not see that information.

These may feel like engineering niceties, but in systematic trading they are risk controls: they prevent you from deploying capital based on mirages.

From Plumbing to Honest Alpha

Contrarian strategies are especially vulnerable to data sins. A late correction in a price series can look like a sharp reversal; a restated earnings surprise can appear to predict past returns; a delisted firm quietly dropped from your universe can transform a mediocre strategy into a stellar one.

By defining "point-in-time" concretely, understanding the behavior of your data sources, and embedding time-awareness into your storage architecture, you make it much harder for such illusions to survive. The rest of this book will build on this foundation: every labeling scheme, model, and backtest assumes that the features it sees are the ones a real trader could have known at the time. Without that, we are not hunting market anomalies—we are hunting ghosts in the data.

2.2 Cleaning, Corporate Actions & Adjustments

In the previous section we insisted that your data must be *point-in-time correct*: the model may only see information that was actually available when the trading decision would have been made. This section tackles the next prerequisite for honest alpha: even if your data is perfectly time-aware, it may still be *wrong*, *noisy*, or *inconsistently adjusted*.

Contrarian strategies, which rely on identifying reversals and extreme moves, are particularly sensitive to these issues. A single bad price, an unadjusted stock split, or a missing delisting return can manufacture apparent reversals or momentum where none exist. Our objective here is to show, step by step, how to transform messy real-world prices into clean, corporate-action-aware histories that preserve genuine economic jumps but remove artifacts.

We proceed in three stages:

- Understanding common defects in market data and why they mimic trading signals.
- Incorporating corporate actions correctly and choosing an adjustment scheme.
- Building a repeatable, auditable cleaning and adjustment pipeline.

How Raw Prices Go Wrong

Real-world trade and quote data is not a tidy sequence of daily closes. It is a stream of messages generated by human traders, algorithms, and exchange systems. Along the way, errors and irregularities appear. If you down-sample this stream into daily bars or returns without care, you can bake those pathologies into your backtest.

Bad Ticks

A *bad tick* is a trade or quote with an obviously incorrect price or size. Causes include:

- Human input errors (extra zero, decimal misplaced).
- Systematic glitches in routing or reporting.
- Trades marked with special conditions (e.g., out-of-sequence, late prints) that are not suitable for your analysis.

For example, suppose a stock trades around $50. In the middle of the day a single erroneous trade prints at $5. If you compute a daily low of $5 and a volume-weighted average that includes that trade, you may create:

- An apparent intraday crash from $50 to $5 and back.
- A huge daily range, inflating volatility estimates.
- A large spurious negative return if you use the bad tick as a close.

A contrarian signal that "buys large losers" could easily pick up such events and appear profitable in backtest, even though no real investor could have executed at the erroneous price for meaningful size.

Practical filters for bad ticks.

Common heuristics for flagging and removing bad ticks include:

- **Range checks:** Reject trades whose price deviates excessively from recent prices or quotes. For example, drop any trade with

  $$\frac{|p_t - \tilde{p}_t|}{\tilde{p}_t} > \theta,$$

  where $\tilde{p}_t$ is a rolling median or mid-quote, and θ is a threshold such as 20%.

- **Cross-check with quotes:** Require that trades occur within (or very close to) the prevailing bid-ask spread; trades far outside are likely misprints.

- **Exchange condition codes:** Many feeds label trades as "corrected", "cancelled", or "non-standard". You can systematically exclude these from bar-building.

The art is to choose filters tight enough to remove obvious errors but not so aggressive that you delete real jumps (e.g., earnings gaps).

Out-of-Order and Stale Events

Even if every trade and quote is individually correct, their *timing* can go wrong in the data:

- Messages can arrive out of chronological order, especially across multiple venues.
- A quote may persist in a feed even though no one is actually willing to trade at that price (a *stale quote*).

Stale quotes are especially damaging to bid-ask spreads and liquidity estimates. A fictional example:

- At 10:00:00, the NBBO is 50.00 / 50.05.
- At 10:00:01, a new quote updates the ask to 50.50 on one venue, but your feed does not receive or process it.
- For several seconds, your system thinks the spread is still 5 cents, while the real spread is 50 cents.

If you compute an intraday "reversion from the bid" signal, stale or misordered quotes can create artificial predictability in mid prices and spreads.

Mitigating stale and out-of-order data.

Key steps include:

- **Sequence numbers and exchange timestamps:** Use exchange timestamps, not arrival timestamps, to order events when possible.

- **Maximum quote age:** Discard quotes that have not been updated for more than a threshold (e.g., 30 seconds) during active hours.
- **Bar-building rules:** When constructing bars (e.g., 1-minute OHLCV), define clear policies: which trades count, how to handle overlapping messages, and how to treat intervals with no trades.

Missing Days and Trading Halts

It is common for a stock to have days with no trades (illiquid securities), holidays, or exchange-specific closures. More problematic are:

- **Partial days:** A stock is halted during part of the session due to news.
- **Vendor gaps:** Your data provider simply omits price records for certain days due to technical issues.

Naively computing returns as:

$$r_t = \frac{P_t - P_{t-1}}{P_{t-1}}$$

assumes that P_{t-1} is the close from the immediately preceding trading day. If your dataset silently skips days, a multi-day move is compressed into a single large return, which may be mistaken for a one-day overreaction.

Best practice is to:

- Maintain a *trading calendar* per venue.
- Track whether each security actually traded or merely carried forward its last price.
- Treat vendor gaps differently from true non-trading days—vendor gaps should be imputed or flagged for exclusion.

Crossed and Locked Markets

In quote data, a *crossed market* occurs when the best bid exceeds the best ask; a *locked market* occurs when they are equal. These situations are usually transient and result from unsynchronized updates across venues.

If you take mid-prices as:

$$m_t = \frac{\text{bid}_t + \text{ask}_t}{2},$$

then crossed markets imply mid-prices that can jump discontinuously even when no trade occurs. A contrarian strategy that reacts to deviations of trade price from mid-quote may interpret these as price jumps.

Filtering rules typically:

- Replace crossed markets with the last non-crossed quotes.
- Enforce a non-negative spread constraint by adjusting whichever side changed last.

Corporate Actions: The Quiet Distorters

Even if your tick-level data is pristine, your time series can still be severely distorted by *corporate actions*. These are events where the firm changes its capital structure or returns value to shareholders, such as:

- Stock splits and reverse splits.
- Cash and stock dividends.
- Rights issues and bonus issues.
- Spin-offs and mergers.
- Delistings (including bankruptcies and acquisitions).

The key challenge is that corporate actions routinely change the price and share count without changing the firm's underlying value in a simple way. If you ignore these mechanics, you fabricate crashes, booms, and volume surges.

Splits and Reverse Splits

A stock split multiplies the share count and divides the price by the same factor (simplifying slightly). For example, in a 2-for-1 split:

- Before: 1 share at $100.
- After: 2 shares at $50 each.

Ignoring the split, you observe a 50% overnight loss:

$$r_{split\ day} = \frac{50 - 100}{100} = -50\%.$$

A contrarian strategy that buys the biggest losers will be all over this "opportunity". But there is no true loss; value is preserved, just sliced differently.

A reverse split (e.g., 1-for-10) has the opposite effect:

- Before: 10 shares at $1.
- After: 1 share at $10.

Ignoring it, you see a 900% gain.

Price adjustment factors.

To create a consistent price history, vendors provide split factors F_t such that:

- For a 2-for-1 split, $F_t = 0.5$ on split date t.
- For a 1-for-10 reverse split, $F_t = 10$.

You can then define an adjusted price series $\tilde{P}_t$ by chaining these factors backward or forward so that splits appear as smooth, economically neutral transitions in the adjusted series.

Dividends and Total Return

Cash dividends reduce the firm's equity value but increase the investor's cash. On the ex-dividend date, the stock price typically drops by roughly the dividend amount (ignoring taxes and frictions):

$$P_{ex} \approx P_{cum} - D,$$

where D is the dividend per share.

If you ignore dividends, you systematically understate returns for high-yield stocks and distort comparisons across securities. For contrarian research this matters in two ways:

- **Mis-measured reversals:** A one-day price drop due to a large dividend may look like an overreaction, prompting false buy signals.
- **Biased performance:** Backtested profits are overstated or understated if you do not properly reinvest or account for dividend cash flows.

A *total-return* series incorporates dividends by adjusting past prices so that:

- The adjusted price path grows by the combined effect of price appreciation and reinvested dividends.
- One-step returns computed on the adjusted series reflect total return, not just capital gains.

Vendors often provide "total return factors" that combine splits and dividends. You can build:

- A **price-only adjusted** series (splits only).
- A **total-return adjusted** series (splits and dividends).

We discuss shortly which one you should feed to a contrarian model.

Rights Issues, Spin-offs, and Complex Events

Beyond simple splits and dividends, complex corporate actions can change the mapping between price, shares, and firm value:

- **Rights issues:** Existing shareholders get the right to buy new shares at a discount. If they exercise, value is preserved; if they do not, they are diluted.
- **Spin-offs:** Part of the company's business is carved out into a new, separately traded entity. Shareholders receive shares in the new company.
- **Mergers and acquisitions:** One company absorbs another, with various cash and stock consideration.

For these, you typically rely on vendor-supplied adjustment factors or detailed corporate action records that specify how values should be re-allocated. The important conceptual point: many sudden price moves around such events are mechanical, not informational. A naive contrarian strategy might repeatedly buy "crashes" that are simply ex-rights adjustments or spin-off mechanics.

Delistings and the Disappearing Losers Problem

Delistings are where survivorship bias and corporate actions meet. A firm can be delisted because:

- It is acquired at a premium.
- It fails to meet exchange listing standards (often after severe price declines).
- It enters bankruptcy or is liquidated.

If your dataset simply stops showing prices after the last trading day, and you treat the last price as the terminal value, you ignore potentially large negative returns realized upon delisting. Contrarian strategies that buy large losers near the end of their life cycle can look fantastic in such a biased world: the worst outcomes have been silently removed.

To handle delistings correctly:

- Use a database that includes *delisting return* information (e.g., CRSP-style delisting returns).
- Incorporate the final cash flow—positive or negative—into your total-return calculations.
- Ensure your investable universe histories do not retroactively drop failing firms.

Adjustment Schemes and Their Consequences

With this background, we can discuss explicit adjustment schemes. There is no single "right" choice; the correct scheme depends on the question you are asking and the strategy you are testing.

Price-Only vs. Total-Return Adjustment

Let P_t be the raw closing price and C_t be the cumulative corporate action factor up to time t. Then:

- **Split-only adjusted price:** $\tilde{P}_t^{split} = P_t \cdot S_t$, where S_t adjusts for splits and similar nominal changes only.
- **Total-return adjusted price:** $\tilde{P}_t^{TR} = P_t \cdot T_t$, where T_t incorporates both splits and dividends (and often other distributions).

If you compute returns as:

$$r_t^{TR} = \frac{\tilde{P}_t^{TR} - \tilde{P}_{t-1}^{TR}}{\tilde{P}_{t-1}^{TR}},$$

you are effectively assuming dividends are reinvested in the stock.

Which series for contrarian signals?

For many contrarian signals:

- **Use split-only adjusted prices for price dynamics.** When measuring short-horizon reversals (1–5 days), your goal is to capture overreaction in *traded prices*, not in a hypothetical dividend-reinvested path. Splits should be neutralized, but cash dividends are part of returns.
- **Use total-return series for performance evaluation.** When you evaluate the P&L of your strategy, you want to include all cash flows—price changes, dividends, delisting payments.

This leads to a dual practice:

- Maintain both split-only and total-return histories.
- Construct labels and features from the series appropriate to the economic question.

Adjusted vs. Unadjusted Volume and Liquidity Measures

Corporate actions also affect volume and share counts. A 10-for-1 split multiplies reported volume in shares by 10, but trading *value* in dollars may be unchanged.

For liquidity and impact-sensitive contrarian strategies, you must be careful:

- **Volume in shares** should be adjusted for splits if you are comparing activity across time.
- **Dollar volume** (price times shares) is invariant to splits, but still affected by other events (e.g., rights issues).

A robust approach is to:

- Store raw, unadjusted volume and share counts from the feed.
- Compute adjusted volume series using the same factors as prices, so that measures such as turnover and participation rate are consistent through time.

A Repeatable Cleaning and Adjustment Pipeline

All of the concepts above must be embedded into a process you can run every day (or every time new data arrives), not a one-off script in a research notebook. The pipeline should be:

- **Automated:** Triggered by new data.
- **Transparent:** Every transformation is logged and reproducible.
- **Conservative:** Prefers to flag suspicious data rather than silently "fix" it.

Typical Pipeline Stages

A daily pipeline for equities might look like this:

- **Ingest raw data.** From exchange or vendor feeds into the raw layer described in the previous section.
- **Pre-cleaning at tick/quote level.**

- Remove obviously bad ticks based on range and quote checks.
- Reorder out-of-sequence events by exchange timestamp.
- Filter non-standard trades (e.g., odd-lots, special conditions) according to your bar-building policy.

- **Bar construction.**

- Build time bars (e.g., 1-minute, daily) with explicit rules for open, high, low, close, and volume.
- Handle intervals with no trades by carrying forward last price or marking them as missing, depending on your convention.

- **Corporate action application.**

- Merge in corporate action data, keyed by your internal security ID and date.
- Compute split factors and total-return factors.
- Generate split-only and total-return adjusted price and volume series.

- **Quality checks.**

- Flag extreme returns that cannot be explained by known corporate actions or news.
- Compare vendor A and vendor B (if available) on overlapping universes; discrepancies above thresholds are flagged.

- **Publish research-ready tables.**

- Store cleaned, adjusted series in the research-ready layer, tagged by snapshot and code versions.
- Update derived features and labels that depend on prices (e.g., short-horizon returns, rolling volatility).

Avoiding Over-Smoothing

While cleaning, there is a constant temptation to "fix" every ugly spike. Over-smoothing is as dangerous as under-cleaning: you can erase real price jumps and understate true risk. Consider:

- A genuine 30% overnight drop after catastrophic earnings.
- A thinly traded small-cap that periodically gaps when a single large order hits the book.

These are precisely the events that contrarian strategies might be designed to exploit or avoid. If your filters ruthlessly delete all large moves, your research will systematically underestimate the frequency and severity of tail events.

A defensible compromise is:

- Use **knowledge-aware** filters: before deleting a large move, check whether there was a split, dividend, or other documented corporate action on or near that date.
- Prefer **flagging** to automatic deletion: mark suspicious returns with a quality flag and allow models or researchers to decide whether to include them.
- Maintain **parallel series**: a minimally cleaned "conservative" series and a more aggressively cleaned one. Compare results across them.

Auditing and Diagnostics

Finally, build diagnostics into your pipeline:

- Histograms of daily returns before and after cleaning; extreme tails should shrink but not disappear.
- Counts and lists of securities with the largest adjustments; inspect a sample regularly.
- Dashboards for corporate actions by type (splits, dividends, delistings) to ensure they are being applied consistently.

These tools are not cosmetic. They are your early-warning system that a vendor changed its feed, a corporate action file shifted convention, or a bug crept into the ETL logic.

Clean Data as a Precondition for Meaningful Anomalies

Contrarian trading is about exploiting mispricings, not exploiting mistakes in your data. A naïve backtest that buys unadjusted split "crashes" or ignores delisting losses is not evidence of market inefficiency; it is evidence of missing engineering.

By understanding the anatomy of raw market data defects, treating corporate actions carefully, and embedding these lessons into a systematic cleaning and adjustment pipeline, you dramatically narrow the gap between your backtests and what a real trading system could have experienced. In the next section we will confront the remaining structural biases—survivorship, look-ahead, and selection—and show how to keep even a well-cleaned dataset from quietly cheating on your behalf.

2.3 Survivorship, Look-Ahead & Selection Bias Controls

By now we have insisted on two pillars of honest alpha. First, your data must be *point-in-time*: no record may claim to exist before it actually arrived. Second, your prices must be *clean and correctly adjusted*: no phantom crashes from splits, no missing delisting losses, no bad ticks masquerading as reversals.

Even with those in place, backtests can still cheat. The danger now is no longer obviously bad data, but subtle *structural* biases in how you define your universe, line up timestamps, and pick which ideas to report. This section focuses on three of the most important:

- **Survivorship bias:** Dropping failed or delisted assets from your universe.
- **Look-ahead bias:** Accidentally using information that was not known at the decision time.
- **Selection bias:** Cherry-picking strategies, universes, or subsamples that "worked" ex post.

We will see how each bias creeps into contrarian research, and how to build concrete defenses into your data infrastructure and code.

Three Ways a Backtest Cheats

Before going into details, it is helpful to visualize where these biases enter the research pipeline. Conceptually, every backtest follows a timeline:

- You define an *universe* of tradable assets.

- You receive and process *data* as time passes.

- You *train* models and run backtests.

Each bias has a natural "insertion point" on this timeline:

- Survivorship bias enters where you define and maintain the universe.

- Look-ahead bias enters where you join and align data with decision times.

- Selection bias enters where you choose which runs and subsamples to report.

The following schematic will serve as a map for the rest of the section.

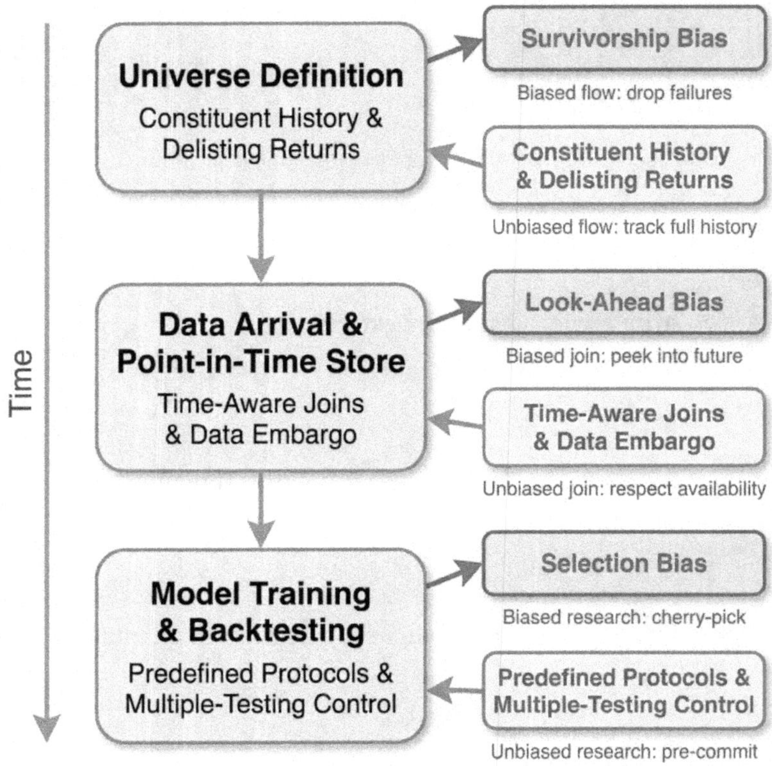

We now examine each bias type, concrete failure modes in contrarian research, and defenses you can encode in your data and code.

Survivorship Bias: The Disappearing Losers

Survivorship bias occurs when your historical universe includes only assets that *survived* to some reference date (often today), omitting those that went bankrupt, were delisted, or simply faded into illiquidity.

How Survivorship Bias Distorts Contrarian Strategies

Consider a simple daily contrarian rule: each day, buy the 10% of stocks with the worst return yesterday and hold for one day. If you run this strategy on a universe defined as "all current index members":

- Firms that crashed and never recovered enough to remain in the index are missing.
- Firms that were acquired at low prices or delisted after poor performance are missing.
- What remains is a selection of firms that, by definition, survived past episodes of distress.

The result is that the "worst losers" in your backtest are, on average, *healthier* than the real-world worst losers at the time. You may see attractive mean reversion in your simulations that would have been wiped out by the missing disasters.

This problem is not limited to indices. Any universe defined as "securities present in the database as of date T" is suspect unless the database explicitly includes dead names and delisting histories.

Maintaining Constituent History

The antidote is to maintain a *constituent history* for each index, exchange, or custom universe:

- For each security, store the full timeline of membership:

$$(\text{security\_id}, \text{universe\_id}, \text{start\_date}, \text{end\_date}).$$

- At any backtest date t, your investable universe is the set of securities for which

$$\text{start\_date} \leq t < \text{end\_date}.$$

This ensures that when you simulate trading on January 15, 2006, you see the index membership as it was known then, including future dropouts and future additions that had not yet occurred.

If you define your own universes (e.g., "top 2000 by market cap"), you must recompute them through time using point-in-time market caps, not by screening today's survivors backward.

Delisting Returns and Final Outcomes

Survivorship bias also hides the final loss (or gain) when a security disappears. As discussed in the previous section, you should:

- Include explicit delisting returns for bankruptcies, liquidations, and acquisitions.
- Treat the delisting date as the final trading date; beyond that, the security is unavailable.

For a contrarian strategy that gravitates toward distressed names, this is crucial. Without delisting returns, the tail of bad outcomes is artificially truncated, making the strategy appear safer and more profitable.

Concrete Implementation Patterns

In practice:

- Store universe membership in a dedicated, point-in-time table in your research-ready layer.
- When constructing daily decision rows, join prices and features only for securities that were alive and in-universe at that date.
- Expose helper functions in your research API that make it easier to request "the investable universe on date t" than to hard-code symbol lists.

The goal is to make the unbiased path the path of least resistance.

Look-Ahead Bias: Peeking into the Future

Look-ahead bias arises when your model uses information that would not have been known at the decision time. The previous chapter on point-in-time data laid the conceptual groundwork; here we focus on how look-ahead sneaks into feature engineering and label construction for contrarian strategies.

Where Look-Ahead Hides

There are three especially common failure modes:

Using end-of-day prices to trade earlier the same day.

Suppose you backtest a daily contrarian rule that buys stocks with large intraday drops and assumes trading at the closing price. You construct features using:

- Today's close-to-close return.
- Today's volume spike.

If you make decisions at the close, these features are not available yet; they include the entire day's trading. Unless your execution assumption explicitly states that you trade on the next day's open, you are using information from the future of your decision time.

Ignoring reporting lags in fundamentals and alternative data.

You compute a "value" contrarian signal using the most recently filed earnings as of calendar date t, but your fundamental table stores only period_end_date. If you join by "last quarter with period end $\leq t$", you implicitly assume earnings were known at the quarter's end, ignoring actual filing and vendor publication dates.

Restated and revised data.

A company restates a prior quarter's results in 2018, and your vendor overwrites the 2017 values. If you use that vendor table in a backtest covering 2017, your models see the restated numbers before they existed.

Time-Aware Joins and Data Embargoes

The main defense is to enforce time-aware joins everywhere:

- For each feature source, maintain an avail_time field representing when the information became tradable in your system.
- When building features at decision time t, require:

  $$\text{avail\_time} \leq t - \Delta,$$

  where Δ is a safety margin for processing and trading latency.

In intraday settings, an additional guard is a *data embargo*: when evaluating a model on a period $[t_0, t_1]$, you exclude nearby periods from training to avoid subtle leakage through overlapping windows or cross-validation folds.

Overlapping Targets and Future Bar Leakage

Contrarian labels often use short-horizon returns, such as "next-day" or "next-5-day" performance. If you define:

$$r_{t,t+5} = \frac{P_{t+5} - P_t}{P_t},$$

and you train on daily observations $\{t\}$, your training examples are heavily overlapping: $r_{t,t+5}$ and $r_{t+1,t+6}$ share four days of price information. This is not, by itself, look-ahead bias, but it does mean that naive cross-validation can leak information across folds.

More subtle is the mistake of using the entire bar (including closing price) both as a feature and to define the label boundary. For example:

- Features for day t computed from bar t (open, high, low, close).
- Label defined as return from close t to close $t + 1$.

If your trading decision is modeled as happening at the close of day t, then using the full-day bar, especially the close itself, as a feature assumes you knew the price at which you are about to trade. Sometimes this is intended (e.g., VWAP strategies that trade throughout the day), but you must make the timing assumption explicit.

Implementation Patterns

To guard against look-ahead:

- Encode decision times explicitly in your feature tables (e.g., decision_time).
- Build features using only data whose availability times are earlier than the decision time.
- For bar-based features, clarify whether the decision is at bar open, within-bar, or at bar close, and adjust which fields are allowed.

- In cross-validation, group samples by time blocks to avoid train/test overlaps that leak future patterns.

These mechanisms complement the point-in-time storage from earlier chapters; they ensure that your modeling code respects the same temporal discipline as your database.

Selection Bias: Cherry-Picking Winners

Selection bias is more diffuse than survivorship or look-ahead. It captures the many ways in which, after running many tests and seeing many results, you end up reporting only the best-looking ones.

In anomaly hunting this is nearly unavoidable: you try many signals, many holding periods, many universes. But if you do not account for this multiplicity, the "best" strategy in your notebook is very likely to be a statistical accident.

How Selection Bias Appears in Practice

Typical patterns include:

- **Universe-tuning:** You start with all stocks, then refine to "mid-caps only", then "mid-caps excluding financials", and so on, until performance looks good.
- **Horizon-tuning:** You try holding periods of 1, 2, 5, 10 days and choose the one with the highest Sharpe ratio.
- **Conditioning on ex-post liquidity or spreads:** You keep only stocks that, in hindsight, traded above a certain volume or below a certain spread, removing difficult-to-trade names that would have hurt live performance.
- **Discarding failed ideas:** Dozens of backtests that produced no edge quietly disappear from the narrative, leaving only the stars.

Each individual choice may seem reasonable, but collectively they amount to *cherry-picking* among many noisy realizations. The more you search, the more likely you are to find something that looks good by chance alone.

Universe Definition vs. Universe Tuning

One of the most pernicious interactions is between universe selection and strategy performance. For example:

- A strategy seems to work only on small caps.
- Then it seems to work only on small caps in a certain region.
- Then it seems to work only during certain years.

There may be a genuine economic reason for such patterns. But if you did not specify these filters before looking at the results, you have *conditioned* on favorable noise.

A disciplined approach is to distinguish:

- **Design time:** Before running large-scale tests, you define a small number of universes that are economically motivated (e.g., "U.S. large and mid-caps with at least $10M of average daily dollar volume").
- **Analysis time:** After seeing results, you may explore heterogeneity across subuniverses, but you treat such findings as hypotheses to be validated out-of-sample, not as final evidence.

Structurally, this means your infrastructure should:

- Store universe definitions and their rationale.
- Tag backtests with the universe used.
- Make it easy to rerun the same strategy across pre-defined universes, but harder to define ad hoc narrow subsets ex post.

Multiple Testing and False Discoveries

From a statistical perspective, running many backtests is a multiple-testing problem. If you run N independent strategies with no true edge, the maximum observed Sharpe ratio across them will be positive with high probability—often temptingly high.

Formally, if S_i is the estimated Sharpe for strategy i, and under the null all S_i are centered around zero, then:

$$\max_{1 \le i \le N} S_i$$

grows with N. Without correction, you are very likely to declare a false discovery.

While a full treatment of multiple-testing control comes later in the book, at the infrastructure level you can already:

- **Log every backtest.** Maintain an experiment registry that records each strategy specification, universe, period, and result. This makes the search space explicit.
- **Separate exploration and confirmation.** Use one time period (or market) for idea generation and another, untouched period for confirmation. Only strategies that survive the second phase move forward.
- **Penalize complexity.** Prefer simpler strategies with fewer tuned parameters; complex rules that fit a particular sample are more likely to be artifacts.

Coding Patterns and Checklists for Bias Control

To make these defenses practical, you need concrete patterns and checks in your research code.

Bias-Resistant Data Access

Design your data access API to enforce good behavior by default:

- Functions that return price and feature panels should require an explicit universe identifier and date range.
- The universe identifier should map to a point-in-time constituent history, not a static symbol list.

- Joins between features and labels should internally apply availability constraints and avoid overlapping training and test windows.

By contrast, providing raw tables and encouraging ad hoc SQL joins is an invitation to subtle look-ahead and survivorship errors.

A Pre-Trade Checklist

Before trusting a backtest result, you can run it through a brief checklist:

- **Universe:**
  - Does the universe include dead and delisted names?
  - Was it defined using only information available at each date?
- **Timing:**
  - For each feature, is the availability time earlier than the decision time?
  - Are labels constructed from non-overlapping future windows, or is any dependence properly handled?
- **Corporate actions:**
  - Are splits, dividends, and delistings handled consistently in both signals and P&L?
- **Search:**
  - How many related strategies and universes were tried?
  - Is there an untouched period or market where the strategy was validated?

You can automate parts of this checklist: for instance, require that any production candidate strategy includes a summary from the experiment registry listing how many siblings were tested.

Embedding Controls into the Research Workflow

Finally, integrate these ideas into your daily research practice:

- **Templates:** Provide notebook or script templates that already include point-in-time data pulls, universe selection, and evaluation routines with proper cross-validation.
- **Education:** Make new team members explicitly aware of survivorship, look-ahead, and selection biases, with concrete examples from your own history where they caused problems.
- **Review:** Treat major new strategies like code changes: require peer review that specifically checks for these biases.

From Clean Data to Credible Evidence

Contrarian strategies often target exactly those segments of the market most exposed to bias: distressed names, thinly traded stocks, and short-horizon reversals that can be magnified by data issues. It is therefore not enough to have sophisticated models; the scaffolding around them must be robust.

In this chapter we have combined three elements:

- Point-in-time data sourcing and storage to prevent future information from leaking backward.
- Cleaning and corporate-action adjustments to remove artifacts and preserve genuine price dynamics.
- Survivorship, look-ahead, and selection bias controls to ensure that your universes, joins, and research process do not quietly tilt the odds in your favor.

Together, these form the "invisible half" of any serious anomaly research program. The next chapter will build on this foundation to define labels and sampling schemes that align what your models learn with trades you can actually execute, completing the data side of the hunt for honest contrarian alpha.

2.4 Labeling Events & Sampling Schemes

Up to this point we have focused on the *inputs* to your models: building point-in-time data stores, cleaning prices, and controlling for structural biases in universes and joins. We now turn to an equally important but often less visible choice: *what exactly you ask the model to predict*, and *when* you ask it to make that prediction.

In machine learning language, this is the problem of **labeling** (defining the target variable) and **sampling** (choosing the observation times). In trading language, it is the problem of deciding:

- Which economic event constitutes a "trade opportunity".
- Over what horizon a contrarian effect is supposed to play out.
- How closely the data clock matches the trading clock.

Labels and sampling clocks are deceptively powerful. Given the same cleaned, unbiased dataset, two different labeling choices can lead one researcher to "discover" strong contrarian effects and another to "prove" they do not exist. To design robust, tradable contrarian signals, you must ensure the labels reflect real trading outcomes and not arbitrary artifacts of how you sliced the time series.

From Price Paths to Prediction Targets

Start with a simple object: the cleaned, corporate-action-aware price path of a stock, say daily close prices $\{P_t\}$. Even this apparently simple sequence can give rise to many different labels:

- Next-day return.
- 5-day cumulative return.
- Whether a profit target or stop-loss barrier is hit first.
- Whether a short-term move is a reversal or a trend continuation.

Each label encodes a particular economic story. For contrarian strategies, the story is usually:

> "When a sufficiently extreme move or imbalance occurs at time t, will the price, over some horizon, tend to revert or continue?"

Translating that into a model-friendly label involves three main design decisions:

- **Event definition:** What counts as a "signal event"? A large negative return? A volatility spike? A jump in order imbalance?
- **Prediction horizon and payoff:** Over what period do you measure outcome, and how do you summarize it (raw return, risk-adjusted return, barrier outcome)?
- **Sampling scheme:** At which times do you create labeled examples, and how do overlapping trades interact?

We will examine these choices step by step.

Fixed-Horizon Return Labels

The simplest and most common label is a fixed-horizon forward return. For a decision at time t, you define:

$$r_{t \to t+H} = \frac{P_{t+H} - P_t}{P_t},$$

where H is a fixed number of time steps (e.g., 1 day, 5 days, 1 hour).

For a contrarian classifier, you might convert this to a sign label:

$$y_t = \begin{cases} +1 & \text{if } r_{t \to t+H} > c_{pos}, \\ 0 & \text{if } |r_{t \to t+H}| \le c_{neut}, \\ -1 & \text{if } r_{t \to t+H} < -c_{neg}, \end{cases}$$

where $c_{pos}, c_{neg}, c_{neut}$ are thresholds that define what counts as a meaningful move versus noise.

Economic Interpretation

In this setup, the model is effectively asked:

> "Conditional on information available at t, will a long (or short) position held for H units produce a positive or negative return beyond transaction costs?"

This aligns naturally with simple trading rules: enter at t, exit at $t + H$. It also aligns with standard backtesting engines that operate on fixed holding periods.

Pitfalls and Remedies

However, there are several subtleties:

Transaction costs. If the average bid-ask spread and fees for your universe are, say, 10 basis points (0.1%), a model that "predicts" a 5 basis point average move is not economically useful. You can handle this by:

- Building transaction-cost estimates directly into the label thresholds $c_\cdot$.
- Or treating raw returns as labels, but later applying cost-aware decision rules.

Volatility scaling. A 1% move in a low-volatility large-cap stock is more remarkable than a 1% move in a highly volatile small-cap. For contrarian signals, you often care about *standardized* returns, e.g.:

$$\tilde{r}_{t\to t+H} = \frac{r_{t\to t+H}}{\hat{\sigma}_t},$$

where $\hat{\sigma}_t$ is an estimate of forward-looking volatility based on history up to t. Labels based on $\tilde{r}$ capture how exceptional the move was, not just its raw size.

Market direction. Contrarian equity strategies often bet on mean reversion in *relative* performance, not in the market level. A large negative stock return during a market crash may be less informative than its performance relative to the market or sector. You can define labels in terms of residual returns:

$$r^{excess}_{t \to t+H} = r_{t \to t+H} - r^{benchmark}_{t \to t+H},$$

and then label based on r^{excess}.

Barrier-Based and Event-Driven Labels

Fixed horizons are simple, but markets do not know your chosen H. A price that reverses sharply in two days and then trends for eight more will look very different depending on whether you choose $H = 2$, $H = 5$, or $H = 10$.

An alternative is to define labels in terms of *barriers*: price levels that represent profit targets or stop-losses. For example:

- An upper barrier at $P_t(1 + u)$.
- A lower barrier at $P_t(1 - d)$.
- An optional time limit H_{max}.

You then track the future path $\{P_{t+1}, P_{t+2}, \dots\}$ until:

- Either the upper barrier is hit (favorable outcome for a long contrarian trade),
- Or the lower barrier is hit (unfavorable outcome),
- Or the time limit is reached without hitting either barrier.

This yields a label such as:

$$y_t = \begin{cases} +1 & \text{if upper barrier hit first,} \\ -1 & \text{if lower barrier hit first,} \\ 0 & \text{if neither hit within } H_{max}. \end{cases}$$

Why Barriers Are Natural for Contrarian Trades

Contrarian strategies often think in terms of:

> "If the price has overreacted today, it will revert by at least $x\%$ with reasonable probability before it moves further against me by $y\%$."

Barrier-based labels match this thinking:

- u and d can be chosen to approximate your desired risk-reward profile.
- The time limit H_{max} caps how long capital can be tied up.

Crucially, barrier labels are less sensitive than fixed-horizon labels to arbitrary choices of H. They focus on "which happens first, a favorable or unfavorable move?" rather than on the exact return at a preset time.

Complex Labels: Reversal vs. Trend Continuation

You can refine the barrier idea to distinguish reversals from continuations. For example, define:

- A short-term barrier capturing immediate reaction (e.g., within 2 days).
- A medium-term barrier capturing subsequent behavior (e.g., days 3–10).

Labels can then encode patterns like:

- "Sharp drop followed by quick bounce" (class: immediate reversal).
- "Sharp drop followed by further decline" (class: continuation).
- "No significant move" (class: neutral).

Such multi-class labels allow models to learn when an apparent overreaction is more likely to be a genuine regime change.

Sampling Clocks: Time, Tick, Volume, Dollar Bars

Once you have a label definition, you still must choose when to sample observations. Financial time series are irregular: trades cluster during active periods and dry up during quiet ones. If you sample on a simple time grid (e.g., every minute or every day), you introduce a bias: active periods contribute many more observations, which can distort models.

Several bar types are commonly used:

- **Time bars:** One observation every fixed time interval (1 minute, 5 minutes, 1 day).
- **Tick bars:** One observation every fixed number of trades.
- **Volume bars:** One observation every time traded volume accumulates to a threshold.
- **Dollar bars:** One observation every time traded dollar value (price $\times$ volume) reaches a threshold.

For contrarian research, the choice of bar type affects:

- How you define "extreme moves" (relative to what baseline).
- The distribution of labels (more or fewer reversals).
- The dependence structure between observations.

Time Bars: Simple but Uneven

Daily or intraday time bars are easiest to work with:

- Align naturally with many institutional processes (closing auctions, risk checks).
- Facilitate integration with fundamental and reference data (often reported daily or quarterly).

However, periods of intense trading produce higher volatility within a bar, while quiet periods produce flat bars. If you define contrarian signals based on time-bar returns, you implicitly weight calm market hours and frantic ones equally.

Volume and Dollar Bars: Equalizing Trading Activity

Volume and dollar bars aim to make each observation represent roughly the same amount of trading activity:

- A volatile period with many trades yields many bars.
- A quiet period yields few bars.

For contrarian strategies based on microstructure effects (e.g., order imbalance, short-term impact), this can be appealing: you treat "units of trading" as the clock, not wall-clock time. Labels like "next-bar reversal" then refer to a future of comparable economic significance (similar traded volume), even if that corresponds to different calendar durations.

At daily horizons, time bars usually suffice, but understanding the bias they introduce helps align your intraday and daily research.

Overlapping Labels and Dependence

A central issue in labeling for time series is **overlap**. If you generate a label at every bar t with a horizon H, then labels for $t, t+1, ..., t+H-1$ share much of the same future path. This creates strong dependence between training examples.

For contrarian strategies, which often use short horizons, overlap is almost unavoidable. But you must account for it when designing models and validation:

- **Inflated sample size:** Treating overlapping labels as independent can lead you to underestimate uncertainty and overstate significance.
- **Leakage in cross-validation:** Randomly splitting overlapping examples into training and test sets allows information about the future price path to leak across the split.

Non-Overlapping Sampling

One simple remedy is to sample only every H-th bar; for horizon H, you might use only times $t = H, 2H, 3H, \ldots$. This ensures non-overlapping label windows, at the cost of fewer examples.

For example, with daily data and $H = 5$, you might sample only every 5th day. This is statistically clean but can be wasteful when you have limited history or want to study conditional effects around specific events (earnings, news).

Event-Driven Sampling

An alternative is event-driven sampling. Instead of labeling every bar, you label only when some triggering event occurs, e.g.:

- The stock's return over the past day is in the bottom 5% cross-sectionally.
- Intraday order imbalance exceeds a threshold.
- A news item or earnings announcement hits the tape.

You then define horizons relative to this event and often avoid overlapping by construction (e.g., do not label again until the previous trade's horizon is complete). This can dramatically reduce redundancy and focus the model on situations where contrarian effects are plausibly strongest.

Aligning Labels with Real Execution

A label is only as meaningful as your ability to trade on it. This requires careful alignment between:

- The decision time t.
- The data available at t (as enforced by your point-in-time store).
- The execution price and horizon.

Decision at Close vs. Open

Two common conventions for daily strategies are:

- **Close-to-close labels:** Decision at (or just before) the close on day t, execution priced at close P_t^{close}, label defined as return to next close P_{t+1}^{close}.
- **Close-to-open labels:** Decision after close t using data up to that close, execution at next day's open P_{t+1}^{open}, label defined accordingly.

The first assumes you can react right at the close with negligible latency. The second is more conservative and often closer to how discretionary desks operate. In each case, your label definition and feature timestamps must match this assumption; otherwise, you are mixing incompatible worlds.

For intraday contrarian strategies (e.g., betting on reversion after midday overreaction), the same logic applies at finer granularity: you must specify whether the model decides and trades within the same bar or on the next one.

Incorporating Execution Constraints

Real trades face:

- Slippage relative to mid-quote or last price.
- Limited participation in thin names.
- Market impact for larger orders.

Labels that ignore these effects may teach the model to identify patterns that are only exploitable at unrealistic sizes or costs. While detailed cost modeling is a separate topic, you can partially integrate these concerns at the labeling stage by:

- Excluding labels where expected costs exceed some fraction of the predicted move.
- Conditioning labels on feasible position sizes (e.g., maximum participation rate).
- Defining outcome in terms of achievable prices (e.g., VWAP over an execution window) rather than idealized closes.

Class Imbalance and Rare Events

Contrarian trades often focus on rare extremes: the worst 5% of returns, the most illiquid sell-offs, the most dramatic intraday reversals. Consequently, labels may be highly imbalanced:

- Only a small fraction of times correspond to extreme events (potential trades).
- Among those, only some produce profitable reversals.

A naive classifier trained on all times might mostly see neutral cases and learn to always predict "no trade" or "no edge", missing the pockets where contrarian effects matter.

To address this:

- Use event-driven sampling to focus the training set on situations where a trade is even considered.
- Consider asymmetric loss functions or class weights that penalize errors on rare but important classes.
- Evaluate models using metrics that reflect trading objectives (e.g., expected return per trade, hit rate in the tails), not just overall accuracy.

Template Labeling Schemes for Contrarian Research

Bringing these ideas together, it is useful to define a small set of template schemes that you and your team reuse. Examples include:

Daily cross-sectional mean-reversion (fixed horizon).

- Universe: liquid equities with point-in-time universe controls.
- Sampling: daily, at close.
- Event filter: all stocks, but features highlight recent extreme losers/winners.

- Label: 1-day or 5-day *excess* return vs. benchmark, computed close-to-close with split-only adjusted prices.

Intraday overreaction reversal (barrier-based).

- Universe: top N most liquid stocks.
- Sampling: 5-minute or dollar bars.
- Event: bar return below a negative threshold relative to recent volatility.
- Label: which is hit first over the next H_{max} minutes—a profit-take barrier (e.g., +0.5%) or stop-loss barrier (e.g., -0.3%).

Earnings surprise drift vs. reversal (multi-horizon).

- Universe: firms with earnings announcements.
- Sampling: event-driven at earnings release time.
- Label: combination of short-horizon (e.g., 1-day) and medium-horizon (e.g., 20-day) excess returns, possibly discretized into reversal vs. continuation categories.

Each template should:

- Be fully specified in terms of decision time, execution assumption, horizon, and cost baseline.
- Be implemented once, carefully, using your point-in-time store and bias controls.
- Serve as a building block for many models and feature sets.

Stress-Testing Labeling and Sampling Choices

Finally, labels and sampling schemes should themselves be treated as hypotheses, not as immutable facts. You can stress-test them by:

- Varying the horizon H or barrier levels slightly and checking whether the qualitative conclusions persist.
- Comparing time bars to volume or dollar bars to see whether apparent edges depend on the sampling clock.
- Shifting decision times (e.g., using previous bar close vs. next bar open) to ensure that results do not hinge on an unrealistic timing assumption.

If a contrarian anomaly vanishes or reverses whenever you tweak the labeling scheme slightly, it is likely an artifact of that particular construction rather than a robust market pattern.

In summary, designing labels and sampling schemes is the step where abstract economic ideas about contrarian behavior meet the concrete demands of machine learning. By grounding your targets in realistic trading horizons, carefully chosen clocks, and event definitions that respect costs and constraints, you greatly increase the chance that what your models learn will correspond to genuine, repeatable trading edges rather than quirks of how you carved up the past.

Chapter 3

Statistical & Time-Series Foundations

Contrarian trading lives and dies on small edges buried in volatile, dependent price data. This chapter arms you with the statistical and time-series foundations needed to separate genuine mean-reversion from illusion: you'll learn how tails really behave, how to test fragile signals without fooling yourself, and how to model reversion dynamics in ways that can actually be traded.

3.1 Probability Distributions & Tail Risk

Contrarian trading is built on a simple empirical observation: prices sometimes move "too far" in the short run and then partially reverse. To turn that sentence into a robust trading rule, you must answer three quantitative questions:

1. How do we define "too far" in a consistent, numerical way?
2. Given that a move looks extreme, how often do such extremes

occur?

3. When they occur, how bad can things get if the move keeps going against us?

All three are questions about *distributions of returns*. This section develops the basic language of distributions, connects it to empirical features of financial data, and then ties those features back to practical decisions about sizing and limits in contrarian strategies.

Random Returns and Distributions

Consider a simple daily close-to-close log-return on an asset:

$$r_t = \log P_t - \log P_{t-1}.$$

Before the market opens on day t, r_t is unknown. We treat it as a *random variable*: a quantity that can take on different values with certain probabilities.

Formally, a random variable R has an associated *probability distribution*. For our purposes you can think of this in two equivalent ways:

- **Discrete view:** There is a set of possible outcomes $r_1, r_2, \ldots$ and probabilities $\mathbb{P}(R = r_i)$ that sum to one.
- **Continuous view:** There is a density function $f(r)$ such that for small intervals

$$\mathbb{P}\big(r \le R \le r + \Delta r\big) \approx f(r)\,\Delta r,$$

  and the total area under f is one.

In finance we usually work with continuous approximations, even though observed returns are discrete at the tick level. The key object for risk management is the *cumulative distribution function (CDF)*,

$$F(r) = \mathbb{P}(R \le r),$$

which tells us the probability that the return is at or below a threshold r. Tail risk lives in the extreme ends of this CDF—very negative r for downside risk and very positive r for upside windfalls.

Moments: Mean, Variance, Skewness, Kurtosis

A distribution is a full, infinite object, but we often summarize its main features with a few *moments*. For contrarian trading, four are particularly important.

Mean (first moment). The mean (or expected value)

$$\mu = \mathbb{E}[R]$$

is the long-run average return if we could sample R many times. For daily equity index log-returns, μ is typically small (e.g., 0.03%–0.05% per day), often negligible over a 1–5 day contrarian horizon. This is why short-horizon contrarian edges of a few basis points matter.

Variance and standard deviation (second moment). The variance

$$\sigma^2 = \mathbb{E}\big[(R-\mu)^2\big]$$

measures the dispersion of returns around the mean; the standard deviation σ is its square root. In practice, contrarian traders often think in terms of *z-scores*:

$$z_t = \frac{r_t - \hat{\mu}}{\hat{\sigma}},$$

where $\hat{\mu}$ and $\hat{\sigma}$ are sample estimates. A move of $z_t = -2$ means the return is two "volatility units" below average. Position-sizing rules and entry triggers are often expressed directly in terms of z.

Skewness (third moment). Skewness captures asymmetry:

$$\text{Skew}(R) = \frac{\mathbb{E}\big[(R-\mu)^3\big]}{\sigma^3}.$$

- Positive skew: long right tail, many small losses and a few big gains.
- Negative skew: long left tail, many small gains and a few big losses.

Many contrarian and option-writing strategies exhibit negative skew: they earn frequent small profits by leaning against moves, but occasionally suffer large losses when trends persist.

Kurtosis (fourth moment). Kurtosis measures tail thickness relative to a normal (Gaussian) distribution:

$$\text{Kurt}(R) = \frac{\mathbb{E}\left[(R-\mu)^4\right]}{\sigma^4}.$$

The normal distribution has kurtosis 3; we often report *excess kurtosis* as $\text{Kurt}(R) - 3$. Financial returns tend to have positive excess kurtosis: more probability in the tails and more mass near zero than a Gaussian with the same μ and σ. This phenomenon is known as *fat* or *heavy* tails.

From a contrarian perspective, high kurtosis means:

- Extreme signals (e.g., $|z_t| > 3$) occur more often than the normal model predicts, providing more entry opportunities.
- But losses when you are on the wrong side of an extreme can be much larger than Gaussian-based risk models suggest.

Gaussian Idealization vs. Fat-Tailed Reality

The normal distribution is appealing because it is mathematically convenient and fully characterized by μ and σ:

$$R \sim \mathcal{N}(\mu, \sigma^2).$$

Under this assumption:

- About 68% of observations lie within $\pm 1\sigma$ of the mean.
- About 95% lie within $\pm 2\sigma$.
- About 99.7% lie within $\pm 3\sigma$.

A -3σ daily move should be a once-in-years event.

Empirically, this is not what we see. Even on large, diversified equity indices, 3σ and 4σ moves occur far more often than the normal model allows. Single stocks and leveraged products are even more extreme. This mismatch is not a minor detail: it directly affects how we set stop-losses, capital at risk, and stress tests.

One way to model fat tails is with the Student-t distribution. A standardized t-distribution with ν degrees of freedom has density

$$f_\nu(r) = \frac{\Gamma\left(\frac{\nu+1}{2}\right)}{\sqrt{\nu\pi}\,\Gamma\left(\frac{\nu}{2}\right)}\left(1+\frac{r^2}{\nu}\right)^{-\frac{\nu+1}{2}}.$$

For large ν, t_ν behaves like a normal; for small ν the tails are much heavier. In practice, daily returns for liquid assets often look roughly Gaussian near the center but t-like in the tails.

Why this matters for contrarian traders. Suppose your entry rule is "go long when $z_t \leq -2$." Under a normal model, this should happen only about 2.3% of days. Under a fat-tailed model, it might happen 4%–6% of days instead. You will trade more frequently and your realized drawdown profile will be dominated by those tail events. A normal-based Value-at-Risk (VaR) will systematically underestimate the worst losses you experience precisely when your positions are largest (because signals are extreme).

Empirical vs. Model Distributions

It is often instructive to compare:

1. The *empirical distribution* of observed returns, summarized by a histogram or kernel density estimate.

2. Fitted parametric models, such as a normal and a Student-t with degrees of freedom chosen to match sample moments.

The histogram reveals what actually happened in your data sample; the model densities tell you what your risk engine assumes will happen in the future. For contrarian strategies, discrepancies in the tails are more important than discrepancies near the center.

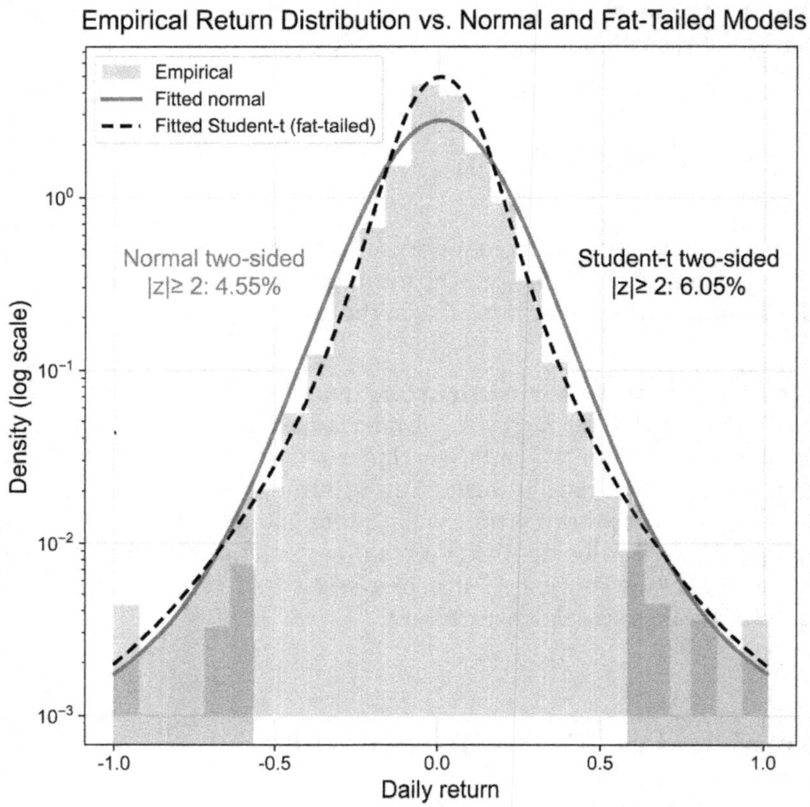

Figure 3.1: Empirical histogram of simulated daily returns with overlaid normal and Student-t (fat-tailed) densities. The log-scale y-axis emphasizes differences in the tails; shaded regions mark the two-sided $|z| \geq 2$ tail under a Gaussian assumption.

Figure illustrates two key points:

1. Near zero, both models track the empirical histogram reasonably well.

2. In the tails, the Student-t density aligns much better with the observed extremes, while the normal density decays too fast.

From a contrarian perspective, you can read this as: "if I use a normal model to decide what is extreme, I will systematically underestimate how often extremes occur and how large they can be."

Tail Risk Measures: VaR, Expected Shortfall, Drawdowns

To connect distributions to trading decisions, we need risk measures that focus on the tails.

Value-at-Risk (VaR). For a given confidence level α (e.g., 95% or 99%) and horizon (e.g., 1 day), the α-VaR is the loss threshold that is exceeded with probability $1-\alpha$:

$$\text{VaR}_\alpha = \inf\{x : \mathbb{P}(L \le x) \ge \alpha\},$$

where L is the loss (negative of P&L). For a normal loss distribution $L \sim \mathcal{N}(\mu_L, \sigma_L^2)$,

$$\text{VaR}_\alpha = \mu_L + z_\alpha \sigma_L,$$

with z_α the α-quantile of the standard normal. Under fat tails, this formula understates the actual loss you see once every 20 or 100 days.

Expected Shortfall (ES). VaR tells you the threshold of bad events, but not how bad things can get once you cross it. Expected Shortfall (also called Conditional VaR) is the average loss given that the loss exceeds VaR:

$$\text{ES}_\alpha = \mathbb{E}\big[L \,\big|\, L \ge \text{VaR}_\alpha\big].$$

For fat-tailed distributions, ES can be much larger (in units of σ) than VaR, whereas under a normal assumption the gap is modest. ES better captures the *shape* of the tail, not just its starting point.

Drawdown distributions. Contrarian traders often think in terms of *equity curve* behavior rather than single-day losses. A drawdown is the drop from a running peak to a subsequent trough. The distribution of maximum drawdowns over a month, quarter, or year is a complex function of the full return distribution, including dependence across days. Nonetheless, a first approximation is that fatter daily tails and negative skew translate into more frequent and deeper drawdowns.

A practical workflow is:

1. Estimate a realistic fat-tailed model for strategy returns (e.g., Student-t residuals).
2. Simulate many paths (Monte Carlo).
3. For each path, compute the maximum drawdown over your horizon.
4. Use the empirical distribution of these drawdowns to inform leverage, margin buffers, and risk limits.

Beyond Correlation: Dependence and Joint Tails

So far we have treated returns as if they were independent draws. In reality, financial data exhibit:

- **Volatility clustering:** large-magnitude returns (both positive and negative) tend to arrive in bursts.
- **Cross-asset dependence:** assets in the same sector, or across risk-on markets, tend to move together, especially in crises.

For a single series, volatility clustering means that extreme contrarian signals are more likely to occur in clusters. If you scale your positions naively by a long-run $\hat{\sigma}$, you will be over-levered just when volatility spikes. For a portfolio of contrarian trades, cross-asset dependence means that many supposedly independent bets can all lose money simultaneously.

The simplest way to summarize dependence between two random variables R_1 and R_2 is the *correlation*:

$$\rho = \frac{\mathbb{E}\big[(R_1 - \mu_1)(R_2 - \mu_2)\big]}{\sigma_1 \sigma_2}.$$

However, correlation has two important limitations:

1. It is symmetric and linear: it captures only average co-movements, not how dependence behaves in the tails.
2. It can be misleading when volatilities change over time; unconditional ρ may mask regime shifts.

Joint tails. For risk sizing, the crucial question is:

$$\mathbb{P}(R_1 \leq r_1,\ R_2 \leq r_2),$$

for large negative r_1 and r_2. This is the probability that both assets or strategies experience extreme losses together. Two strategies may have low or moderate correlation in normal times, but exhibit strong co-crashes in stressed markets. This feature is called *tail dependence.*

A useful conceptual tool here is the *copula,* which separates:

- The marginal distributions of each asset (how heavy their individual tails are).
- The dependence structure linking them (how often extremes coincide).

You do not need to implement copulas to benefit from the intuition: it is not enough to know individual VaRs; you must consider how losses stack up across positions in joint tail events.

Practical implications for contrarian portfolios.

- **Diversification illusions:** Many mean-reversion signals built on similar underlying risk factors (e.g., equity value vs. equity quality spreads) may all blow up together when the equity risk premium reprices. Counting them as independent because their daily correlations are 0.3–0.4 is dangerous.
- **Position limits by cluster:** Instead of sizing each trade in isolation, group trades by underlying driver (asset class, sector, risk factor) and set aggregate limits by cluster, informed by joint tail behavior in historical stress episodes.
- **Volatility and correlation regimes:** Use rolling or regime-dependent estimates of volatility and dependence, rather than a single unconditional covariance matrix, to adjust leverage and gross exposure when markets become turbulent.

From Distributional Insights to Sizing and Limits

The goal of distributional thinking is not theoretical elegance; it is to make more informed, quantitatively consistent decisions about how much risk to take when you lean against extremes.

Here is a concrete checklist linking concepts in this section to trading practice:

1. **Define signals in standardized units.** Use rolling estimates of μ_t and σ_t to compute z-scores for prices, spreads, or returns. Trigger entries at thresholds like $|z| \geq 2$ or $|z| \geq 2.5$, but recognize that under fat tails these events are more common than Gaussian theory suggests.

2. **Estimate fat-tailed models, not just Gaussians.** Fit simple Student-t or mixture-normal models to your residual returns. Use them to compute VaR and ES that reflect empirically observed tail behavior, rather than blindly applying normal formulas.

3. **Translate tail metrics into position sizes.** For each strategy, choose a capital-at-risk limit (e.g., "1-day $\text{ES}_{97.5\%}$ must not exceed x% of NAV") and back out the leverage factor that satisfies this limit under your fat-tailed model.

4. **Account for volatility clustering.** Base $\hat{\sigma}_t$ on recent data (e.g., exponentially weighted volatility or a GARCH forecast) so that your notion of a "2σ move" adapts to current conditions. In high-vol regimes, entry thresholds in raw return units widen automatically, and position sizes per unit of z shrink.

5. **Incorporate dependence into portfolio limits.** Use historical stress episodes to estimate how often multiple signals are simultaneously in the tail, and by how much. Set tighter gross and net exposure limits during regimes where joint tail risk is high.

6. **Simulate drawdowns under realistic tails.** Given your estimated distribution (including fat tails and dependence), run Monte Carlo simulations of the full portfolio. Examine the distribution of maximum drawdowns and time-under-water. Use these outputs to calibrate investor expectations and to enforce hard stop-out rules at the portfolio level.

By grounding your contrarian strategy in realistic distributions—with heavy tails, volatility clustering, and joint extremes—you move from loosely defined "overreactions" to a precise language of probabilities and losses. This, in turn, provides the foundation on which the next sections will build: formal statistical inference about edges, multiple-testing corrections, and time-series models that capture temporal dependence in a disciplined way.

3.2 Statistical Inference & Hypothesis Testing

The previous section introduced distributional thinking: we described how returns are spread out, how fat the tails are, and how dependence shapes risk. That perspective is descriptive. In this section, we turn to an inferential perspective: given historical data, what can we credibly say about the existence and size of a *trading edge*?

For contrarian strategies, this task is especially delicate:

- Signals are often weak (Sharpe ratios between 0.3 and 1 on realistic capital).
- Samples are effectively small, because regimes change and we cannot rely on decades of stationary data.
- Observations are dependent, with overlapping positions, volatility clustering, and slow-moving spreads.

We therefore need a pragmatic framework: one that respects textbook statistics but also adapts it to the messy realities of financial time series.

From Data to Estimates: Point Estimation

Suppose you have a candidate contrarian strategy and a backtest that produces a time series of returns $\{r_t\}_{t=1}^{T}$ at some horizon (daily, intraday, weekly). The most basic question is: what is the *average* return?

The natural estimator of the mean is the sample average:

$$\hat{\mu} = \frac{1}{T}\sum_{t=1}^{T} r_t.$$

If you scale to annualized Sharpe, you might compute

$$\widehat{\text{Sharpe}} = \frac{\hat{\mu}}{\hat{\sigma}}\sqrt{K},$$

where $\hat{\sigma}$ is the sample standard deviation of $\{r_t\}$ and K is the number of return periods per year (e.g., $K = 252$ for daily data).

IID textbook world

In an idealized setting, we assume that returns are *independent and identically distributed* (IID) draws from some distribution with mean μ and variance σ^2. Under IID assumptions, the variance of the sample mean is

$$\text{Var}(\hat{\mu}) = \frac{\sigma^2}{T},$$

and we estimate it by plugging in $\hat{\sigma}^2$:

$$\widehat{\text{Var}}(\hat{\mu}) = \frac{\hat{\sigma}^2}{T}.$$

The standard error (SE) of $\hat{\mu}$ is

$$\text{SE}_{IID}(\hat{\mu}) = \frac{\hat{\sigma}}{\sqrt{T}}.$$

This gives us a first sense of precision: doubling the backtest length reduces the standard error by about $1/\sqrt{2}$, and strategies with volatile returns (large $\hat{\sigma}$) require longer samples to estimate their mean accurately.

Dependent, heteroskedastic reality

Financial returns rarely satisfy IID assumptions:

- *Autocorrelation*: strategy returns often exhibit serial correlation due to partial position overlaps, execution delays, and slow-moving spreads.

- *Heteroskedasticity*: volatility clusters over time; some periods are much more volatile than others.

Under dependence, the variance of $\hat{\mu}$ is no longer σ^2/T. For a stationary time series with autocovariance function $\gamma(k) = \mathrm{Cov}(r_t, r_{t-k})$, one can show:

$$\mathrm{Var}(\hat{\mu}) \approx \frac{1}{T}\left(\gamma(0) + 2\sum_{k=1}^{\infty}\gamma(k)\right).$$

Define the *long-run variance* (LRV)

$$\omega^2 \equiv \gamma(0) + 2\sum_{k=1}^{\infty}\gamma(k).$$

Then

$$\mathrm{Var}(\hat{\mu}) \approx \frac{\omega^2}{T}, \qquad \mathrm{SE}(\hat{\mu}) \approx \frac{\omega}{\sqrt{T}}.$$

Autocorrelation inflates ω^2 relative to $\sigma^2 = \gamma(0)$. Intuitively, if your daily returns are positively correlated, 1,000 days contain much less information than 1,000 independent draws. The "effective sample size" is smaller.

Practical takeaway. If you apply IID formulas to dependent strategy returns, you will usually:

- Underestimate the standard error of your mean return and Sharpe ratio.
- Overstate the strength and statistical significance of your edge.

To address this, we need *robust* standard errors that respect dependence and heteroskedasticity.

Robust Standard Errors and Long-Run Variance Estimation

In practice, we do not know the true autocovariances $\gamma(k)$, nor how far the dependence extends. Instead, we estimate ω^2 from data.

One widely used approach is the *Heteroskedasticity and Autocorrelation Consistent* (HAC) estimator, also known as Newey–West. The idea is:

$$\hat{\omega}^2 = \hat{\gamma}(0) + 2\sum_{k=1}^{K} w_k \hat{\gamma}(k),$$

where:

- $\hat{\gamma}(k)$ are sample autocovariances at lag k,
- w_k are weights that taper off as k increases (often triangular or similar),
- K is a maximum lag that grows slowly with T.

Then the robust standard error of $\hat{\mu}$ is

$$\text{SE}_{HAC}(\hat{\mu}) = \frac{\hat{\omega}}{\sqrt{T}}.$$

Conceptually:

- If your returns are close to IID, $\hat{\gamma}(k)$ for $k \geq 1$ are small and $\hat{\omega}^2 \approx \hat{\sigma}^2$.
- If your returns exhibit strong positive autocorrelation, the sum of $\hat{\gamma}(k)$ increases $\hat{\omega}^2$, widening your confidence intervals and making you more cautious about declaring a discovery.

In code, Newey–West-type estimators are available in most econometrics libraries and are straightforward to implement yourself.

Interval Estimation: How Big Is the Edge?

Point estimates like $\hat{\mu}$ are not enough; we need to know how uncertain they are. This is the role of confidence intervals.

Under mild conditions (including weak dependence), a central limit theorem implies that

$$\frac{\hat{\mu} - \mu}{\text{SE}(\hat{\mu})} \approx \mathcal{N}(0, 1)$$

for large T. This leads to an approximate $(1-\alpha)$ confidence interval:

$$\hat{\mu} \pm z_{1-\alpha/2} \cdot \mathrm{SE}(\hat{\mu}),$$

where $z_{1-\alpha/2}$ is the corresponding normal quantile (e.g., $z_{0.975} \approx 1.96$ for 95%).

Interpretation in trading terms. A 95% confidence interval for μ of, say,

$$[-0.01\%, 0.05\%] \quad \text{per day}$$

means:

> Given our model and data, a wide range of true daily edges—from slightly negative to moderately positive—is consistent with what we observed. We cannot rule out that the true edge is essentially zero.

Even if $\hat{\mu}$ is positive, a confidence interval that includes zero tells you that the evidence is weak. This is particularly common in small-sample backtests or for strategies with noisy returns.

For contrarian traders, it is helpful to think of confidence intervals as *plausible bands on Sharpe* rather than precise estimates. For example, a point estimate of Sharpe $= 1.0$ with a 95% interval of $[0.2, 1.8]$ is very different from a point estimate of Sharpe $= 1.0$ with interval $[0.8, 1.2]$.

Hypothesis Testing in the Language of Trading

Hypothesis testing formalizes the question: "Is this edge real, or could it be random noise?"

Null and alternative

We typically frame tests in terms of a *null hypothesis* H_0 and an *alternative hypothesis* H_1.

For a contrarian strategy, a natural choice is:

$$H_0 : \mu \leq 0 \quad (\text{"no edge"}), \qquad H_1 : \mu > 0 \quad (\text{"positive edge"}).$$

Equivalently, you might test $H_0 : \mu = 0$ vs. $H_1 : \mu > 0$ for simplicity.

Test statistic and t-ratio

We use the sample mean $\hat{\mu}$ as our statistic, standardized by its standard error:

$$t = \frac{\hat{\mu} - 0}{\text{SE}(\hat{\mu})}.$$

Here, $\text{SE}(\hat{\mu})$ should be a robust estimate (e.g., HAC), not the naive IID version, when returns are dependent.

Under H_0 and for large T, t is approximately standard normal. For a one-sided test at level α (e.g., $\alpha = 0.05$), we reject H_0 in favor of H_1 if

$$t > z_{1-\alpha}.$$

Type I and Type II errors

Two kinds of mistakes are possible:

- **Type I error (false positive):** rejecting H_0 when it is actually true—believing you found a positive edge when there is none.
- **Type II error (false negative):** failing to reject H_0 when H_1 is true—missing a genuine edge.

The significance level α controls the probability of a Type I error. Setting $\alpha = 0.05$ means you accept a 5% chance of mistakenly concluding that a non-existent edge is real, *for a single test.* (The multiple-testing section later in the chapter will revisit what happens when you run many such tests.)

The *power* of a test is the probability of correctly rejecting H_0 when a specific alternative is true. High power requires:

- A reasonably strong true edge (large μ relative to volatility),
- A long enough sample T,
- A well-chosen test that accounts properly for dependence.

Weak signals and short samples imply low power. In practice this means that many potentially valuable contrarian edges will not show up as "statistically significant" at conventional levels when tested in isolation.

The p-value

The p-value summarizes the evidence against H_0:

$$p = \mathbb{P}\left(\text{Test statistic under } H_0 \geq \text{observed } t\right).$$

For a one-sided test with approximate normality,

$$p = 1 - \Phi(t),$$

where Φ is the standard normal CDF. Small p-values indicate that the observed t would be unlikely if H_0 were true.

Practical interpretation. In trading research:

- A p-value is *not* the probability that H_0 is true.
- It is a measure of how surprising your data are under H_0.
- A p-value of 0.03 means that if there were truly no edge, you would see a t as large as observed (or larger) about 3% of the time.

Given the prevalence of data mining in quant research, it is wise to treat p-values as tools for skepticism rather than confirmation: large p-values (say > 0.1) are strong evidence *against* a large edge, but small p-values are not, by themselves, proof of a robust anomaly. Later sections will add multiple-testing and out-of-sample tools to strengthen your conclusions.

Complications: Overlapping Returns and Clustered Dependence

Many contrarian strategies use holding periods longer than one return interval. For example, you might compute 1-day returns but hold trades for 5 days. If you measure performance at the daily frequency, your return series will have *overlapping* components: today's P&L depends partly on positions opened yesterday, the day before, and so on.

Overlapping returns induce strong autocorrelation:

- A k-day overlapping return constructed from daily data has autocorrelation at lags $1, 2, \ldots, k-1$ even if underlying one-day returns are IID.

- If you naively treat overlapping returns as independent, you will multiply effective sample size by roughly k, seriously exaggerating your evidence.

Similarly, if you run cross-sectional strategies (e.g., daily mean reversion across 500 stocks) and then aggregate to a single portfolio return, the cross-sectional overlap in names and the common market shocks can induce *clustered dependence* across days.

What to do in practice.

- When feasible, switch to *non-overlapping* return series matched to your holding period (e.g., use 5-day returns for a 5-day holding strategy). You get fewer observations, but they are more independent.

- If you must use overlapping returns, treat them as a time series with autocorrelation and use robust (HAC) standard errors that extend the lag window beyond the overlap length.

- For clustered dependence (e.g., returns clustered by week or month), cluster-robust standard errors can be used: they allow arbitrary dependence within clusters but treat clusters as independent units.

The key is to align your statistical assumptions with how trades actually evolve over time.

Bootstrap and Monte Carlo Methods

Parametric formulas for standard errors and p-values rely on assumptions about distributions and dependence. When these are questionable—which is often in financial data—resampling methods provide a flexible alternative.

Bootstrap confidence intervals

The bootstrap approximates the sampling distribution of an estimator by resampling from observed data. For time series, we must preserve dependence, so we use variants like the block bootstrap.

A simple block bootstrap procedure:

1. Choose a block length B (e.g., 5 or 10 days).
2. Partition your return series into overlapping or non-overlapping blocks of length B.
3. Construct many bootstrap samples by drawing blocks with replacement and concatenating them until you reach length T.
4. For each sample, compute the estimator of interest (e.g., $\hat{\mu}^*$ or $\widehat{\text{Sharpe}}^*$).
5. Use the empirical distribution of $\hat{\mu}^*$ across bootstrap samples to form confidence intervals.

The block structure retains local dependence and volatility clustering while randomizing the ordering of blocks. This yields more realistic uncertainty estimates than IID resampling, while remaining nonparametric.

Monte Carlo tests for trading rules

For a specific trading rule, you can design a Monte Carlo test tailored to the null hypothesis of "no edge." For example:

- Randomly permute the signal time series while keeping the return series fixed, thereby breaking any real signal-return linkage but preserving the distribution and dependence of returns.
- Randomly shift the time alignment of signals relative to returns.
- Generate synthetic signals from a null model (e.g., white noise) with the same distribution as your actual signal.

In each Monte Carlo draw, recompute the strategy return series and its performance metrics. The fraction of simulations whose performance exceeds the observed performance provides a Monte Carlo p-value.

This approach is particularly powerful when the structure of your strategy is complex (e.g., with stop-losses, non-linear payoffs) and analytic formulas for sampling distributions are intractable.

Putting It Together: A Pragmatic Workflow

To close, let us outline a practical inference workflow for a single contrarian signal, acknowledging weak signals, small effective samples, and dependence:

1. **Specify the estimand.** Decide what you want to infer: mean daily return, annualized Sharpe, information ratio vs. a benchmark, or something more tailored (e.g., expected P&L per trade).

2. **Compute point estimates.** Calculate $\hat{\mu}$ and $\widehat{\text{Sharpe}}$ from your backtest, using returns aligned with your actual holding period to avoid unnecessary overlap.

3. **Diagnose dependence.** Inspect autocorrelation plots of returns, squared returns, and possibly residuals from simple models. Identify the presence and approximate range of serial correlation.

4. **Estimate robust standard errors.** Use HAC or cluster-robust methods to obtain $\text{SE}(\hat{\mu})$ and $\text{SE}(\widehat{\text{Sharpe}})$ that reflect dependence and heteroskedasticity.

5. **Form confidence intervals.** Construct $(1 - \alpha)$ intervals for μ and Sharpe. Interpret them as ranges of plausible edges, not precise truths.

6. **Perform hypothesis tests carefully.** Test $H_0 : \mu \leq 0$ vs. $H_1 : \mu > 0$ using robust t-statistics, and compute p-values. Use small p-values as a reason to investigate further, not as a license to lever up.

7. **Use bootstrap or Monte Carlo checks.** Where dependence is strong or model assumptions are fragile, complement analytic results with block bootstrap intervals and Monte Carlo null distributions specific to your strategy design.

8. **Document and prepare for multiple testing.** Log your tests, including failed ideas and variations. This record will be crucial when we address multiple testing and false discovery control in the next section.

This framework does not eliminate uncertainty; it makes uncertainty explicit and quantifiable. For contrarian anomaly hunters operating in noisy, dependent environments, that is a central competitive advantage: you are less likely to overreact to noisy backtests, and more likely to allocate capital to signals whose strength is supported by both data and disciplined inference.

3.3 Multiple Testing & False Discovery Control

In the previous section, we treated statistical inference as if you were testing a single trading rule: one signal, one backtest, one p-value. Real quantitative research is very different. You will:

- Try many variations of a contrarian idea (different lookbacks, rebalancing frequencies, asset universes).
- Tweak filters, risk targets, transaction cost models, and execution assumptions.
- Explore entirely different anomaly families (short-term reversals, long-term reversals, factor spreads, cross-asset signals).

Each attempt implicitly or explicitly involves a statistical test. If you look at enough noisy backtests, some will look surprisingly good *by chance alone*. This is the essence of the multiple-testing problem.

This section explains how to reason about that problem and how to use error-rate control tools—such as Bonferroni corrections and

Benjamini–Hochberg (BH) procedures—to limit the number of *false discoveries* you promote into production.

The Explosion of False Positives

Suppose you test a single null hypothesis H_0: "this contrarian rule has no edge" at a significance level $\alpha = 5\%$. Under H_0, you will incorrectly reject it (a false positive) with probability 0.05.

Now suppose you test m independent strategies, all of which are in reality noise (no edge). The probability that *none* of them looks significant at the 5% level is

$$\mathbb{P}(\text{no false positives}) = (1 - \alpha)^m.$$

Therefore, the probability of at least one false positive is

$$\mathbb{P}(\text{at least one false positive}) = 1 - (1 - \alpha)^m.$$

For small m, this is close to $m\alpha$. For larger m, it quickly saturates near 1.

For example:

m (number of tests)	α (per-test)	$\mathbb{P}(\geq$ 1 false positive)
10	0.05	$\approx 40\%$
100	0.05	$\approx 99.4\%$
1,000	0.05	$\approx 100\%$

If you run hundreds or thousands of tests—typical in systematic strategy research—it becomes almost certain that some strategy will show an apparently great Sharpe or tiny p-value even if every signal is pure noise. If you then select the "winners" based on backtest performance, you have data-mined illusions.

Error Rates: FWER vs. FDR

To address multiple testing, we need to formalize what error we want to control.

Family-wise Error Rate (FWER)

Given a family of m hypotheses $H_0^{(1)}, \ldots, H_0^{(m)}$, the *family-wise error rate* (FWER) is

$$\text{FWER} = \mathbb{P}(\text{at least one false rejection in the family}).$$

Controlling FWER at level α means: among all the tests you run, the probability you make *any* false positive is at most α.

FWER control is stringent. It is appropriate when:

- The cost of even a single false discovery is very high (e.g., a large strategic allocation).
- The number of hypotheses m is modest.

False Discovery Rate (FDR)

In large-scale factor or signal searches, you might be willing to tolerate some false positives as long as they are a small fraction of what you select. This motivates the *false discovery rate* (FDR).

Let:

- R be the number of rejections (signals you decide are "discoveries"),
- V be the number of those rejections that are actually false (no real edge),
- So the proportion of false discoveries is $\frac{V}{R}$ (define this as 0 when $R = 0$).

Then the FDR is the expected proportion of false discoveries:

$$\text{FDR} = \mathbb{E}\left[\frac{V}{R}\right].$$

Controlling FDR at level q means: on average, no more than a fraction q of your selected signals are false. For example, with $q = 10\%$, if you select 20 strategies, you expect about 2 to be false discoveries and 18 to be real (on average).

In the context of systematic anomaly hunting across many signals, FDR control is often a more suitable objective than FWER. It allows more power (more discoveries) while keeping the fraction of bogus signals in check.

Simple Corrections for FWER: Bonferroni and Holm

The simplest way to control FWER is to make each individual test more stringent.

Bonferroni correction

The Bonferroni rule says: to control FWER at level α across m tests, use a per-test significance level of α/m.

Concretely:

1. Test each hypothesis $H_0^{(i)}$ separately and compute its p-value p_i.
2. Reject $H_0^{(i)}$ only if
$$p_i \leq \frac{\alpha}{m}.$$

By the union bound,

$$\mathbb{P}(\text{any false rejection}) \leq \sum_{i=1}^{m} \mathbb{P}(\text{false rejection of } H_0^{(i)}) \leq m \cdot \frac{\alpha}{m} = \alpha.$$

Example. If you test $m = 100$ variants of a contrarian rule and you want FWER $\leq 5\%$, Bonferroni requires $p_i \leq 0.0005$ to declare significance. That is much stricter than the usual 0.05 threshold.

Pros and cons.

- Pro: very simple, valid under minimal assumptions.
- Con: often too conservative—especially when m is large and tests are correlated—leading to low power (few or no discoveries).

Holm's step-down procedure

Holm's method is a stepwise improvement over Bonferroni: it controls FWER at α, but is less conservative.

Procedure:

1. Order the p-values: $p_{(1)} \leq p_{(2)} \leq \cdots \leq p_{(m)}$.

2. For $k = 1$ to m:
   - Compare $p_{(k)}$ to $\alpha/(m-k+1)$.
   - If $p_{(k)} > \alpha/(m-k+1)$, then *stop* and do not reject $H_{(k)}$ or any $H_{(j)}$ with $j > k$.
   - Otherwise, reject $H_{(k)}$ and move to $k+1$.

Holm always rejects at least as many hypotheses as Bonferroni and often more, while still controlling FWER. For most trading audiences, Holm is a better default than plain Bonferroni when FWER control is the target.

Controlling FDR: The Benjamini–Hochberg Procedure

When you test dozens, hundreds, or thousands of contrarian signals, FDR control is usually more relevant than FWER. The classic tool is the Benjamini–Hochberg (BH) procedure.

Fix a desired FDR level q (e.g., $q = 10\%$). Given m p-values $p_1, \ldots, p_m$:

1. Order the p-values from smallest to largest:

$$p_{(1)} \leq p_{(2)} \leq \cdots \leq p_{(m)}.$$

2. For each rank k, compute the BH critical value:

$$\tau_k = \frac{k}{m}q.$$

3. Find the largest $k^\star$ such that

$$p_{(k^\star)} \leq \tau_{k^\star}.$$

4. Reject all hypotheses $H_{(1)}, \ldots, H_{(k^\star)}$ (those with $p_{(k)} \leq p_{(k^\star)}$).

Intuition:

- For small k, the threshold τ_k is small; BH is strict about the very smallest p-values.

- As k grows, τ_k increases, allowing more liberal thresholds for larger p-values if many strong candidates are present.

- By tying thresholds to ranks, BH adapts to the overall shape of the p-value distribution.

Under mild assumptions (e.g., independent tests), BH guarantees that the expected fraction of false discoveries among all rejections is at most q. Even with dependent tests (as in correlated strategy returns), BH is often robust in practice, though some theoretical adjustments exist.

Visualizing BH vs. Bonferroni

It is useful to visualize how BH and Bonferroni differ in practice.

Imagine you have computed $m = 100$ p-values from testing many contrarian strategies. You sort them and plot $p_{(k)}$ against their rank k. On the same chart, you overlay:

- The Bonferroni threshold: a flat horizontal line at α/m (e.g., 0.0005 for $\alpha = 0.05$).

- The BH curve: a line from $(1, q/m)$ up to (m, q), representing $\tau_k = (k/m)q$.

Strategies whose $p_{(k)}$ fall below a threshold line are selected under that rule.

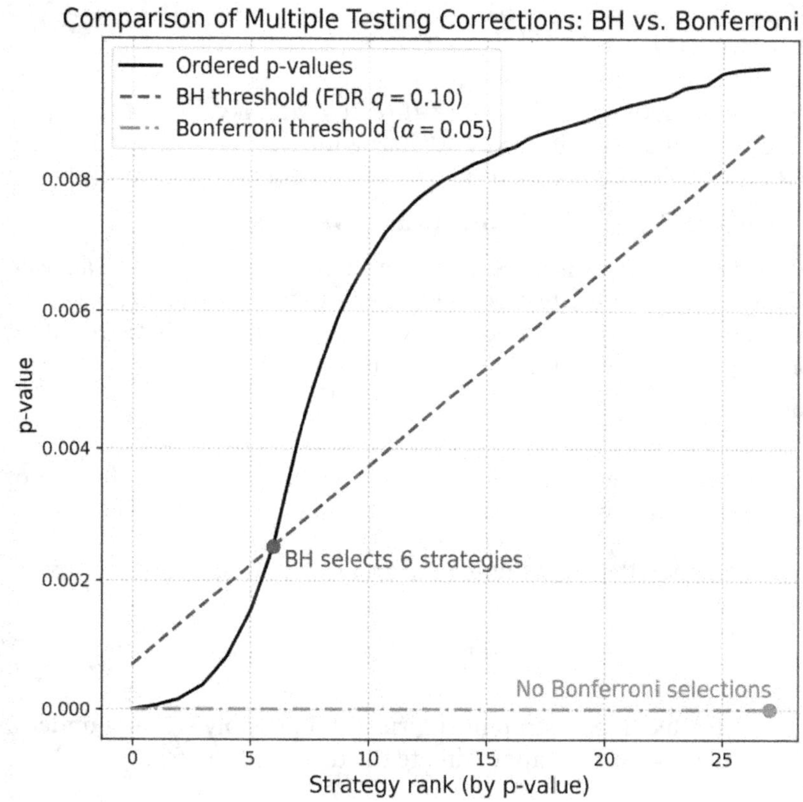

Figure 3.2: Ordered p-values from many strategy tests, with Bonferroni (FWER) and Benjamini–Hochberg (FDR) thresholds. BH typically selects more strategies while controlling the expected proportion of false discoveries.

Figure illustrates a typical outcome:

- The Bonferroni line is very low; often no p-values fall below it, leading to zero selected strategies.
- The BH threshold rises with rank and intersects the p-value curve at a higher $k^{\star}$, allowing you to select more strategies while explicitly managing the false discovery rate.

Beyond Thresholds: Reality Checks and Sharpe Discounting

While Bonferroni and BH work directly with p-values, trading researchers often think in terms of Sharpe ratios. There are procedures that effectively *discount* Sharpe ratios to account for data mining.

White's reality check (conceptual overview)

White's reality check is a bootstrap-based method designed to answer: "Given a set of candidate models (strategies), is the performance of the best one significantly better than that of a benchmark, after accounting for the fact that we picked the best ex post?"

The idea is:

1. Compute the performance (e.g., average return or Sharpe) of each strategy and of a benchmark (e.g., zero or a market index).
2. Consider the maximum performance difference across strategies:
$$T = \max_{i=1,\dots,m} \left(\widehat{\text{perf}}_i - \widehat{\text{perf}}_{\text{benchmark}} \right).$$
3. Use a block bootstrap of returns (and possibly signals) under a null of no edge to approximate the distribution of T.
4. Calculate a p-value: the fraction of bootstrap samples in which the bootstrapped maximum $T^{\star}$ exceeds the observed T.

If this p-value is large, the apparent winner looks impressive only because you tried many alternatives. If it is small, you have evidence that *even after* accounting for the search, the top-performing strategy is genuinely better than the benchmark.

Sharpe ratio discounting

An easier, more heuristic approach is to apply a penalty to in-sample Sharpe ratios based on the number of tests and the degree of overfitting. For example:

- Suppose you tested m variants of a strategy family.

- You can simulate under a null of no edge to see how large the maximum in-sample Sharpe tends to be after m trials.
- The difference between this "null maximum" and your observed Sharpe provides a discount or haircut.

The exact formulas depend on assumptions, but the guiding principle is straightforward: the more you searched, the less you should trust the raw in-sample Sharpe of the best-performing variant.

Practical Research Habits to Limit False Discoveries

Formal corrections are important, but your daily research habits are just as critical in protecting you from data-mined illusions.

Log everything: build a test ledger

Maintain a log or database of all tests you run:

- Strategy family and idea description.
- Parameter settings (lookbacks, thresholds, universes).
- Sample period and data sources.
- Performance metrics and p-values.

This ledger lets you approximate the total number of implicit and explicit tests (m), which is essential for any multiple-testing correction. It also disciplines you against retroactively editing history by forgetting failed attempts.

Separate exploration and confirmation

Adopt a two-stage process:

1. **Exploration stage:** Freely search for patterns and tune parameters on a designated *research sample*. Here you accept that p-values are exploratory, not confirmatory.

2. **Confirmation stage:** Lock in a small set of candidate strategies and test them *once* on a separate *holdout* or *out-of-sample* period. Apply standard single-test inference or mild multiple-testing corrections appropriate for the reduced candidate set.

This is analogous to the train/validation/test split in machine learning and greatly reduces the effective number of tests contaminating your final inference.

Control complexity and degrees of freedom

Each tunable parameter (lookback length, entry threshold, volatility target, filter rule) is a degree of freedom that can soak up noise. To reduce multiple-testing burden:

- Keep parameter grids coarse rather than exploring hundreds of tiny increments.
- Prefer simple, interpretable rules over highly flexible ones.
- When possible, pre-specify reasonable parameter ranges based on economic intuition or previous literature instead of letting the data suggest arbitrary values.

Fewer degrees of freedom mean fewer implicit tests and, therefore, less aggressive corrections.

Use FDR-aware selection pipelines

When you run a large-scale scan over thousands of candidate signals (e.g., cross-sectional factors, alternative data features), treat it explicitly as an FDR problem:

1. Compute p-values (or other test statistics) for each candidate effect.
2. Apply BH or related FDR procedures to select a subset of signals that pass the desired FDR level.
3. Within that subset, apply further filters based on stability, turnover, and implementability.

This approach blends statistical discipline with practical concerns and leads to leaner, more trustworthy signal sets.

Summary and Outlook

Multiple testing is unavoidable in systematic anomaly hunting: experimentation is your job. What you can control is how rigorously you discount apparent edges for the search process itself.

Key messages from this section:

- Testing many signals without correction virtually guarantees false discoveries.
- FWER control (Bonferroni, Holm) offers strong guarantees but can be too conservative in large-scale searches.
- FDR control (Benjamini–Hochberg) is better aligned with the needs of factor discovery, balancing power and reliability.
- Bootstrap-based tools like White's reality check and Sharpe discounting methods help adjust for data mining in a more customized way.
- Good research hygiene—logging tests, separating exploration from confirmation, limiting degrees of freedom, and building FDR-aware pipelines—is as important as any formal correction.

Armed with these tools and habits, you can approach the next stages of the book—time-series modeling and machine-learning-based signal discovery—with a disciplined perspective on what constitutes real evidence of an anomaly and what is likely just noise dressed up as alpha.

3.4 Time-Series Dependence & Stationarity

Up to this point we have treated returns largely as a collection of random draws: we talked about their distributions, tails, and how to infer an edge from noisy data. But contrarian strategies are explicitly *temporal.* They bet that what happened recently—a sharp move, a widening spread, an abnormal pattern—will be followed by partial reversal.

To design and diagnose such strategies, we must understand how returns (or prices, or spreads) evolve over time. This is the domain of *time-series analysis*. In this section, we introduce the core concepts:

- Time series and dependence.
- Stationarity: when the statistical environment is "stable enough" to model.
- Autocorrelation and the autocorrelation function (ACF).
- Unit roots and random walks.
- Seasonality and calendar effects.

Our focus is not on sophisticated models yet, but on intuition and diagnostics that tell you whether a series is a promising candidate for mean reversion and how trustworthy your backtests are.

What Is a Time Series?

A *time series* is a sequence of observations indexed by time:

$$\{X_t\}_{t=1}^{T} = X_1, X_2, \ldots, X_T,$$

where t might represent days, minutes, or trades. In finance:

- X_t could be a price level (e.g., P_t for a stock).
- It could be a return (e.g., $r_t = \log P_t - \log P_{t-1}$).
- It could be a spread (e.g., the difference between two cointegrated prices).

Unlike in IID setups, the order of observations matters: X_t is typically *dependent* on past values $X_{t-1}, X_{t-2}, \ldots$.

Stationarity: A Stable Statistical Environment

Many time-series tools assume some form of *stationarity*. Intuitively, a time series is stationary if its statistical properties do not change over time.

There are several flavors; here we use *weak stationarity* (also called covariance stationarity). A time series $\{X_t\}$ is weakly stationary if:

1. The mean is constant over time: $\mathbb{E}[X_t] = \mu$ for all t.
2. The variance is finite and constant: $\text{Var}(X_t) = \sigma^2$ for all t.
3. The covariance between X_t and X_{t-k} depends only on the lag k, not on calendar time t:

$$\text{Cov}(X_t, X_{t-k}) = \gamma(k).$$

Stationarity is crucial for contrarian modeling because:

- It allows you to use past data to estimate features (means, variances, autocorrelations) that are relevant for the future.
- It implies that deviations from the mean are meaningful: if a spread is typically near zero, a value of 3σ above zero is rare and may revert.

Nonstationary series (like raw prices in a growing economy) tend to wander, with changing means and variances; they typically *do not* provide straightforward mean-reversion opportunities without transformation.

Autocovariance and Autocorrelation

To quantify dependence over time, we define the *autocovariance* at lag k:

$$\gamma(k) = \text{Cov}(X_t, X_{t-k}) = \mathbb{E}\big[(X_t - \mu)(X_{t-k} - \mu)\big].$$

The lag-0 autocovariance $\gamma(0) = \sigma^2$ is the variance. For $k \geq 1$, $\gamma(k)$ describes how deviations from the mean at time t relate to deviations k periods earlier.

We often work with the standardized version, the *autocorrelation function* (ACF):

$$\rho(k) = \frac{\gamma(k)}{\gamma(0)}.$$

By construction, $\rho(0) = 1$, and $|\rho(k)| \leq 1$.

Intuition for autocorrelation.

- If $\rho(1) > 0$ and reasonably large, then positive deviations from the mean tend to follow positive deviations, and negative follow negative: the series has *momentum* at that horizon.
- If $\rho(1) < 0$, then a positive deviation tends to be followed by a negative one and vice versa: the series has *mean reversion* at that horizon.
- If $\rho(k) \approx 0$ for all $k \geq 1$, the series is approximately serially uncorrelated (like white noise).

For contrarian trading, we are especially interested in negative autocorrelation of *returns* or of some transformed series (e.g., a residual, spread, or z-score). But even when raw returns show little autocorrelation, other derived series—like squared returns or volatility proxies—often show strong positive autocorrelation, reflecting volatility clustering.

Random Walks vs. Mean-Reverting Processes

To see how stationarity and autocorrelation shape time-series behavior, it is useful to contrast two archetypes:

1. A *random walk* (nonstationary, no mean reversion).
2. A *mean-reverting* process (stationary, tends to return to a long-run level).

Random walk

A simple random walk is defined by

$$X_t = X_{t-1} + \varepsilon_t,$$

where ε_t are IID shocks with mean zero and variance σ_ε^2.

Properties:

- X_t has no fixed mean: its expected value depends on the starting point.
- The variance grows linearly with time: $\text{Var}(X_t) = t\sigma_\varepsilon^2$ (if $X_0 = 0$).
- The distribution of X_t spreads out indefinitely; there is no restoring force pulling it back.

Prices of liquid assets are often modeled as random walks (possibly with drift) over short to medium horizons. They are nonstationary series: trends and levels change over time.

Mean-reverting process

A simple discrete-time mean-reverting process is the AR(1) model:

$$X_t = \phi X_{t-1} + \varepsilon_t,$$

where $|\phi| < 1$ and ε_t are IID with mean zero. If $|\phi| < 1$, the process is stationary with:

$$\mathbb{E}[X_t] = 0, \qquad \text{Var}(X_t) = \frac{\sigma_\varepsilon^2}{1 - \phi^2},$$

and autocorrelation

$$\rho(k) = \phi^k.$$

If $0 < \phi < 1$, shocks persist but decay geometrically. If ϕ is negative, the process oscillates around the mean, displaying short-term reversals.

Many contrarian signals are built on series that either behave like an AR(1) (e.g., deviations of a pair from equilibrium, normalized spreads) or can be approximated as such over limited horizons.

Visualizing Stationarity and Autocorrelation

To build intuition, compare:

- A random walk: nonstationary, drifting level, persistent shocks.
- A stationary AR(1) process: fluctuating around a stable mean, with decaying autocorrelation.

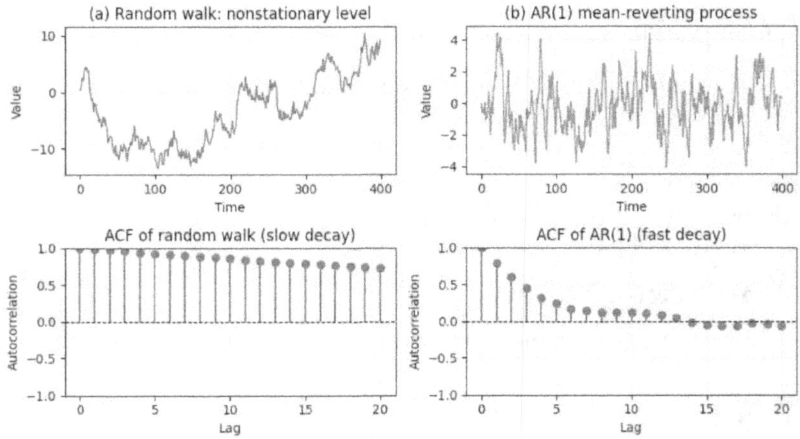

Figure 3.3: Comparison of a nonstationary random walk and a stationary AR(1) mean-reverting process. Top panels: time series paths. Bottom panels: sample autocorrelation functions (ACFs). The random walk exhibits a wandering level and very slow decay in autocorrelation; the mean-reverting process fluctuates around a stable mean with faster autocorrelation decay.

Figure shows that:

- The random walk drifts without a clear long-run level; its ACF decays very slowly, reflecting persistent dependence in levels.
- The AR(1) series stays around a stable mean; its ACF decays faster, roughly geometrically at rate ϕ^k.

Contrarian opportunities usually live in series that look more like the right-hand side: they have a notion of "fair value" (long-run mean) and visible reversion dynamics.

Unit Roots and Testing for Nonstationarity

The random walk can be seen as an AR(1) with $\varphi = 1$:

$$X_t = X_{t-1} + \varepsilon_t.$$

This is called a *unit root* process because the autoregressive root is at 1. When $|\phi| < 1$, the process is stationary; when $\phi = 1$, it is nonstationary with a unit root.

Why does this matter for contrarian trading?

- If a price series has a unit root (behaves like a random walk), its level is not stationary. Buying because price is "below its historical average" is not justified statistically; the concept of a fixed historical mean is ill-defined.
- However, the *differences* (returns) of a unit root series are often stationary. Contrarian strategies on returns, or on spreads that remove a common stochastic trend, can be well grounded.

Basic unit root tests (ADF and KPSS, conceptually)

Two families of tests help assess whether a series is stationary or unit-root-like:

Augmented Dickey–Fuller (ADF) test.

- Null hypothesis H_0: the series has a unit root (nonstationary).
- Alternative H_1: the series is stationary (around a constant or trend).

ADF essentially estimates a regression of ΔX_t on X_{t-1} (and lagged differences) and tests whether the coefficient on X_{t-1} is zero (unit root) or negative (stationary).

KPSS test.

- Null hypothesis H_0: the series is stationary (around a level or trend).
- Alternative H_1: the series has a unit root (nonstationary).

In practice, many traders use both tests together: if ADF rejects unit root and KPSS accepts stationarity, you have stronger evidence for stationarity; if both point towards nonstationarity, you treat the series as trend-like.

Practical workflow.

1. For candidate mean-reversion signals (e.g., pair spreads, factor spreads), run unit root tests on the level series.
2. If tests suggest nonstationarity, consider transforming the series (e.g., differencing, cointegration residuals) instead of trading on the raw level.
3. Remember that tests have limited power in finite samples; combine statistical evidence with visual inspection and economic logic.

Seasonality and Calendar Effects

Stationarity requires that the statistical properties of a series do not change over time. But many financial time series exhibit systematic, time-dependent patterns known as *seasonality* or *calendar effects*. Examples include:

- Day-of-week effects in equity returns.
- Month-end or quarter-end flows affecting bonds or FX.
- Intraday patterns: strong mean reversion or momentum during specific hours (e.g., open vs. close).

Seasonality creates a structured form of nonstationarity: the mean or variance may depend on the time index in a predictable way, such as

$$\mathbb{E}[r_t \mid \text{day-of-week}] \neq \text{constant}.$$

For contrarian trading, ignoring such patterns can lead to:

- Spurious signals: what looks like mean reversion might simply be a recurring calendar effect.

- Overstated edge: you might unintentionally exploit a day-of-week effect that disappears once widely known or arbitraged.

Handling seasonality.

- Include seasonal dummies (e.g., indicators for day-of-week, month-end) in models and work with residuals that have seasonality removed.
- Apply separate analyses for different intraday segments (opening auction, midday, close) when building intraday contrarian strategies.
- Test whether your signal survives after de-seasonalizing the data.

The goal is to focus on genuine mean reversion in the underlying process, not on arbitrary calendar regularities that may not be robust.

Stationary Transforms of Nonstationary Series

A central theme in building contrarian strategies is that while *prices* may be nonstationary, appropriately transformed quantities can be stationary and mean reverting:

- **Returns:** If prices follow a random walk with drift, log-returns are often modeled as stationary around a small mean.
- **Spreads between cointegrated assets:** If two price series share a common stochastic trend, a linear combination (spread) can be stationary. Trading this spread (pairs trading) is a classic mean-reversion strategy.
- **De-meaned or de-trended series:** Removing deterministic trends or slow-moving components (e.g., via rolling means) can yield approximately stationary residuals.

Before committing capital to a contrarian signal, always ask: *What is the stationary object here?* Are you betting on reversion to a well-defined mean, or on a level that drifts unpredictably?

Diagnosing Mean-Reversion Candidates

Putting the pieces together, here is a practical checklist for diagnosing whether a series is a plausible mean-reversion candidate:

1. **Visual inspection.** Plot the series over time:
   - Does it wander without apparent bounds (like a random walk), or does it fluctuate around a relatively stable level?
   - Are there obvious structural breaks (e.g., regime shifts, jumps in level) that violate stationarity?
2. **ACF and PACF.** Examine the autocorrelation and partial autocorrelation functions:
   - A stationary, mean-reverting series often has ACF that decays to zero reasonably quickly.
   - Strong, persistent autocorrelation at many lags may indicate unit-root-like behavior or long memory in levels.
3. **Unit root tests.** Run ADF and KPSS (or similar) tests:
   - If ADF rejects unit root and KPSS does not reject stationarity, that supports stationarity.
   - If both suggest nonstationarity, consider differencing or alternative transforms.
4. **Seasonality checks.** Stratify the series by calendar features:
   - Check whether mean or variance differs by day-of-week, month, or intraday segment.
   - If so, either model these effects explicitly or remove them before testing for mean reversion.
5. **Economic rationale.** Ensure that there is a plausible mechanism for mean reversion:
   - Inventory or liquidity effects in microstructure.
   - Rebalancing flows or risk limits that force reversals.
   - Long-run equilibrium relationships between assets (for spreads).

Only after a series passes these basic checks does it make sense to fit more sophisticated models (ARIMA, GARCH, cointegration, OU) and build contrarian rules on top of them—the topic of the next section.

Time-series dependence and stationarity are the backbone of mean-reversion trading:

- *Autocorrelation* measures how current values relate to the past and helps distinguish momentum from mean reversion.
- *Stationarity* ensures that past behavior is informative about the future and that a notion of "fair value" or equilibrium level exists.
- *Unit roots* and random walks characterize nonstationary dynamics of prices; often we must model returns or spreads instead of raw levels.
- *Seasonality* introduces predictable, time-dependent patterns that need to be accounted for or removed.

With these concepts in hand, you can begin to interpret time-series plots, ACFs, and unit root tests not as abstract statistics, but as concrete tools for deciding which series are worthy of contrarian attention and how to model their dynamics in a disciplined way.

3.5 Parametric & Mean-Reverting Models

The previous section introduced time-series dependence and stationarity at a conceptual level: we distinguished random walks from stationary processes, discussed autocorrelation, and highlighted the importance of unit roots and seasonality. We now turn to concrete modeling frameworks that operationalize those ideas for contrarian trading.

Our goal is pragmatic: develop models that help you (i) identify and quantify mean reversion in tradable series and spreads, and (ii) turn that structure into forecasts and position-sizing rules. We focus on four widely used families:

- ARIMA models for linear dependence and trends.
- GARCH models for time-varying volatility.
- Cointegration for long-run relationships between assets.
- Ornstein–Uhlenbeck (OU) processes for continuous-time mean reversion.

Throughout, keep in mind that these are tools, not religions: simple specifications, well-understood and stress-tested, typically outperform ornate models that fit in-sample noise.

AR and ARIMA Models: Linear Mean Dynamics

We begin with autoregressive (AR) models, which extend the AR(1) intuition from the previous section.

AR(p) models

An AR(p) model for a (weakly) stationary series $\{X_t\}$ has the form

$$X_t = \phi_1 X_{t-1} + \phi_2 X_{t-2} + \cdots + \phi_p X_{t-p} + \varepsilon_t,$$

where $\{\varepsilon_t\}$ are zero-mean shocks (often assumed uncorrelated with constant variance), and the parameters $\phi_1, \ldots, \phi_p$ satisfy stability conditions ensuring stationarity.

Intuitively:

- X_t depends linearly on its last p values.
- The coefficients ϕ_j encode the pattern of autocorrelation and mean reversion.

For contrarian trading, you might let X_t be:

- A return or excess return series, capturing short-term reversal or momentum.
- A normalized spread (e.g., z-score of a pair spread), capturing mean-reversion speed.

Mean reversion in AR(p). If the AR polynomial has roots outside the unit circle, the process is stationary and shocks eventually die out. In AR(1),

$$X_t = \phi X_{t-1} + \varepsilon_t,$$

we saw that $|\phi| < 1$ implies stationarity. The closer $|\phi|$ is to 1 (from below), the *slower* the mean reversion: shocks persist longer.

For contrarian applications:

- Strong mean reversion: ϕ (or dominant roots) relatively small in magnitude; deviations decay quickly, suggesting shorter holding periods.
- Weak mean reversion: ϕ close to 1; deviations take longer to fade and may be swamped by noise and costs.

ARIMA: trends and differencing

Many raw financial series (especially prices and indices) are nonstationary with trends. ARIMA models generalize AR by applying differencing to induce stationarity.

An ARIMA(p, d, q) model for a series $\{Y_t\}$ can be summarized informally:

1. Difference the series d times to obtain

   $$X_t = \Delta^d Y_t,$$

   where $\Delta Y_t = Y_t - Y_{t-1}$.
2. Model $\{X_t\}$ as an ARMA(p, q) process, i.e., AR(p) plus a moving-average (MA(q)) component in the shocks.

For example:

- ARIMA$(0, 1, 0)$ is a random walk: $Y_t = Y_{t-1} + \varepsilon_t$.
- ARIMA$(1, 1, 0)$ implies that *changes* in Y_t follow an AR(1):

  $$\Delta Y_t = \phi\,\Delta Y_{t-1} + \varepsilon_t.$$

In contrarian contexts, ARIMA is most useful when:

- You want to model and forecast returns or spread changes that exhibit serial correlation.
- You wish to remove deterministic trends or slow drifts before applying mean-reversion logic to residuals.

Model identification and diagnostics

A typical AR/ARIMA modeling cycle involves:

1. **Preprocessing.**
   - Decide whether to work with prices, log-prices, returns, or spreads.
   - Apply transformations (e.g., differencing, de-meaning, deseasonalizing) to make the series approximately stationary.
2. **Identification.**
   - Inspect the ACF and partial ACF (PACF) to get a sense of suitable p and q.
   - Use information criteria (AIC, BIC) to balance fit and parsimony across candidate orders.
3. **Estimation.**
   - Fit the model (e.g., via maximum likelihood) to estimate ϕ_j and MA parameters.
4. **Diagnostics.**
   - Analyze residuals: they should resemble white noise (no significant autocorrelation).
   - Re-estimate or simplify the model if residual structure remains.

In trading practice, you rarely need high-order ARIMA models. AR(1) or AR(2) (sometimes with an MA component) often suffice to capture the main mean-reversion pattern. Overfitting higher orders tends to create fragile signals that fail out of sample.

GARCH Models: Time-Varying Volatility for Risk Scaling

So far we have treated residual shocks ε_t as homoskedastic (constant variance). Empirically, financial returns exhibit *volatility clustering*: periods of high volatility cluster together, as do periods of calm. GARCH models provide a convenient framework for this.

Basic GARCH(1,1)

Consider a return series $\{r_t\}$ modeled as:

$$r_t = \mu + \sigma_t z_t,$$

where:

- z_t are IID innovations with mean zero and variance one (often Gaussian or Student-t),
- σ_t^2 is the conditional variance (volatility) at time t, evolving as

  $$\sigma_t^2 = \omega + \alpha r_{t-1}^2 + \beta \sigma_{t-1}^2,$$

  with $\omega > 0$, $\alpha \geq 0$, $\beta \geq 0$, and $\alpha + \beta < 1$ for stationarity.

Interpretation:

- Volatility responds to recent squared returns (r_{t-1}^2) and to its own past level (σ_{t-1}^2).
- Large shocks (positive or negative) increase σ_t^2, making future returns more volatile.

Why GARCH matters for contrarian strategies

Mean reversion and volatility dynamics interact in several important ways:

- **Signal scaling.** A 2% price move on a quiet day may be a huge outlier; on a crisis day, it may be routine. By forecasting σ_t with GARCH (or simpler rolling measures), you can standardize signals:

  $$z_t^{\text{signal}} = \frac{X_t - \hat{\mu}_t}{\hat{\sigma}_t},$$

making entry/exit thresholds more consistent across regimes.

- **Risk-based position sizing.** Position size can be made inversely proportional to forecasted volatility (e.g., target volatility or risk parity across signals). In a GARCH world, this means down-sizing in high-vol regimes and up-sizing in calm periods.
- **Tail risk.** Since GARCH captures volatility clustering, simulations from a fitted GARCH model yield more realistic drawdown distributions than constant-volatility models, especially for portfolios of contrarian trades whose risk is concentrated in turbulent regimes.

In practice, you might:

1. Fit a simple GARCH(1,1) (or related) model to residual returns of your strategy.
2. Use $\hat{\sigma}_{t+1}$ as your forecast of next-period volatility.
3. Scale notional exposure so that expected risk per trade or per day is approximately constant over time.

Cointegration: Mean-Reverting Spreads Between Assets

Many of the most intuitive contrarian trades are *spread trades*: long one asset, short another, betting on convergence. Cointegration provides a formal framework for identifying spreads that are stationary even when the underlying prices are not.

Conceptual idea

Suppose you have two nonstationary price series, $P_t^{(1)}$ and $P_t^{(2)}$, both of which behave roughly like random walks. Individually, neither $P_t^{(1)}$ nor $P_t^{(2)}$ has a stable long-run mean.

However, if there exists a linear combination

$$S_t = P_t^{(1)} - \beta P_t^{(2)},$$

that is stationary, then we say $P_t^{(1)}$ and $P_t^{(2)}$ are *cointegrated* with cointegrating vector $(1, -\beta)^\top$.

- S_t is a spread that fluctuates around a stable mean.
- Deviations of S_t from its mean tend to be temporary and thus natural targets for mean-reversion trades:
  - Go long the spread when S_t is unusually low.
  - Go short the spread when S_t is unusually high.

Economically, cointegration encodes a long-run equilibrium relationship (e.g., two share classes, ETF and its underlying, closely related commodities) where arbitrage forces or shared fundamentals tie prices together.

Testing for cointegration

The workflow typically involves:

1. **Unit root tests on individual series.**
   - Confirm that each price series is nonstationary (e.g., I(1)).
2. **Estimation of cointegrating vector.**
   - Regress $P_t^{(1)}$ on $P_t^{(2)}$:
     $$P_t^{(1)} = \alpha + \beta P_t^{(2)} + u_t,$$
     and treat the residuals $\hat{u}_t$ as an estimate of S_t.
   - More generally, for multiple assets, you can use Johansen's method to estimate several cointegrating relationships.
3. **Stationarity test on residuals.**
   - Apply unit root tests (e.g., ADF) to $\hat{u}_t$.
   - If residuals are stationary, this supports cointegration.

Error-correction representation

When series are cointegrated, short-run dynamics often follow an *error-correction model*:

$$\Delta P_t^{(1)} = \lambda\,(P_{t-1}^{(1)} - \beta P_{t-1}^{(2)}) + \text{short-run terms} + \varepsilon_t.$$

Here:

- The term $(P_{t-1}^{(1)} - \beta P_{t-1}^{(2)})$ is the lagged spread.
- λ measures how strongly deviations of the spread from equilibrium are corrected in the next period.

For a pairs trading strategy, λ is effectively a mean-reversion speed: larger $|\lambda|$ suggests faster convergence and shorter expected holding periods.

Ornstein–Uhlenbeck Processes: Continuous-Time Mean Reversion

In high-frequency or derivatives contexts, it is often convenient to model mean reversion in continuous time. The Ornstein–Uhlenbeck (OU) process is the canonical continuous-time mean-reverting model.

Definition and properties

An OU process $\{X_t\}$ satisfies the stochastic differential equation (SDE)

$$dX_t = \kappa(\theta - X_t)\,dt + \sigma\,dW_t,$$

where:

- θ is the long-run mean level.
- $\kappa > 0$ is the mean-reversion speed.
- $\sigma > 0$ is the volatility parameter.
- W_t is a standard Brownian motion.

Interpretation:

- When X_t is below θ, the drift term $\kappa(\theta - X_t)$ is positive, pushing it upwards; when X_t is above θ, the drift is negative.
- The stochastic term $\sigma\, dW_t$ injects random shocks.

Key properties (under stationarity):

- The stationary distribution of X_t is normal with mean θ and variance $\sigma^2/(2\kappa)$.
- Autocorrelation decays exponentially: $\rho(\tau) = e^{-\kappa\tau}$ for time lag τ.

Discretization and connection to AR(1)

If we sample the OU process at discrete times separated by Δt, we obtain

$$X_{t+\Delta t} = \theta + e^{-\kappa\Delta t}(X_t - \theta) + \eta_t,$$

where η_t is Gaussian noise with variance depending on σ, κ, and Δt. This is an AR(1) process with coefficient

$$\phi = e^{-\kappa\Delta t}.$$

Thus, estimating a discrete-time AR(1) on a spread S_t effectively gives you OU-like parameters:

- $\hat{\phi}$ from AR(1) $\Rightarrow \hat{\kappa} \approx -\frac{1}{\Delta t}\ln\hat{\phi}$,
- Long-run mean $\hat{\theta}$ from intercept and $\hat{\phi}$.

Trading interpretation of OU parameters

For a contrarian strategy on a stationary spread modeled as OU:

- **Mean-reversion speed κ:** Controls how quickly the spread is expected to revert.
  - A common metric is the *half-life* of mean reversion:

    $$\text{Half-life} = \frac{\ln 2}{\kappa},$$

    the expected time for a deviation to shrink by half. This guides holding-period expectations.

- **Volatility σ:** Determines the typical scale of random fluctuations and thus the dispersion of potential profits and losses between entry and exit.
- **Long-run mean θ:** Provides the anchor around which entry and exit bands are defined.

A simple OU-inspired trading rule might be:

- Enter long when $X_t < \theta - k \cdot \hat{\sigma}_\infty$.
- Enter short when $X_t > \theta + k \cdot \hat{\sigma}_\infty$.
- Exit (or reduce) positions as X_t reverts towards θ.

where $\hat{\sigma}_\infty = \sigma/\sqrt{2\kappa}$ is the stationary standard deviation and k is an entry multiple (e.g., $k = 1$ or 2).

Choosing the Right Model Complexity

With ARIMA, GARCH, cointegration, and OU processes at your disposal, it is tempting to build highly parameterized models. However, from an anomaly-hunting and trading perspective, a few guiding principles help keep you grounded:

- **Start simple.** Begin with low-order AR models for returns or spreads. Only add complexity (MA terms, higher lags, GARCH components) when residual diagnostics show clear, stable structure that simpler models miss.
- **Align frequency and horizon.** The sampling frequency of your model should match the holding period and decision frequency of your strategy. For a 5-day contrarian trade, modeling daily dynamics in exquisite intraday detail may not add value.
- **Exploit economic structure.** Use cointegration and OU-like mean reversion where you have clear economic reasons to expect equilibrium relationships (e.g., dual-listed shares, ETF vs. index, related commodities).

- **Respect regime shifts.** Stationarity is always an approximation; markets change. Periodically re-estimate models, watch for parameter drift, and use rolling windows or regime indicators where appropriate.

- **Integrate with inference and multiple-testing controls.** Model parameters and implied Sharpe ratios should be subjected to robust inference and false discovery control (as in prior sections) before you trust them for capital allocation.

This section has sketched the core parametric tools for modeling mean reversion in financial time series:

- AR and ARIMA models capture linear dependence and, after differencing, allow you to describe and forecast stationary components of prices, returns, or spreads.
- GARCH models describe time-varying volatility, vital for scaling contrarian positions and understanding when tail risk is elevated.
- Cointegration formalizes long-run equilibrium relations between assets and provides stationary spreads that are natural substrates for mean-reversion trades.
- Ornstein–Uhlenbeck processes offer a continuous-time perspective on mean reversion, closely related to discrete-time AR(1) and useful for parameterizing trading rules (e.g., half-life, entry bands).

These models, combined with the distributional and inferential tools from earlier sections, form the quantitative backbone of the anomaly-hunting framework that the rest of this book builds on-whether you ultimately implement signals with traditional time-series econometrics or more flexible machine-learning methods.

Chapter 4

Machine Learning Pipeline for Contrarian Signals

Machine learning does not fail in finance because the algorithms are weak-it fails because the pipeline is sloppy. In contrarian trading, where edges are microscopic and decay quickly, any leakage, look-ahead bias, or overfitting instantly turns a clever model into an expensive random number generator. In this chapter you will design a battle-tested ML pipeline specifically for hunting market anomalies: defining robust targets, enforcing strict temporal discipline, tuning models without data snooping, and choosing architectures that respect the structure of financial time series. By the end, you will have a blueprint for turning raw, noisy price data into contrarian signals that can survive first contact with live trading.

4.1 Supervised Learning Workflow & Regularization

In previous chapters we focused on the economics of contrarian strategies: why temporary mispricings arise, what market frictions they must overcome, and how to express them as systematic rules. We now take the next step and formalize contrarian signal construction as a supervised machine learning (ML) problem.

The core idea is simple: we want a model that, at each decision time t, takes in information available *at or before* t (prices, volumes, fundamentals, order book states, factor returns, ...) and outputs a prediction about what will happen over some future horizon $(t, t + H]$. That prediction is then translated into a trading action (long, short, or flat).

This section describes the supervised learning loop that makes this possible:

- Designing labels that encode the contrarian hypothesis.
- Choosing loss functions that reflect trading goals.
- Evaluating predictions with metrics connected to P&L.
- Using regularization, feature scaling, and leakage control to keep models stable in noisy financial data.

Throughout, keep in mind that financial prediction is a *low signal-to-noise* problem: most small patterns are spurious. The purpose of a disciplined workflow is not to squeeze every last drop out of the in-sample data, but to identify patterns that are likely to survive contact with the real market.

From Financial Intuition to Labels

A contrarian strategy starts with an intuition such as:

> "If a stock drops sharply in a day without major news, its expected return over the next few days is positive."

Supervised learning requires that we turn this verbal hypothesis into a numerical *label* y_t defined at each decision time t, and a corresponding *feature vector* $\mathbf{x}_t$ summarizing available information.

Basic return-based labels

Let p_t denote the price at time t and $r_{t+1} = \frac{p_{t+1}-p_t}{p_t}$ the single-period return. For a horizon of H periods, define the *future horizon return* at time t as

$$R_{t\to t+H} = \sum_{h=1}^{H} r_{t+h},$$

possibly adjusted for transaction costs, funding, and benchmark returns.

Common label designs include:

- **Signed return (regression label).**

$$y_t = R_{t\to t+H}.$$

  Here the model predicts a real-valued expected return. Trading rules may then go long if $\hat{y}_t > \theta^+$, short if $\hat{y}_t < \theta^-$, and flat otherwise.

- **Binary reversal indicator (classification label).**

$$y_t = \begin{cases} 1, & \text{if } R_{t\to t+H} > c, \\ 0, & \text{otherwise,} \end{cases}$$

  where c might be zero or a small positive threshold to cover costs. The model estimates the probability of a "profitable reversal" event.

- **Ternary long/flat/short label.** For more direct mapping to actions,

$$y_t \in \{-1, 0, +1\}$$

  indicates whether an idealized contrarian would take a short, flat, or long position at time t.

These are all ways of encoding the same intuition: we believe that extreme negative moves today are associated with positive returns over the next window. The choice among them is driven by your downstream use case (regression vs classification model classes, risk constraints, interpretability) and by data properties (class imbalance, noise).

Horizon choice and overlap

The length H of the horizon is economically important. Contrarian strategies are usually short-horizon: a day to a few weeks. But from an ML perspective, H also controls how noisy labels are:

- Very short horizons (e.g., one bar in intraday data) produce labels dominated by microstructure noise.
- Very long horizons dilute the specific contrarian effect you are targeting.

In practice, you will often use rolling horizons, so labels overlap in time: both $R_{t\to t+H}$ and $R_{t+1\to t+1+H}$ include many of the same returns. This overlap is not a problem by itself, but it has consequences for validation and leakage prevention (treated in detail in the next chapter). Here, it is enough to note that labels are rarely i.i.d.; temporal dependence must be respected throughout the pipeline.

Including costs and constraints in labels

If transaction costs, borrowing fees, or risk limits are significant, it can be helpful to bake them into the label:

$$y_t = R_{t\to t+H} - \text{Cost}_t,$$

or

$$y_t = \mathbb{1}\left\{R_{t\to t+H} - \text{Cost}_t > 0\right\}.$$

This focuses learning directly on *post-cost* profitability instead of raw price movements, which can materially change which patterns appear attractive.

The Supervised Learning Loop

Once you have labels and features, you can set up the supervised learning workflow:

- Split the time-ordered data into train, validation, and test segments.

- Engineer features and fit models on the training set.

- Use the validation set to tune hyperparameters and diagnose problems.

- Reserve the test set as a final, untouched estimate of real-world performance.

This loop is not a single pass; you will iterate many times. Each iteration should respect *chronology*: information from the future must never influence the past.

A High-Level Workflow Diagram

To fix ideas, Figure summarizes the main components of a supervised contrarian signal pipeline, emphasizing the steps where leakage is most likely.

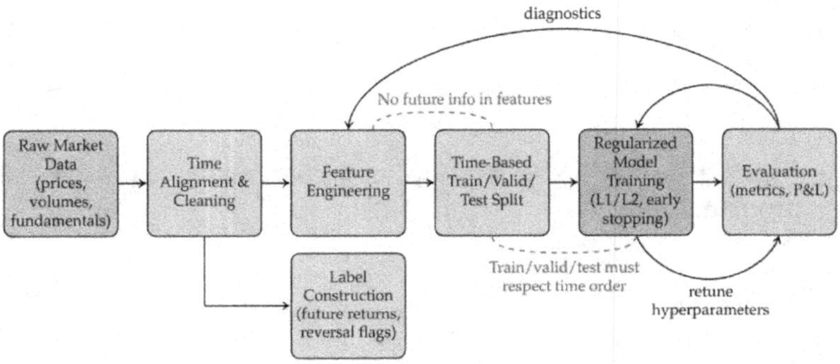

We will now unpack each modeling component in more detail.

Loss Functions Aligned with Trading Goals

A loss function measures how "wrong" a prediction is. In ML, we minimize average loss on the training set. In trading, *implicit* loss functions such as negative P&L, drawdown, or missed opportunities also matter, but they are rarely differentiable or easy to optimize directly. The art is to choose a statistical loss that is both tractable and well aligned with your trading objective.

Squared error for regression

For real-valued labels y_t (e.g., future returns), the most common choice is mean squared error (MSE):

$$\mathcal{L}_{MSE} = \frac{1}{N}\sum_{t=1}^{N}(y_t - \hat{y}_t)^2.$$

MSE penalizes large deviations heavily. In low-signal environments this can be useful: it discourages the model from making wild predictions. However, MSE is symmetric: overpredicting and underpredicting are treated equally, while in trading we often care more about specific types of errors (e.g., false positives after costs).

Logistic loss for event prediction

For binary labels $y_t \in \{0, 1\}$ indicating whether a profitable reversal occurs, we can model the probability

$$p_t = \mathbb{P}(y_t = 1 \mid \mathbf{x}_t)$$

and use logistic loss:

$$\mathcal{L}_{log} = -\frac{1}{N}\sum_{t=1}^{N}\left[y_t \log p_t + (1 - y_t)\log(1 - p_t)\right].$$

Logistic loss implicitly encourages well-calibrated probabilities: the predicted p_t should match the empirical frequency of positive outcomes in similar situations. This is valuable when signals feed into portfolio optimizers or risk models that treat probabilities explicitly.

Asymmetric and custom losses

Contrarian strategies typically face:

- **Class imbalance:** profitable reversals may be rare.
- **Cost asymmetry:** entering a bad trade can be substantially worse than skipping a good one, especially when turnover and costs are high.

To reflect this, we can weight different errors unequally. For binary labels,

$$\mathcal{L}_{wlog} = -\frac{1}{N}\sum_{t=1}^{N}\left[w_1 y_t \log p_t + w_0(1 - y_t)\log(1 - p_t)\right],$$

where w_1 and w_0 upweight underrepresented or more costly mistakes.

Even when using standard library loss functions, you can shape the effective loss via:

- **Sample weighting:** give more weight to regimes or assets that matter more to your strategy.
- **Label transformation:** for regression, predict a monotone transform of returns (e.g., clipped or rank-transformed returns) to reduce sensitivity to outliers.

The key principle is: choose a loss that penalizes the kinds of prediction errors that hurt your P&L the most, while staying within the realm of well-understood ML objectives.

Evaluation Metrics Connected to Trading

Minimizing a loss on the training set is necessary but not sufficient. We need metrics that tell us whether a model is attractive as a *trading signal.* The standard ML metrics—accuracy, precision, recall, R^2—can be informative but must be interpreted through a financial lens.

Hit rate and payoff asymmetry

For binary or ternary labels, the *hit rate* is the fraction of trades with positive outcome:

$$\text{Hit rate} = \frac{\#\text{profitable trades}}{\#\text{total trades}}.$$

Hit rate alone is misleading if gains and losses are asymmetrical. A contrarian strategy can be profitable with a hit rate below 50% if the average gain per winner exceeds the average loss per loser. Therefore you should always examine:

- Distribution of trade P&L (median, tails).
- Average profit conditional on a positive prediction.
- Average loss conditional on a negative outcome.

Ranking quality and concentration of alpha

Many production strategies do not trade all positive predictions, but instead allocate to the *top-ranked* opportunities by predicted return or probability. In that case, the quality of the *ranking* matters more than the absolute accuracy.

Useful diagnostics include:

- **Information coefficient (IC):** correlation between predicted scores and realized returns.
- **Bucketed returns:** sort assets into quantiles by predicted score and compute average realized return per bucket. A contrarian signal should show monotone improvement across buckets.

This connects naturally to portfolio construction: a model that ranks well (high IC) can be scaled and combined more flexibly than one that only rarely emits strong long/short signals.

Operational metrics: turnover and slippage sensitivity

Because contrarian strategies often trade frequently, it is crucial to track:

- **Turnover:** how much the portfolio changes per unit time, given your chosen thresholding of model outputs.
- **Slippage sensitivity:** how quickly performance degrades as you widen execution costs or tighten trading constraints.

In low-signal regimes, even a slight underestimation of costs can flip expected alpha from positive to negative. When evaluating models, always simulate performance under conservative cost assumptions.

Regularization: Embracing Simpler Models in Noisy Markets

Financial datasets often feature many candidate predictors but relatively few truly independent observations. Without constraints, flexible models can fit the noise instead of the signal. *Regularization* addresses this by explicitly penalizing complexity.

L2 regularization (Ridge)

In linear regression, we estimate

$$\hat{\boldsymbol{\beta}} = \arg\min_{\boldsymbol{\beta}} \left[\frac{1}{N} \sum_{t=1}^{N} (y_t - \boldsymbol{\beta}^\top \mathbf{x}_t)^2 + \lambda \|\boldsymbol{\beta}\|_2^2 \right],$$

where $\lambda \geq 0$ is a hyperparameter. The ℓ_2 penalty shrinks coefficients toward zero, especially those associated with weak or noisy predictors. This reduces variance at the cost of a little bias—an excellent trade in most financial settings.

L1 regularization (Lasso)

L1 regularization uses the ℓ_1 norm:

$$\hat{\boldsymbol{\beta}} = \arg\min_{\boldsymbol{\beta}} \left[\frac{1}{N} \sum_{t=1}^{N} (y_t - \boldsymbol{\beta}^\top \mathbf{x}_t)^2 + \lambda \|\boldsymbol{\beta}\|_1 \right].$$

The ℓ_1 penalty favors *sparse* solutions, where many coefficients are exactly zero. For contrarian strategies, this is especially valuable:

- It automates feature selection, often revealing a small subset of indicators that drive most of the predictive power.
- It reduces model sensitivity to small changes in the data, improving robustness across market regimes.

Elastic Net and beyond

Elastic Net combines both penalties:

$$\mathcal{L} = \frac{1}{N} \sum_{t=1}^{N} (y_t - \boldsymbol{\beta}^\top \mathbf{x}_t)^2 + \lambda_1 \|\boldsymbol{\beta}\|_1 + \lambda_2 \|\boldsymbol{\beta}\|_2^2.$$

This is often a good default in finance, particularly when features are correlated (as many technical indicators are). The L2 part stabilizes coefficients across correlated predictors, while the L1 part encourages sparsity.

In nonlinear models such as gradient-boosted trees and neural networks, regularization takes other forms: limiting tree depth, shrinkage (learning rate), dropout, early stopping. The unifying idea is to constrain the model so that it cannot react too aggressively to idiosyncrasies of the training sample.

Underfitting is often safer than overfitting.

Because apparent in-sample Sharpe ratios can be vastly inflated by luck, a slightly underfit model that leaves some alpha on the table is usually preferable to a highly optimized model that collapses out of sample. When in doubt, choose the simpler specification that still delivers economically meaningful performance on validation data.

Feature Scaling: Making Regularization and Optimization Work

Most regularization techniques implicitly assume that features are on comparable scales. For example, L1 and L2 penalties treat a one-unit change in any coefficient equally. If one feature ranges between 0 and 1 while another ranges between 0 and 1,000, the unscaled model will treat them very differently.

Standardization and normalization

A common remedy is to transform each continuous feature $x^{(j)}$ by subtracting its mean and dividing by its standard deviation:

$$\tilde{x}_t^{(j)} = \frac{x_t^{(j)} - \mu^{(j)}}{\sigma^{(j)}}.$$

In time-series contexts, $\mu^{(j)}$ and $\sigma^{(j)}$ must be computed using *only past data* relative to each time point to avoid look-ahead bias. In practice, we approximate this by fitting the scaler on the training set and applying the same transformation to validation and test sets. More refined approaches use rolling-window statistics.

Feature scaling improves:

- Numerical stability of optimization algorithms.

- Effectiveness of regularization (penalties treat all coefficients comparably).
- Interpretability of linear models (coefficients can be compared across features).

Leakage Control: Guarding the Boundary Between Past and Future

Leakage occurs when information from the future leaks into the training process, directly or indirectly, making performance look much better than it will be in reality. In financial ML, leakage is a frequent and deadly flaw. Examples include:

- Using full-sample statistics (means, standard deviations, PCA loadings) computed over the entire dataset to transform features at early time points.
- Including features that are functions of future prices or volumes, mislabeled as "current" indicators.
- Performing random cross-validation shuffles that mix future and past observations indiscriminately.

Chronology-respecting preprocessing

Any transformation that must be *estimated* from data (standardization, PCA, clustering, feature selection) should be fitted on the training period only, then applied unchanged to validation and test periods. This rule applies recursively whenever you move the training window forward in time.

For example, a correct standardization pipeline for a single split is:

- On training data only, compute $\mu_{train}^{(j)}$ and $\sigma_{train}^{(j)}$.
- Transform both training and validation/test features using these training statistics.

Never recompute scaling parameters using validation or test data; doing so lets future information subtly guide feature magnitudes and model fit.

Avoiding target leakage

Target leakage occurs when labels (or their near equivalents) are smuggled into features. Obvious examples are rare, but subtle variants abound:

- Using realized volatility over $(t, t+H]$ as a feature at time t while also using returns over the same window in the label.
- Using future analyst revisions or accounting restatements that would not have been known at time t.

The safeguard is conceptual: at each decision time t, imagine taking a snapshot of everything your trading system *could know in real time*. Features must come from that snapshot or earlier; labels must come from the future. There should be a clean separation between the two, as highlighted by the red leakage boundaries in Figure.

Putting It All Together

The supervised learning workflow for contrarian signals is not fundamentally different from that in other domains, but the economic context raises the stakes. Labels must faithfully encode the anomaly you are pursuing, loss functions and metrics must reflect trading realities, and every preprocessing and modeling choice must respect the arrow of time.

Regularization and feature scaling are not just technicalities; they are core risk controls in a world where apparent patterns are cheap and genuine anomalies are rare. Leakage control, in turn, is about intellectual honesty: ensuring that your backtests are a fair representation of what could have been known and done in real time.

In the following sections, we will deepen this pipeline by developing time-aware cross-validation schemes that make the notion of "out of sample" precise in a temporal setting, and by exploring hyperparameter optimization and model families suitable for hunting contrarian opportunities.

4.2 Time-Aware Cross-Validation & Leakage Prevention

In the previous section we treated contrarian signal construction as a supervised learning problem: we defined labels, chose loss functions, and stressed the importance of regularization and chronology-respecting preprocessing. We now focus on the layer that often makes or breaks a strategy in practice: *validation*.

Validation asks a simple question: *given the model and features we have designed, how well should we expect them to perform on data we have not yet seen?* In other words, what is the realistic out-of-sample Sharpe ratio, hit rate, and drawdown profile?

In ordinary machine learning, this is often answered with random train/test splits or standard K-fold cross-validation. For time-series contrarian strategies, these methods can be dangerously misleading because they ignore temporal dependence and label overlap. This section develops time-respecting schemes—walk-forward and purged K-fold with embargo—that produce performance estimates closer to what you would observe in live trading.

Why Standard Cross-Validation Fails for Time Series

Classical cross-validation relies on an i.i.d. worldview:

- Each observation is assumed to be independent of the others.
- The joint distribution of data is assumed to be stationary over time.

Under these assumptions, it is legitimate to shuffle observations at random and split them into training and validation folds. But contrarian signals violate both assumptions.

Temporal dependence

Financial returns and features are time-ordered. A shock today often affects returns tomorrow and the day after. If you randomly shuffle timestamps, a model may be trained on data from 2019 and validated on data from 2010. This allows *future regimes* to influence estimates used when predicting the past, which is impossible in live trading.

Overlapping labels

Contrarian labels are typically defined over rolling windows:

$$y_t = R_{t \to t+H} = \sum_{h=1}^{H} r_{t+h}.$$

Then y_t and y_{t+1} share most of their underlying returns. If you randomly assign t to the training set and $t+1$ to the validation set, the two labels are highly correlated, and more importantly, they depend on many of the *same* future returns. The model can effectively learn about the validation labels from their near-duplicates in the training set, leading to overoptimistic estimates.

Regime shifts

Markets undergo structural changes: monetary policy regimes, microstructure innovations, crises. Standard cross-validation that mixes all periods together hides the model's sensitivity to these shifts. You might obtain a seemingly robust average Sharpe ratio that is really driven by a single, favorable subperiod.

Validation Schemes at a Glance

Before diving into implementation, it is useful to compare the main options: random K-fold (what we should avoid), simple temporal split, walk-forward validation, and purged K-fold with embargo. Figure summarizes these visually along a time axis.

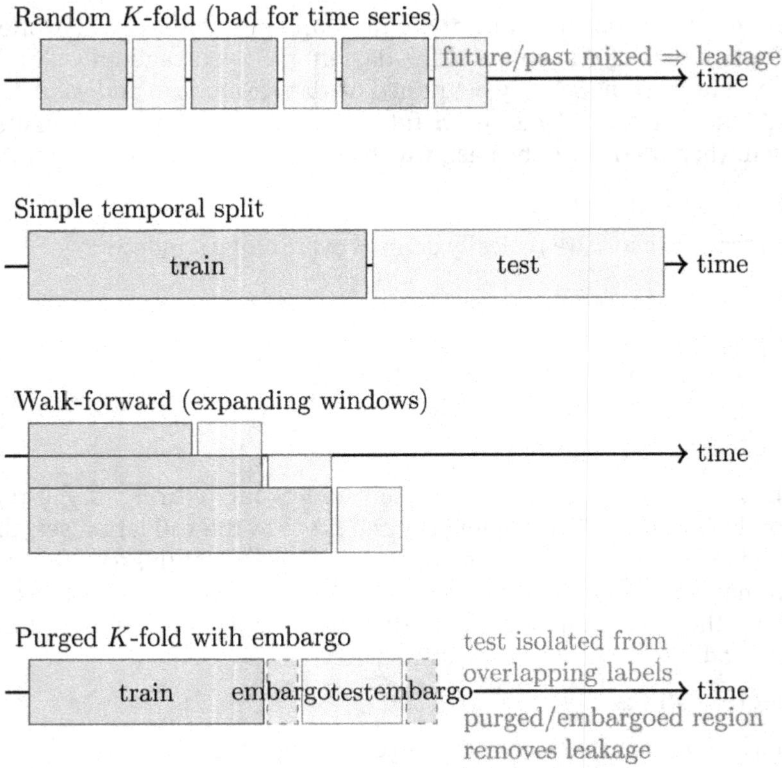

We now examine the time-aware methods in more detail, and show how they interact with label overlap and leakage.

Simple Temporal Train/Test Splits

The simplest time-respecting approach is a single split:

- Train on data up to time T_{train}.
- Test on data from $T_{train} + 1$ onwards.

This mirrors the natural experiment: you design your strategy using historical data up to a certain date, then deploy it going forward.

Advantages

- **Respects chronology.** No future data influences model training.
- **Operationally simple.** Easy to implement, easy to explain to stakeholders.
- **Realistic deployment scenario.** Particularly suitable when your intention is to fit a model once and then run it unchanged for a long period.

Limitations

- **Single split sensitivity.** Results may depend heavily on where you place T_{train}. A slightly different split could give a different Sharpe ratio.
- **Limited insight into regime robustness.** A single train/test split does not show how performance varies across different market environments.

Simple temporal splits are a good starting sanity check but are rarely sufficient on their own for serious model selection, especially when labels overlap and markets exhibit strong regime variation.

Walk-Forward Validation

Walk-forward validation addresses the shortcomings of a single split by mimicking how a model would be *retrained* as time passes. Instead of one train/test split, you construct a sequence of expanding (or rolling) windows:

Fold 1:	Train on $[t_0, t_1]$,	Test on $(t_1, t_2]$.
Fold 2:	Train on $[t_0, t_2]$,	Test on $(t_2, t_3]$.
Fold 3:	Train on $[t_0, t_3]$,	Test on $(t_3, t_4]$,
etc.		

In an *expanding window*, the training set grows as you move forward. In a *rolling window*, you keep the training window length fixed (e.g., last three years) and roll it forward.

Why walk-forward is powerful

- **Multiple pseudo out-of-sample periods.** Each test segment plays the role of a future period not seen during its corresponding training. Aggregating performance across folds provides a more stable estimate of generalization.
- **Regime coverage.** By placing test windows in different market regimes (e.g., pre-crisis, crisis, recovery), you see how the model behaves under varied conditions.
- **Operational realism.** The process closely mirrors live deployment: train using data to date, trade for a period, then retrain with the new history.

For contrarian strategies with overlapping labels, walk-forward validation already avoids the most egregious leakage: you never train on data from the same or later calendar dates as your test labels. However, it does not automatically prevent *label window* overlap around boundaries, which is where purged K-fold and embargo come in.

Purged K-Fold Cross-Validation

Purged K-fold cross-validation is designed specifically for time-series with labels that depend on intervals rather than single points. To motivate it, recall that for a horizon H, label y_t depends on returns over $(t, t+H]$. If you are careless when splitting data, the label windows for training and test observations can overlap in time, letting future information seep into the model.

Event-time representation

A convenient way to think about this is to associate each observation at time t with an *event interval*:

$$[t, t + H].$$

Two observations i and j have potentially leaking labels if their intervals overlap:

$$[t_i, t_i + H] \cap [t_j, t_j + H] \neq \emptyset.$$

Purged K-fold proceeds by splitting data into K contiguous time blocks (folds) along the time axis, but then *purging* from the training set any observation whose label interval overlaps with that of the test fold.

Algorithm sketch

For each fold $k = 1, \dots, K$:

- Define a contiguous test time block $\mathcal{T}_k = [a_k, b_k]$.
- Define a candidate training set as all observations outside $\mathcal{T}_k$.
- **Purge:** remove from the training set any observation with label interval intersecting $\mathcal{T}_k$. Concretely, drop any t such that

$$[t, t + H] \cap [a_k, b_k] \neq \emptyset.$$

- Train the model on the remaining observations; evaluate on $\mathcal{T}_k$.

This ensures that the model is never trained on returns that contribute to test labels, even indirectly through overlapping intervals. You then aggregate performance across folds as usual.

Embargo: Adding a Safety Buffer

Purging removes observations whose label windows overlap directly with the test interval. In practice, we may also want to avoid using data that is *too close* to the test interval, even if it does not strictly overlap. This is particularly relevant when:

- Your features evolve slowly, so information near the boundary is highly correlated.
- There are market microstructure effects or delayed reactions that persist beyond H.

An *embargo* implements a buffer around the test fold: a period before and after $\mathcal{T}_k$ from which we also exclude training observations.

Formally, for a chosen embargo length E:

- Embargoed interval around test fold k is
$$[a_k - E, b_k + E].$$
- Any observation whose *timestamp* falls inside this embargoed interval is excluded from training for that fold.

Purging and embargo work together:

- **Purging** looks at *label intervals* and ensures no overlapping labels across train and test.
- **Embargo** looks at *time proximity* and removes observations near folds to further reduce dependence.

In Figure, the red dashed embargo blocks around the green test segment illustrate this idea. The remaining blue training region is separated in time and in label windows from the test.

Choosing Between Walk-Forward and Purged K-Fold

Both walk-forward and purged K-fold with embargo are time-aware and leakage-conscious. Which should you use?

Walk-forward: when deployment structure dominates

Walk-forward is most natural when:

- Your strategy will be retrained on a fixed calendar schedule (e.g., monthly, quarterly).
- You care strongly about the path of cumulative performance over time: how the strategy would have evolved if you had been running it historically.
- Label horizons are short relative to evaluation windows, so label overlap is less problematic.

Here, each fold's test segment is a realistic simulation of a deployment period.

Purged K-fold: when label overlap is central

Purged K-fold with embargo is particularly valuable when:

- Labels are defined over long or variable horizons (e.g., event-driven strategies where exits occur on triggers rather than fixed H).
- Overlapping labels are pervasive, and you want precise control over dependence structures.
- You need to exploit data efficiently across many assets and events, making multiple non-overlapping walk-forward segments less practical.

Because purged K-fold reuses data across folds while carefully eliminating overlapping label contamination, it often delivers a good compromise between statistical efficiency and bias control.

In practice, sophisticated shops use *both*: walk-forward validation to understand time-path behavior and regime robustness, and purged K-fold with embargo as a rigorous tool for model comparison and hyperparameter tuning.

Diagnostics: Detecting Residual Leakage

Even with time-aware schemes in place, leakage can sneak in through other channels: preprocessing, feature engineering, or inadvertent peeking at future data.

You should routinely run diagnostics such as:

- **Performance vs. embargo length.** Increase the embargo length and observe how estimated Sharpe ratio and hit rate change. If performance collapses as you widen the buffer, your original estimate likely relied on boundary leakage.
- **Performance vs. horizon H.** Extremely short horizons that appear extremely profitable are suspect; often they are exploiting microstructure patterns that would vanish once realistic costs or latency are accounted for.
- **Temporal stability.** Plot cumulative performance across folds in chronological order. Strategies that look too smooth or too uniformly good in all regimes warrant extra scrutiny.

Additionally, verify that your preprocessing pipeline respects time:

- Scaling, PCA, and feature selection should be fitted separately within each training window of each fold.
- Any parameter estimated using both train and test data (even innocently, as when you preprocess the whole sample at once) is a potential leakage vector.

Connecting Validation to Live Trading Reality

Ultimately, validation is useful only insofar as it approximates the uncertainty you face when you deploy capital. For contrarian strategies, this means:

- **Respecting time.** Never let the model see the future, directly or through preprocessing.
- **Respecting label structure.** Treat labels as intervals, not points, and ensure intervals do not overlap across train and test.
- **Respecting costs and constraints.** Apply realistic transaction costs, borrow fees, and liquidity filters in every validation fold, not just in a final backtest.

Time-aware cross-validation and careful leakage prevention do not guarantee that a strategy will work; markets can and do change. But they *do* ensure that when you decide to allocate capital, you are not basing that decision on artifacts of your backtest.

In the next section we will build on these validation concepts to discuss hyperparameter optimization and model selection: how to search over model specifications without "p-hacking" Sharpe ratios, and how to judge which models exhibit genuine robustness rather than overfitting to the historical record.

4.3 Hyperparameter Optimization & Model Selection

By now we have described how to express contrarian ideas as supervised learning problems, and how to evaluate them with time-aware cross-validation while guarding carefully against leakage. The next step is to decide *which* model, with *which* settings, you should trust with real capital.

This is the domain of *hyperparameter optimization* and *model selection*. Hyperparameters govern model complexity and behavior but are not learned directly from the loss function in the way ordinary parameters are. For contrarian strategies, the way you choose hyperparameters can easily turn a marginal signal into what appears to be a spectacular backtest—without adding any real predictive content. This section develops principled search schemes (grid, random, Bayesian) and shows how to embed them into nested, time-aware cross-validation so that model choice reflects genuine robustness rather than data-mined luck.

What Are Hyperparameters, Exactly?

Parameters are quantities learned from data by minimizing a loss: regression coefficients, tree split points, neural network weights. Hyperparameters, in contrast, are configuration knobs you set *before* training:

- For penalized linear models (Ridge, Lasso, Elastic Net): regularization strengths λ_1, λ_2.
- For tree-based models: maximum depth, minimum samples per leaf, learning rate, number of trees.
- For neural sequence models: number of layers, hidden units, dropout rates, sequence length, optimizer settings.

In contrarian trading, these knobs control not just statistical fit, but also economically relevant properties:

- Sharper or smoother signals (affects turnover and costs).
- Sensitivity to specific regimes (overfitting vs stability).
- Latency and computational overhead in production.

Choosing hyperparameters is therefore a multi-criteria problem: you seek settings that deliver good risk-adjusted performance *and* satisfy operational constraints, under a validation scheme that respects time and overlapping labels.

The Danger of Naive Hyperparameter Tuning

Suppose you define a validation procedure (say, a walk-forward scheme) and then:

1. Enumerate hundreds or thousands of hyperparameter combinations.
2. For each combination, run the full validation and record its Sharpe ratio.
3. Pick the combination with the highest Sharpe ratio and declare success.

Even if your validation folds are perfectly time-aware and leakage-free, this procedure can severely overstate performance, for two reasons.

Implicit multiple testing

Each hyperparameter configuration is, in effect, a different model. When you test many models on the same validation data, some will look good *by luck alone*. The more configurations you try, the higher the chance that one of them will overfit the validation set.

This is analogous to multiple hypothesis testing: if you run enough experiments, you will eventually find a high Sharpe ratio even when there is no underlying signal. Without proper control, you are "p-hacking the Sharpe."

Leakage through re-use of the validation set

Repeatedly using the same validation set to guide your choices allows information from that set to accumulate in your decisions. Over time, your modeling process becomes implicitly conditioned on the quirks of the validation period, making its performance estimate optimistic.

To mitigate these issues, you need two ingredients:

- **Time-aware inner validation loops** to evaluate candidate hyperparameters fairly.
- **A separate outer test layer** to estimate generalization after hyperparameters and models have been chosen.

This is the essence of nested cross-validation for time series.

Nested, Time-Aware Cross-Validation

Nested cross-validation creates two distinct roles for your historical data:

- **Inner loop:** hyperparameter tuning and model comparison.
- **Outer loop:** final performance estimation, untouched by tuning decisions within each outer fold.

Conceptual structure

Think of your full time span $[T_{min}, T_{max}]$ being split into several large, contiguous outer folds. For outer fold k:

- The outer training window covers an earlier period $[T_{min}, T^{(k)}_{train,end}]$.
- The outer test window covers a subsequent period $(T^{(k)}_{train,end}, T^{(k)}_{test,end}]$.

Inside each outer training window, you run a time-aware *inner* validation procedure: an expanding walk-forward scheme, or purged K-fold with embargo, that evaluates each candidate hyperparameter configuration. For that outer fold, you:

1. Use only the inner folds to pick the best hyperparameters (e.g., by average information ratio across inner folds).
2. Refit the model with the chosen hyperparameters on the entire outer training window.
3. Evaluate the refitted model once on the outer test window.

You repeat this for each outer fold, obtaining multiple outer test performances. Aggregating them yields an estimate of out-of-sample behavior that accounts for both model fitting and hyperparameter selection.

Respecting time at both levels

Time-awareness must be preserved at both levels:

- **Inner loop:** Walk-forward or purged K-fold with embargo, constructed wholly within the outer training window. No inner test leakage from outer test.
- **Outer loop:** Each outer test segment is strictly in the future relative to its outer training segment, with purging or embargo if needed for overlapping labels.

In effect, the outer loop simulates different historical start dates for your research process: “what if we had stopped our research at this date, picked hyperparameters using only prior data, and then traded the next period?”

Hyperparameter Search Strategies

Within this nested structure, we must still decide *how* to explore the hyperparameter space: which combinations to try, and in what order. Three broad strategies are widely used.

Grid search

Grid search defines a discrete set of candidate values for each hyperparameter and evaluates all combinations. For example, for a Lasso regression you might specify:

$$\lambda \in \{10^{-4}, 10^{-3}, 10^{-2}, 10^{-1}, 1\}.$$

For a tree-based model, you might form a grid over

$$\text{max\_depth} \in \{2, 3, 4\},$$
$$\text{learning\_rate} \in \{0.05, 0.1\},$$
$$\text{n\_estimators} \in \{100, 300\}.$$

This yields $3 \times 2 \times 2 = 12$ combinations; each is evaluated in the inner loop and compared.

Advantages

- **Transparency.** Easy to explain and replicate; natural when you have strong priors about sensible ranges.
- **Coarse exploration.** Works reasonably well when there are few hyperparameters or they operate on log-scales.

Disadvantages

- **Curse of dimensionality.** The number of combinations grows exponentially with the number of hyperparameters.
- **Rigid granularity.** You may waste many evaluations on unimportant parameters while under-exploring critical ones.

In contrarian settings, grid search is appropriate for small, structured spaces: e.g., exploring a few regularization strengths or short lists of depth/learning-rate pairs.

Random search

Random search specifies distributions over hyperparameters and draws a fixed number of random samples. For instance:

- $\log_{10} \lambda \sim \text{Uniform}(-5, 0)$ for regularization strength.
- max_depth $\sim \{2, 3, 4, 5, 6\}$ with equal probability.
- learning_rate $\sim \text{LogUniform}(0.01, 0.3)$.

You then sample, say, 50 or 100 combinations and evaluate each via inner validation.

Why random search is often better

In high-dimensional spaces, different hyperparameters typically differ in *importance*. A small subset has large impact on performance; others matter little within broad ranges. Grid search spends equal effort on all dimensions, while random search implicitly focuses more on exploring diverse combinations of the important ones.

For contrarian models, where data is scarce and each evaluation (full inner validation) is expensive, random search gives better coverage per evaluation. It also facilitates:

- **Anytime behavior.** You can stop early and still have a diverse set of configurations tried.
- **Exploration of wide ranges.** Useful when you do not know appropriate scales a priori.

Bayesian optimization and adaptive methods

Bayesian optimization goes one step further: instead of sampling blindly, it models the mapping from hyperparameters to performance (e.g., average inner-fold Sharpe) as an unknown function. After each evaluation, it updates a surrogate model (often a Gaussian process or tree-based regressor) and chooses the next hyperparameter set where expected improvement is high.

Intuitively, Bayesian optimization learns from past trials:

- It explores promising regions more densely.
- It avoids spending many evaluations on clearly poor regions.

For contrarian strategies, where each full inner-validation run can be computationally heavy (especially with purged K-fold across many assets), Bayesian methods can be very efficient, provided that:

- You keep the search space reasonably low-dimensional and bounded.
- You are disciplined about the total number of iterations to avoid over-conditioning on a single validation architecture.

Other adaptive schemes (e.g., successive halving, Hyperband) allocate more resources to promising configurations progressively, pruning weak ones quickly. These are attractive when you can define cheap proxies for full evaluation (e.g., fewer inner folds, shorter history) and then refine the best candidates on the full setup.

Practical Design of the Search Space

Regardless of search strategy, the choice of hyperparameter *ranges* is crucial. In contrarian problems:

- **Favor strong regularization.** Start with relatively large penalties (strong shrinkage, shallow trees, small networks) and test whether relaxing them genuinely improves *outer* performance, not just inner metrics.
- **Use log-scales for positive hyperparameters.** Regularization strengths, learning rates, and some scale parameters often span orders of magnitude; log-uniform sampling or grids are more natural.

- **Respect operational constraints.** Exclude regions that would produce impractical models: depths that cause unacceptable latency, or a number of factors that risk overloading downstream risk systems.

Keep the space as small as you can while still including materially different model behaviors. The more extravagant your search, the larger the multiple-testing burden and the greater the temptation to cherry-pick.

Model Selection Across Families and Feature Sets

Hyperparameter tuning is not limited to a single model class; in practice, you often compare several:

- A sparse linear model (e.g., Elastic Net) on standardized anomaly features.
- A gradient-boosted tree ensemble on richer, possibly nonlinear interactions.
- A lightweight neural sequence model on return histories or order-book snapshots.

Model selection means deciding which combination of model family, feature set, and hyperparameters you should deploy. A principled approach considers several criteria beyond raw performance.

Stability across folds and regimes

A model whose outer-fold Sharpe ratio is high but erratic (positive in some folds, severely negative in others) is risky. Look at:

- The distribution (mean, median, dispersion) of outer-fold metrics.
- Performance by regime: crisis vs calm, bull vs bear, high vs low volatility.

Preference should usually go to models whose performance is *consistently* acceptable, even if not spectacular in any one fold.

Sensitivity to hyperparameter perturbations

A brittle model is one whose performance collapses when you change a hyperparameter slightly. To assess robustness:

- Take the best configuration and perturb each hyperparameter within a small neighborhood.
- Re-evaluate on the same outer folds (without reusing them to retune).

If small changes flip Sharpe from positive to strongly negative, the model is overfit to quirks of the data or the validation procedure. You may still extract insight from such a model (which features are repeatedly selected), but deploying it with capital is risky.

Interpretability and risk management

Trading is not only about statistical fit; it is also about understanding and controlling risk. Simpler or more interpretable models (e.g., sparse linear models, shallow trees) have advantages:

- Easier to debug when behavior changes.
- More straightforward to justify to investment committees and risk officers.
- Easier to monitor for regime drift (e.g., coefficients changing sign).

When two models deliver comparable outer-fold performance, the more interpretable one is often preferable, particularly early in a research program.

Avoiding Data-Mined Luck

Even with nested, time-aware validation and careful search strategies, it is still possible to fall prey to data-mined luck. A few additional habits help guard against this:

- **Hold back a final "lockbox" period.** Reserve the most recent years (or most relevant regime) as an untouched test set that you only use once, after settling on model class and hyperparameters via nested procedures on earlier data.
- **Simulate research path dependence.** Ask: "If I had stopped my research three years earlier or later, would I have reached the same conclusions?" This can be approximated by shifting the outer folds and repeating the selection.
- **Document decisions.** Keep a log of which hyperparameter ranges and model classes you tried, and why. This makes it easier to see when you are drifting into unprincipled search.

Remember that markets do not reward clever backtests; they reward robust edges that survive after costs, latency, and slippage. The goal of principled hyperparameter optimization and model selection is not to maximize in-sample or even cross-validated Sharpe, but to identify models that are likely to continue working when the data-generating process inevitably evolves.

In the next section we will survey concrete model families—linear, tree-based, and neural sequence models—and examine how the hyperparameter and selection principles developed here apply to each in the specific context of hunting contrarian anomalies.

4.4 Model Families: Linear, Tree-Based & Neural Sequence Models

The previous sections built a disciplined pipeline: we defined contrarian labels, enforced time-aware validation, and tuned hyperparameters within nested cross-validation to avoid data-mined luck. We now turn to the concrete algorithms that sit inside this pipeline.

There is no single "best" model for contrarian strategies. Instead, each family—sparse linear models, tree-based ensembles, neural sequence models, and unsupervised clustering methods—offers a different balance of flexibility, interpretability, data requirements, and operational complexity. This section surveys these families with a focus on:

- What kinds of anomaly structures each is good at capturing.
- How they behave in the low signal-to-noise regime typical of financial markets.
- How to integrate them into the supervised learning and validation framework already developed.

Sparse Linear Models: A Robust Baseline

Sparse linear models such as Lasso, Ridge, and Elastic Net are the workhorses of many successful quantitative strategies. They start from an assumption that is simultaneously simple and powerful:

> Expected returns over the chosen horizon are approximately a *linear* function of a relatively small subset of features.

Basic formulation

Let $\mathbf{x}_t \in \mathbb{R}^p$ be a vector of features for asset or event t and y_t the corresponding contrarian label (e.g., future excess return). A linear model posits

$$\mathbb{E}[y_t \mid \mathbf{x}_t] \approx \beta_0 + \boldsymbol{\beta}^\top \mathbf{x}_t,$$

with $\boldsymbol{\beta}$ estimated by minimizing a penalized loss:

$$\min_{\beta_0, \boldsymbol{\beta}} \frac{1}{N} \sum_{t=1}^{N} \ell(y_t, \beta_0 + \boldsymbol{\beta}^\top \mathbf{x}_t) + \lambda_1 \|\boldsymbol{\beta}\|_1 + \lambda_2 \|\boldsymbol{\beta}\|_2^2.$$

Here ℓ can be squared error (for regression) or logistic loss (for a reversal classifier), while λ_1 and λ_2 control L1 and L2 regularization, respectively.

Why linear models are well-suited to contrarian signals

Interpretability. Each coefficient β_j measures the marginal effect of feature $x^{(j)}$ on expected return, holding others constant. For example, a positive coefficient on a "previous-day drawdown" feature directly encodes the contrarian idea that larger drops today predict higher returns tomorrow.

This makes it straightforward to:

- Explain model behavior to non-technical stakeholders.
- Relate results back to economic theory and anomaly literature.
- Monitor for regime changes (e.g., coefficients switching sign).

Built-in feature selection. With L1 or Elastic Net, many coefficients are driven exactly to zero. This sparsity is valuable in low signal-to-noise markets:

- It reduces overfitting by limiting the number of active predictors.
- It highlights which signals actually matter in the presence of others.
- It simplifies downstream portfolio construction: you are not juggling dozens of tiny, noisy effects.

Good behavior in small samples. With appropriate regularization and feature scaling, sparse linear models can perform reasonably well even when the number of candidate features p is comparable to, or larger than, the effective number of independent observations. This is exactly the regime of high-frequency or multi-asset contrarian strategies.

Integrating sparse linear models into the pipeline

Sparse linear models fit naturally into the supervised learning workflow laid out earlier:

- **Features.** Include key contrarian predictors: short-term returns, moving-average deviations, liquidity and spread measures, volatility states, and cross-sectional ranks.
- **Preprocessing.** Standardize features using training-only statistics; handle outliers via clipping or robust transforms.
- **Validation.** Use walk-forward or purged K-fold with embargo, as appropriate to your label structure.
- **Hyperparameters.** Tune λ_1, λ_2 over log-scaled grids or via random/Bayesian search within the nested cross-validation framework.

As a rule of thumb, you should almost always include a sparse linear baseline in your model family comparison. It sets a high bar that more complex models must clear by a meaningful margin, not just by a small bump in backtested Sharpe.

Tree-Based Ensembles: Capturing Interactions and Thresholds

While linear models assume additive effects, many contrarian patterns are intrinsically nonlinear. For example:

> A previous-day crash predicts a rebound *only* when volatility is moderate and volume is elevated; in extreme volatility, the same crash may signal momentum continuation.

Tree-based methods—random forests and gradient-boosted trees—excel at capturing such interactions and threshold effects with minimal feature engineering.

Decision trees in a nutshell

A single decision tree recursively partitions feature space into regions and assigns a prediction (e.g., mean return or event probability) to each leaf. Splits are of the form "if $x^{(j)} \leq c$, go left; else go right," naturally modeling interactions and non-additive behavior.

However, individual trees are often unstable and prone to overfitting. Ensembles improve stability and performance.

Random forests

Random forests build many trees on bootstrapped samples of the data and average their predictions. They introduce randomness in:

- **Data:** each tree sees a different bootstrap sample.
- **Features:** at each split, only a random subset of features is considered.

Key hyperparameters include:

- Number of trees.
- Maximum tree depth.
- Minimum samples per leaf.

For contrarian strategies, random forests are useful when:

- You suspect nonlinearities but prefer a relatively robust, low-tuning model.
- Interpretability at the individual tree level is less important than understanding feature importance and general patterns.

Gradient-boosted trees

Gradient boosting builds trees *sequentially*, each new tree correcting errors made by the existing ensemble. This yields highly accurate, flexible models but increases the risk of overfitting if not carefully regularized.

Typical hyperparameters include:

- Learning rate (shrinkage).
- Number of trees (iterations).
- Maximum depth or number of leaves per tree.
- Regularization parameters (L1/L2 on leaf weights, subsampling rates).

In contrarian anomaly hunting, gradient boosting is powerful when:

- You have a rich feature set with plausible nonlinear interactions (e.g., interactions between return history, volatility, order-book imbalance).
- Data volume is sufficient to estimate these interactions under time-aware validation.

Strengths and weaknesses for contrarian signals

Strengths.

- **Nonlinear interactions.** Trees readily capture "only when" conditions and thresholds (e.g., signals that activate only beyond certain volume or volatility levels).
- **Mixed data types.** They handle numeric, categorical, and even missing values gracefully, often reducing preprocessing burden.
- **Feature importance measures.** Ensembles provide estimates of how much each feature contributes to reducing loss, guiding both model interpretation and feature pruning.

Weaknesses.

- **Overfitting risk.** Deep trees and many boosting iterations can memorize noise, especially in low signal-to-noise financial data.
- **Complex hyperparameter space.** Many knobs must be set, increasing the scope for accidental p-hacking.
- **Less transparent than linear models.** While global variable importance is accessible, local predictions are harder to reason about economically.

Integrating tree-based ensembles into the pipeline

To use tree-based models responsibly in our framework:

- Start with *shallow* trees and modest learning rates; treat deeper or more aggressive configurations as stress tests.
- Use nested, time-aware cross-validation to tune depth, learning rate, and number of trees, monitoring not just average Sharpe but dispersion across folds.
- Examine feature importance and partial dependence plots to ensure that learned patterns align with plausible contrarian mechanisms, rather than exploiting artifacts (e.g., survivorship bias).

In many workflows, tree-based ensembles are the natural "next step" after a sparse linear baseline: if they fail to deliver materially better, stable performance, there is little justification for added complexity.

Neural Sequence Models: Learning Directly from Time Order

Most of the models discussed so far operate on *snapshot* features at time t: engineered summaries of recent behavior. Neural sequence models instead ingest entire sequences (e.g., a window of returns, order-book states, or factor spreads) and learn temporal patterns automatically.

Main families include recurrent neural networks (RNNs), long short-term memory networks (LSTMs), gated recurrent units (GRUs), and temporal convolutional networks (TCNs).

Why sequences matter for contrarian trading

Contrarian behavior often depends not only on the most recent move but on the path that led there. For example:

- A sudden drop after a long rally may have different implications than the same drop following a choppy, mean-reverting period.
- Reversal strength may depend on the build-up of order-flow imbalance over multiple bars.

Sequence models can, in principle, capture:

- Patterns of acceleration or deceleration in returns.
- Duration of overbought/oversold states.
- Multiscale temporal dependencies (e.g., intraday vs multi-day patterns).

Architectural considerations

Recurrent models (RNNs, LSTMs, GRUs). These process sequences step-by-step, maintaining a hidden state h_t that aggregates information from past observations. LSTMs and GRUs introduce gating mechanisms to better handle long-range dependencies and vanishing gradients.

Temporal convolutional networks (TCNs). These use 1-D convolutions along the time axis with causal padding (no future leakage) and often dilation (skipping steps) to efficiently capture long horizons.

For contrarian applications, the architectural goal is not sophistication but *discipline*:

- Enforce causality (no future steps in receptive fields).
- Limit depth and width to control capacity.
- Combine strong regularization (dropout, weight decay) with early stopping under time-aware validation.

When neural sequence models make sense

Neural sequence models are attractive when:

- You have high-frequency or richly structured time-series data where path-dependence is intuitively important (e.g., tick-level quotes, detailed order flow).
- Linear and tree-based models on snapshot features hit a performance ceiling, but diagnostic plots suggest residual temporal structure.
- Data volume is large enough to support more parameter-rich architectures under proper validation (many independent sequences across assets and time).

However, they come with notable challenges:

- **Overfitting risk.** High capacity and flexible function classes can easily fit noise in thin financial signals.
- **Operational complexity.** Training and serving sequence models can be more resource-intensive and latency-sensitive.
- **Reduced transparency.** Inspecting why a network produced a given signal is often harder than for linear or tree-based models.

Given these trade-offs, sequence models should generally be considered *second-generation* tools in a research program: deployed after simpler families have been exhausted and only when clear, well-validated incremental value is demonstrated.

Unsupervised Clustering as a Complement

While not a predictive model family in the same sense, unsupervised clustering methods (e.g., k-means, Gaussian mixtures, hierarchical clustering) play a useful supporting role in anomaly hunting.

Regime and state identification

Clustering can be applied to features describing:

- Market-wide conditions: volatility level, cross-sectional dispersion, liquidity, macro indicators.
- Asset-specific states: recent volatility, spread, turnover, market cap.

The resulting clusters can be interpreted as regimes or liquidity/volatility states. This information can:

- Inform regime-dependent models (train separate contrarian models per regime).
- Condition execution rules (e.g., scale down exposure in illiquid or stressed clusters).
- Enhance risk overlays (e.g., avoid regimes where historical contrarian performance is weak).

Feature-space structuring

Clustering can also be used to structure the feature space:

- Identify groups of highly similar assets or events to form cross-sectional validation blocks.

- Guide the design of cross-sectional contrarian signals that treat clustered assets similarly.

All unsupervised steps must, as before, respect chronology: if clustering is based on statistical properties estimated from data, those estimators must be fit on training periods only within each fold, then held fixed when applied to validation or test.

Building a Coherent Model Stack

Rather than searching for a single winner, it is often helpful to think in terms of a *model stack* or hierarchy within the pipeline:

- **Start simple:** Build and validate a sparse linear model on well-designed contrarian features. Use it as both a production candidate and a benchmark.
- **Add nonlinear structure:** Introduce tree-based ensembles to capture interactions and thresholds. Retain the linear model as a fallback when tree-based gains are marginal or fragile.
- **Escalate to sequences only when justified:** Explore neural sequence models if the data genuinely merits them and simple models leave systematic structure unexplained.
- **Use unsupervised tools as glue:** Employ clustering to organize regimes and states, then plug that structure into the supervised models (e.g., regime-specific models, regime-aware position sizing).

At each stage, the same discipline applies:

- Time-aware, leakage-free validation.
- Nested hyperparameter tuning.
- Robustness checks across folds and regimes.
- Preference for simpler, more interpretable models when performance is comparable.

The result is not a black box, but a layered, transparent system for hunting contrarian anomalies: one where each model family is used for the kind of structure it handles best, and where statistical sophistication is always subordinated to economic intuition and rigorous out-of-sample testing.

Chapter 5

Feature Engineering & Alpha Design

Contrarian trading lives or dies on the quality of its signals: the market may be noisy, but mispricings often leave a precise numerical fingerprint. In this chapter, we turn trading ideas into features that a machine can understand-systematically encoding overreaction, liquidity stress, and behavioral bias into robust alpha signals rather than ad hoc indicators.

5.1 Price-Based Features for Reversion

In the previous chapters we discussed why market anomalies—and contrarian anomalies in particular—can exist at all, and how to think about returns as noisy realizations of an underlying stochastic process. We now turn to the practical question: *how do we turn raw prices into numerical features that a machine learning model can use to detect short-term overreaction and mean reversion?*

This section develops a compact but rigorous toolkit of price-based transformations. Everything here is designed with three constraints in mind:

- Features must be *causal*: they may use only information available at the prediction time (no look-ahead).
- Features should be as close to *stationary* as possible: their distribution over time should be reasonably stable.
- Features should map cleanly onto plausible *reversion mechanisms*: we want quantities that meaningfully express "overextended" versus "normal" states.

We proceed step by step: returns, multi-horizon structure, rolling statistics and z-scores, volatility scaling, and finally a practical recipe for a feature set that integrates them.

From Prices to Returns

Let P_t denote the price of an asset at time t. The raw price level is not a convenient object for modeling short-term mean reversion; different stocks trade at very different nominal levels, and prices are typically nonstationary. Instead we work with *returns*, which summarize relative changes.

The *simple* (or *discrete*) return from time $t-h$ to t is

$$R_t^{(h)} = \frac{P_t - P_{t-h}}{P_{t-h}} = \frac{P_t}{P_{t-h}} - 1.$$

For h equal to one day, $R_t^{(1)}$ is the familiar daily return:

$$R_t \equiv R_t^{(1)} = \frac{P_t - P_{t-1}}{P_{t-1}}.$$

A closely related concept is the *log return*:

$$r_t^{(h)} = \log\left(\frac{P_t}{P_{t-h}}\right) = \log P_t - \log P_{t-h}.$$

For small returns, $R_t^{(h)} \approx r_t^{(h)}$, but log returns have two advantages:

- They *add* across time: $r_t^{(h_1+h_2)} = r_{t-h_2}^{(h_1)} + r_t^{(h_2)}$.

- When modeling, it's often reasonable (though not exactly correct) to approximate log returns as Gaussian.

In practice, you can work in either simple or log returns as long as you are consistent. Many practitioners compute features in log space but report performance and P&L in simple returns.

Horizon Choice and Reversion Mechanisms

The horizon h is not a technical detail; it encodes the economic story behind the anomaly you are trying to capture. A 5-minute reversal signal reflects microstructure frictions and temporary order-flow pressure. A 5-day reversal signal is more likely related to investor overreaction to news or flows and subsequent correction.

We therefore treat returns over multiple horizons as separate features:

$$r_t^{(1)}, \quad r_t^{(5)}, \quad r_t^{(20)}, \quad \text{etc.}$$

Here, 1 might denote one day, 5 one trading week, and 20 one trading month. For intraday strategies, the units could be minutes or ticks.

- **Very short horizons** (seconds to minutes): features pick up microstructure noise, bid–ask bounce, and short-lived liquidity imbalances.
- **Short horizons** (hours to days): features capture delayed reaction to information, margin or risk limits, and small behavioral overreactions.
- **Medium horizons** (weeks to months): features begin to overlap with value/momentum cycles and position unwinds.

When you build a contrarian model, you typically choose one or two target horizons for your forecasts (e.g., next day or next hour), then engineer lagged return features over a *range* of backward-looking windows. The model learns which lags and horizons carry predictive content for mean reversion.

Rolling Statistics: Moving Averages and Volatility

Single-period returns are noisy. To measure whether an asset is currently "stretched," we compare its recent price or return to its own recent history. This leads naturally to rolling (or moving) statistics computed on a window of the last N observations.

Rolling Mean of Price or Returns

The *rolling mean price* over the last N periods is

$$\overline{P}_t^{(N)} = \frac{1}{N} \sum_{i=0}^{N-1} P_{t-i}.$$

More commonly in trading, we refer to this as a moving average (MA). Short windows (e.g., $N = 5$ or $N = 20$) track the current price closely; long windows (e.g., $N = 100$ or $N = 200$) capture a slow-moving trend or "fair value" anchor.

Similarly, the *rolling mean return* is

$$\overline{r}_t^{(N)} = \frac{1}{N} \sum_{i=1}^{N} r_{t+1-i}.$$

For high-frequency data, you might use returns over seconds and N in the hundreds or thousands; for daily data, typical values are $N \in \{20, 60, 126, 252\}$ (about 1, 3, 6, and 12 months).

Rolling Volatility

To judge how extreme a move is, we also need a sense of the recent variability of returns. The *rolling variance* of returns over window N is

$$\widehat{\sigma}_t^2(N) = \frac{1}{N-1} \sum_{i=1}^{N} \left(r_{t+1-i} - \overline{r}_t^{(N)}\right)^2,$$

and the corresponding *rolling volatility* is

$$\widehat{\sigma}_t(N) = \sqrt{\widehat{\sigma}_t^2(N)}.$$

Intuitively, $\widehat{\sigma}_t(N)$ says how "jumpy" the asset has been recently. If volatility is high, large returns are less informative about overreaction; if volatility is low, the same-size return is more surprising.

In intraday settings, you might compute volatility on returns sampled every k seconds. For daily strategies, you might compute $\widehat{\sigma}_t^{(daily)}(20)$ and then scale it to an annualized volatility by multiplying with $\sqrt{252}$, the approximate number of trading days in a year:

$$\widehat{\sigma}_t^{(ann)}(20) \approx \widehat{\sigma}_t^{(daily)}(20)\sqrt{252}.$$

Z-Scores: Measuring How "Stretched" We Are

Combining the rolling mean and volatility, we can form a standardized measure of how far the current price or return is from its recent average. This is the *z-score.*

Price Z-Score

One way to judge overextension is to ask: how many recent standard deviations is the current price away from its moving average? Define the *price z-score* as

$$Z_t^{(P)}(N) = \frac{P_t - \overline{P}_t^{(N)}}{\widehat{\sigma}_t^{(P)}(N)},$$

where $\widehat{\sigma}_t^{(P)}(N)$ is a rolling standard deviation of prices, computed similarly to that of returns.

A value of $Z_t^{(P)}(N) = +2$ means that P_t is two standard deviations above its N-period moving average. In many reversion strategies, such an overextension triggers a short signal, betting that the price will drift back toward the mean.

Return Z-Score

Alternatively, you can standardize returns. The *return z-score* over horizon h is

$$Z_t^{(r,h)}(N) = \frac{r_t^{(h)} - \overline{r}_t^{(h)}(N)}{\widehat{\sigma}_t^{(h)}(N)},$$

where $\overline{r}_t^{(h)}(N)$ and $\widehat{\sigma}_t^{(h)}(N)$ are rolling mean and volatility of h-horizon returns over the past N observations.

For short-horizon contrarian trading, both price and return z-scores are useful:

- Price z-scores emphasize *level* overextension relative to a local mean.
- Return z-scores emphasize *change* overextension—“an unusually large move” relative to typical moves.

A simple but surprisingly effective idea is: very large negative z-scores on short horizons (e.g., daily or hourly) often lead to partial bounce-backs as liquidity providers and value-motivated traders step in.

Visualizing Overextension and Reversion

Figure illustrates the core idea. We plot a synthetic price series, its rolling mean, and the z-score of price. During a sharp run-up, the price diverges from the moving average and the z-score enters an extreme region, shaded in the chart. Shortly thereafter, the price mean-reverts toward the moving average, and the z-score falls back toward zero.

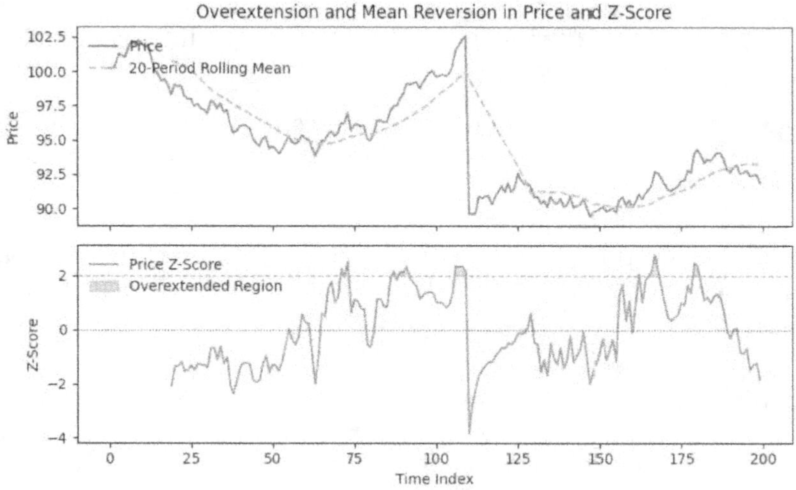

Volatility Scaling and Heteroskedasticity

Financial time series exhibit *heteroskedasticity*: their volatility changes over time. If you ignore this, reversal strategies can appear unstable. A $+3\%$ move might be huge in a calm regime but ordinary in a turbulent regime. To compare signals across time and assets, we often *volatility-scale* returns.

Volatility-Scaled Returns

Given a short-horizon return r_t and an estimate of its current volatility $\widehat{\sigma}_t$, define the volatility-scaled return

$$\tilde{r}_t = \frac{r_t}{\widehat{\sigma}_t}.$$

If $\widehat{\sigma}_t$ is computed over a recent window, then $\tilde{r}_t$ says how many volatility units the latest move represents. This is essentially the same as a z-score, but often $\widehat{\sigma}_t$ is a pure volatility estimate (e.g., from an exponentially weighted moving average or realized volatility formula) instead of a full standard deviation around a mean.

Volatility scaling serves two purposes:

- It makes signals more *comparable* across assets with different risk levels. A 2% move in a utility stock is very different from 2% in a volatile biotech name.
- It encourages more *stationary* features, as the unconditional distribution of $\tilde{r}_t$ is often closer to a fixed shape than that of raw returns.

In machine learning models, $\tilde{r}_t$ and its lags are often more effective inputs than raw returns, especially in cross-asset or cross-sectional settings.

Realized Volatility Estimation

To compute $\widehat{\sigma}_t$ for volatility scaling, we can use several standard estimators. For daily data sampled at close prices, a simple realized volatility proxy on a window of length N is

$$\widehat{\sigma}_t^{(rv)}(N) = \sqrt{\sum_{i=1}^{N} (r_{t+1-i})^2}.$$

For intraday data,

$$\widehat{\sigma}_t^{(rv)}(N) = \sqrt{\sum_{i=1}^{N} (r_{t+1-i}^{\Delta})^2},$$

where r^{Δ} are intraday returns over a fixed interval Δ (e.g., 5 minutes) and N spans, say, one day of such intervals.

Compared to the rolling standard deviation, realized volatility ignores the mean and directly accumulates squared returns. For short horizons, the mean is typically close to zero anyway, so this often suffices.

Classic Overreaction Measures

With returns, rolling means, and volatility scaling in hand, we can define some classic price-based contrarian indicators. These are not complete trading rules, but they are building blocks for alpha features.

Short-Horizon Losers vs. Winners

One of the oldest and most robust anomalies is that short-horizon losers often outperform short-horizon winners in the subsequent period, a pattern interpreted as temporary overreaction.

In a cross-sectional setting, at each date t:

- Compute recent returns (or volatility-scaled returns) $r_{i,t}^{(h)}$ for each asset i over horizon h (e.g., 1 day or 5 days).
- Rank assets into quantiles based on $r_{i,t}^{(h)}$ (e.g., deciles).
- Define features that encode where each asset lies in that ranking:

$$\text{RankFeature}_{i,t} = \frac{\text{rank of } r_{i,t}^{(h)}}{\text{number of assets}}.$$

A machine learning model can learn that very low-ranked (recent losers) assets tend to mean-revert and that very high-ranked (recent winners) assets tend to underperform in the short run, controlling for other features.

Multi-Day Reversal After Large Moves

Another staple pattern: very large one-day or multi-day moves often see partial reversal over the next few days, particularly when not clearly justified by fundamental news.

We can codify this with a *large-move flag*. For example, for daily data:

$$\text{BigMoveFlag}_t = \begin{cases} +1 & \text{if } Z_t^{(r,1)}(N) \leq -z_{th}, \\ -1 & \text{if } Z_t^{(r,1)}(N) \geq +z_{th}, \\ 0 & \text{otherwise,} \end{cases}$$

where z_{th} is a threshold such as 2 or 3. This creates a feature that explicitly marks days when the asset experienced a statistically large negative or positive move, in volatility-adjusted units.

A learning algorithm can then pick up patterns like: following $\text{BigMoveFlag}_t = +1$, the next-day return has a positive bias (bounce-back); following $\text{BigMoveFlag}_t = -1$, the next-day return tends to be negative (give-back).

Gap-Reversal Patterns at the Open

For daily bars, a *gap* is the overnight move between yesterday's close and today's open:

$$r_t^{gap} = \log\left(\frac{P_t^{open}}{P_{t-1}^{close}}\right).$$

Daytime return is

$$r_t^{day} = \log\left(\frac{P_t^{close}}{P_t^{open}}\right).$$

Empirically, large opening gaps, especially those not accompanied by high volume or obvious news, often see partial intraday reversal. A straightforward feature set here includes:

- Volatility-scaled gap return: $\tilde{r}_t^{gap} = r_t^{gap} / \widehat{\sigma}_t^{gap}$.
- Gap direction indicator: $\mathbb{1}\{r_t^{gap} > 0\}$.
- Gap size buckets (e.g., small/medium/large in absolute z-score).

These can be fed to a model predicting r_t^{day} or next-day returns, allowing it to learn when gaps reverse and when they continue.

A Practical Feature Recipe for Price-Based Reversion

We now summarize a coherent feature set that you can implement directly and hand to a machine learning model, with minimal risk of look-ahead bias. Assume we are predicting a target return over some horizon h^* (e.g., next day) for each asset.

Lagged Returns Across Horizons

Include lagged returns at multiple horizons as raw signals:

$$\{r_{t-k}^{(1)}, r_{t-k}^{(5)}, r_{t-k}^{(20)}\}_{k=0}^{K},$$

with K chosen to cover the relevant history length for your strategy (e.g., $K = 5$ for daily data, giving up to one week of overlapping windows).

If using intraday data, you might have analogous sets over 5-minute, 30-minute, and daily horizons.

Normalized Distance to Moving Averages

For each asset and for each choice of moving-average window N, compute the *normalized price distance*:

$$D_t^{(N)} = \frac{P_t - \overline{P}_t^{(N)}}{\overline{P}_t^{(N)}}.$$

This is a dimensionless measure of how far price is above or below its recent mean in relative terms. You can also use the more aggressively standardized price z-score $Z_t^{(P)}(N)$ discussed earlier.

Typical choices:

- Short-term: $N \in \{5, 10, 20\}$.
- Medium-term: $N \in \{60, 126\}$.

These features allow the model to learn contrarian rules such as: when $D_t^{(20)}$ is extremely positive and the short-term return has been strongly positive, the next return tends to be negative.

Volatility-Adjusted Returns and Shock Flags

Include volatility-scaled returns:

$$\tilde{r}_t^{(h)} = \frac{r_t^{(h)}}{\widehat{\sigma}_t^{(h)}},$$

as well as their lags. In addition, create simple *shock flags* based on z-scores or $\tilde{r}_t^{(h)}$ crossing thresholds:

$$\text{ShockUp}_t^{(h)} = \mathbb{1}\{\tilde{r}_t^{(h)} \geq z_{th}\}, \qquad \text{ShockDown}_t^{(h)} = \mathbb{1}\{\tilde{r}_t^{(h)} \leq -z_{th}\}.$$

These categorical indicators help non-linear models (e.g., tree ensembles) capture behavior in extreme tails of the distribution without having to infer implicit thresholds from scratch.

Regime Flags and Volatility State

Finally, it is often useful to indicate the current *volatility regime*. For example, define

$$\text{VolState}_t = \begin{cases} \text{Low} & \text{if } \widehat{\sigma}_t \leq \text{low quantile of past } \widehat{\sigma}, \\ \text{Medium} & \text{if } \widehat{\sigma}_t \text{ is in middle range}, \\ \text{High} & \text{if } \widehat{\sigma}_t \geq \text{high quantile of past } \widehat{\sigma}. \end{cases}$$

Encode this as one-hot flags (e.g., $\mathbb{1}\{\text{VolState}_t = \text{High}\}$, etc.). Many reversal effects are conditional on volatility: mean reversion after extreme moves can be sharper in calm regimes (shocks stand out) and more delayed or noisy in crisis regimes.

Implementation and Leakage Considerations

When computing these features, it is crucial to avoid *look-ahead bias*. Every statistic at time t must be computed using only data up to and including t, not future information. This implies:

- If predicting $r_{t+1}^{(1)}$ at the close of day t, you may use P_t, $r_t^{(h)}$, and rolling statistics up to t, but not P_{t+1} or any volume/price data from day $t+1$.
- Rolling windows should be implemented as trailing windows ending at t, not centered windows that use both past and future observations.
- When evaluating models, ensure that any normalization (e.g., z-scoring across the cross-section) is also done in a causal way, using only contemporaneous or past data.

With these safeguards, the price-based features constructed in this section form a solid, interpretable input space for machine learning models to hunt for short-term mean-reversion opportunities. In subsequent sections, we will extend this toolkit with microstructure, event-driven, seasonal, and pairwise features that further sharpen our view of transient mispricings.

5.2 Microstructure-Driven Features

In the previous section we built contrarian signals using only bar data: prices, returns, and volatility over daily or intraday horizons. Many mean-reversion opportunities, however, are born *inside* the bar, in the mechanics of order submission and trade execution. These are microstructure effects: temporary dislocations caused by imbalanced order flow, transient spread widening, or sudden changes in depth.

Our goal in this section is to transform rich tick-level data—quotes, trades, and the limit order book—into a compact set of features that tell us *who is in a hurry*, how strong that pressure is, and when it is likely to revert. We proceed in four steps:

- Introduce the core objects: bid, ask, spread, depth, and trades.
- Build order-flow imbalance (OFI) features that summarize buying vs. selling pressure.
- Construct spread- and depth-based measures that capture temporary illiquidity and crowding.
- Discuss implementation choices (sampling, aggregation, bias control) to make these features stable and usable in machine learning pipelines.

Throughout, we maintain the same principles as in the price-based section: causality (no look-ahead), approximate stationarity, and clear economic interpretation.

A Brief Tour of the Limit Order Book

Most modern electronic markets are organized around a *limit order book* (LOB). At any point in time, the book contains standing buy and sell limit orders:

- A *bid* is an order to buy at or below a specified price.
- An *ask* (or *offer*) is an order to sell at or above a specified price.

For each side, orders are grouped by price level, and within a price level by arrival time (price–time priority). The *best bid* B_t is the highest bid price outstanding at time t, and the *best ask* A_t is the lowest ask price. Their difference,

$$\text{Spread}_t = A_t - B_t,$$

is the *quoted (bid–ask) spread.* The quantities available at the best bid and best ask, Q_t^B and Q_t^A, are the *top-of-book depths.* Deeper levels (second best bid, third best ask, etc.) provide additional depth further from the mid-price.

The *mid-price* at time t is

$$M_t = \frac{B_t + A_t}{2}.$$

For many microstructure-driven strategies, M_t is a more stable notion of price than last-traded price because it is less affected by bid–ask bounce.

Aggressive vs. Passive Orders and Trades

When a market participant wants to trade *immediately*, they submit a *market order* (or aggressively priced limit order) that executes against standing liquidity at the opposite side of the book:

- A *buy market order* consumes volume from the ask side, potentially walking up the ask ladder.
- A *sell market order* consumes volume from the bid side.

These aggressive orders generate *trades*. Each trade can be signed as buyer-initiated or seller-initiated, based on whether it hits the ask or the bid. The cumulative effect of these aggressive orders over short intervals is a key driver of short-lived price pressure and subsequent mean reversion.

Diagram: A Stylized Limit Order Book

The following schematic illustrates a snapshot of a simple limit order book. On the left we show bid levels and depth; on the right, ask levels and depth. Arrows indicate how we aggregate volumes and prices into order-flow imbalance and spread features that we will define next.

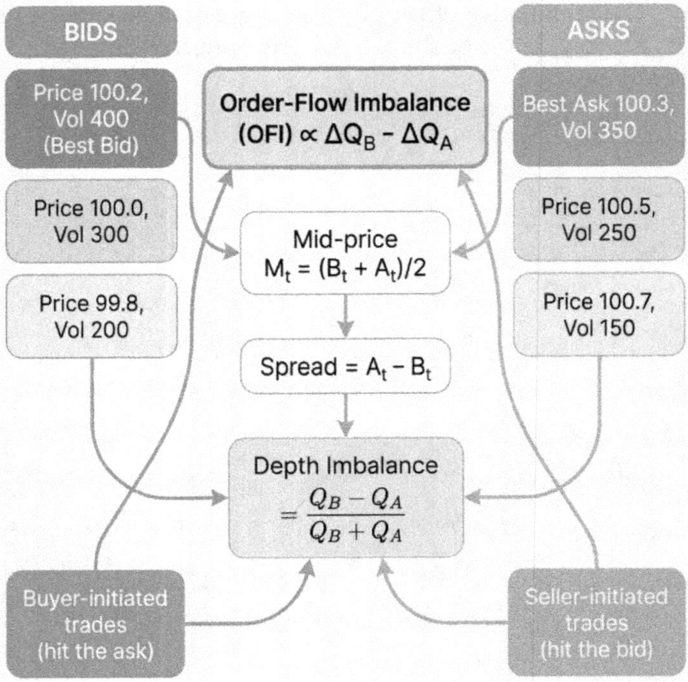

This stylized ladder highlights the essential inputs for our features: prices and quantities at several bid and ask levels, and the direction of recent trades. We now formalize how to convert these into numerical indicators of transient pressure.

Order-Flow Imbalance: Measuring Who Is in a Hurry

Order-flow imbalance (OFI) attempts to quantify which side—buyers or sellers—has been more aggressive over a short time window, and by how much.

Trade-Based OFI

Let us partition time into short intervals, e.g., $\Delta t = 1$ second or 100 milliseconds. Over each interval $[t, t + \Delta t)$, we observe a sequence of trades indexed by j, each with signed volume v_j:

$$v_j = \begin{cases} +q_j & \text{if trade } j \text{ is buyer-initiated (hits the ask),} \\ -q_j & \text{if trade } j \text{ is seller-initiated (hits the bid).} \end{cases}$$

The trade-based order-flow imbalance over the interval is

$$\text{OFI}_{t,\Delta t}^{trade} = \sum_{j \in [t, t+\Delta t)} v_j.$$

If positive, aggressive buying dominates; if negative, aggressive selling dominates.

To make OFI more comparable across time and assets, we often normalize it, for example by total traded volume in the interval:

$$\widetilde{\text{OFI}}_{t,\Delta t}^{trade} = \frac{\sum_{j \in [t,t+\Delta t)} v_j}{\sum_{j \in [t,t+\Delta t)} |v_j| + \varepsilon},$$

where ε is a small constant to avoid division by zero when no trades occur. The normalized OFI lies approximately in $[-1, 1]$, where $+1$ means purely buyer-initiated volume, and -1 purely seller-initiated.

Quote-Based OFI

Trade-based OFI ignores informative changes in the book when no trades occur. For example, liquidity may silently withdraw from one side, widening the spread and signaling future price impact even before any trade prints.

A complementary approach uses changes in top-of-book depth. Let Q_t^B and Q_t^A be the bid and ask volumes at the best prices B_t and A_t. Over a small time step, we can define quote-based OFI as

$$\text{OFI}_t^{quote} = \Delta Q_t^B - \Delta Q_t^A,$$

where $\Delta Q_t^B = Q_t^B - Q_{t^-}^B$ and $\Delta Q_t^A = Q_t^A - Q_{t^-}^A$, with t^- denoting the last time stamp before t.

Intuitively:

- Increases in Q^B (more depth at the best bid) count as positive OFI: more willingness to buy.
- Increases in Q^A count as negative OFI: more willingness to sell.
- Decreases in Q^B or Q^A have the opposite effect, reflecting cancellations or trades depleting depth.

Again, we can aggregate quote-based OFI over intervals and normalize it, for example by average depth and spread, to obtain dimensionless, stationary features.

Why OFI Predicts Mean Reversion

In the short run, an excess of buyer-initiated volume typically pushes prices up: best ask quotes are consumed, the mid-price moves higher, and the spread may briefly widen. However, such bursts of buying pressure are often temporary. Once the urgency to buy subsides, two forces promote mean reversion:

- Liquidity providers and contrarian traders step in on the sell side, attracted by the higher prices.
- Natural sellers who were waiting for better prices begin to submit offers, restoring depth and compressing the spread.

Thus, a large, positive OFI over a short window often precedes a partial reversal in subsequent returns, particularly in the absence of obvious news. Our goal in feature engineering is not to hand-code a specific threshold-based rule, but to provide appropriately scaled OFI measures to a model, which can then learn when and how strongly such patterns play out.

Spread-Based Features: Temporary Illiquidity and Normalization

The bid–ask spread is a direct measure of transaction cost and liquidity. Sudden, temporary widenings of the spread are typically signs of stress or information asymmetry. When that stress is transient, spreads tend to normalize, and mid-prices often mean-revert as liquidity re-enters.

Quoted and Effective Spreads

At time t, the *quoted spread* is

$$s_t^{quoted} = A_t - B_t,$$

or in relative terms

$$s_t^{rel} = \frac{A_t - B_t}{M_t}.$$

A second notion is the *effective spread*, which uses actual transaction prices P_j^{trade}:

$$s_j^{eff} = 2\,|P_j^{trade} - M_{t_j}|,$$

where t_j is the time of trade j, and M_{t_j} is the prevailing mid-price just before the trade. This captures how far the trade price is from the mid, which reflects realized cost and slippage.

We can form interval features by averaging or summing these spreads over a window:

$$\bar{s}_{t,\Delta t}^{rel} = \frac{1}{N_{quotes}} \sum_{q \in [t, t+\Delta t)} s_q^{rel}, \qquad \bar{s}_{t,\Delta t}^{eff} = \frac{1}{N_{trades}} \sum_{j \in [t, t+\Delta t)} s_j^{eff}.$$

Normalized Spread and Spread-Widening Indicators

Raw spreads vary substantially across assets and regimes. To focus on *abnormal* behavior, we normalize spreads relative to their recent history, in the same spirit as z-scores for prices.

For example, define the rolling mean and standard deviation of the relative spread:

$$\overline{s}_t^{rel}(N) = \frac{1}{N}\sum_{i=0}^{N-1} s_{t-i}^{rel}, \qquad \widehat{\sigma}_t^{(s)}(N) = \sqrt{\frac{1}{N-1}\sum_{i=0}^{N-1}(s_{t-i}^{rel} - \overline{s}_t^{rel}(N))^2}.$$

The *spread z-score* is then

$$Z_t^{(s)} = \frac{s_t^{rel} - \overline{s}_t^{rel}(N)}{\widehat{\sigma}_t^{(s)}(N)}.$$

Large positive values of $Z_t^{(s)}$ indicate unusually wide spreads. We can encode this as features:

- The continuous $Z_t^{(s)}$ itself.
- Indicator flags for abnormal widenings, e.g. $\mathbb{1}\{Z_t^{(s)} > z_{th}\}$.
- Rolling counts of how long the spread has been in a "stressed" state.

After transient widenings—for example, around the release of minor news or following a brief volatility spike—spreads tend to compress back, and mid-prices may revert toward their pre-stress levels. Models that observe both spread z-scores and OFI can learn to distinguish between persistent information-driven re-pricings and temporary liquidity gaps.

Depth and Queue Features: Short-Term Crowding

Beyond the best bid and ask, the full depth of the book contains information about how crowded each side is and how much buffer exists against incoming market orders.

Depth Imbalance

The simplest depth feature at the top of the book is the *depth imbalance*:

$$\mathrm{DI}_t = \frac{Q_t^B - Q_t^A}{Q_t^B + Q_t^A}.$$

Values near $+1$ indicate much more bid depth than ask depth; values near -1 indicate the opposite.

The interpretation is intuitive:

- When DI_t is strongly positive, the buy side is "thick" and the sell side "thin". Modest sell pressure may have less impact than buy pressure of similar size.
- When DI_t is strongly negative, a small burst of sell market orders can walk through the thin bids, moving prices quickly downward, but that very move may attract opportunistic buyers, generating a subsequent bounce.

As with other microstructure variables, we often compute rolling statistics and z-scores for DI_t to identify unusually crowded or unusually fragile configurations.

Multi-Level Depth and Slope

Top-of-book depth can be unstable, especially in highly electronic markets where orders are constantly being added and cancelled. To smooth this, we can look at cumulative depth up to level L on each side:

$$D_t^B(L) = \sum_{\ell=1}^{L} Q_t^B(\ell), \qquad D_t^A(L) = \sum_{\ell=1}^{L} Q_t^A(\ell),$$

where $Q_t^B(\ell)$ is the bid quantity at the ℓ-th best bid price, and similarly for asks.

We can then construct:

- A multi-level depth imbalance

$$\mathrm{DI}_t(L) = \frac{D_t^B(L) - D_t^A(L)}{D_t^B(L) + D_t^A(L)},$$

which is more robust to fleeting cancellations.

- A *depth slope*, which compares depth near the top to depth further down, to indicate whether additional liquidity is available if the price moves one or two ticks.

These features are especially useful for very short-horizon strategies (sub-second to seconds), where the immediate liquidity landscape around the mid-price heavily influences the next price move and its tendency to mean-revert after shocks.

From Microstructure Signals to Machine Learning Features

We now summarize a practical, microstructure-based feature set that naturally complements the price- and volatility-based signals from the previous section.

Assume that we sample the LOB and trades at regular *clock times* (e.g., every second, or every 5 seconds). For each sampling time t, we construct:

- **Signed trade volume features**
  - Normalized trade OFI over the last k seconds:

$$\widetilde{\mathrm{OFI}}^{trade}_{t,[t-k,t)}.$$

  - Separate buyer- and seller-initiated volumes, each normalized by total volume and by average volume for that time of day.
- **Quote and depth features**
  - Depth imbalance at top of book: DI_t.

  - Multi-level depth imbalance $\mathrm{DI}_t(L)$ for one or two values of L.
  - Rolling averages and z-scores of these depth measures to highlight unusually crowded or one-sided books.

- **Spread features**
  - Relative quoted spread s_t^{rel} and its rolling z-score $Z_t^{(s)}$.
  - Effective spread measures averaged over the last k seconds, capturing realized transaction costs and price impact.
  - Flags for abnormal spread widening or narrowing.

- **Regime and activity indicators**
  - Instantaneous or short-horizon volatility of mid-price changes (e.g., realized variance over the last few seconds).
  - Order arrival intensity: counts of new limit orders, cancellations, and trades.
  - One-hot indicators for special microstructure regimes, such as opening and closing auctions, lunch breaks in some markets, or halts.

For all of these, we maintain the discipline of using only information available up to time t when predicting returns over a future horizon (e.g., the mid-price move over $[t, t + \tau]$). Any cross-sectional normalization (e.g., ranking OFI across a universe of stocks at time t) must also be done contemporaneously to avoid look-ahead.

These microstructure features are particularly powerful at very short horizons, where traditional price-based indicators may be too slow or blunt. But they also add value at longer horizons by indicating whether a recent large move was driven by persistent informed trading (sustained OFI, structurally wider spreads, thin opposite-side depth) or by a short-lived liquidity squeeze (brief OFI burst, transitory spread widening, quick depth restoration). In the latter case, the odds of mean reversion are far higher.

In the next section we will move beyond the tape and the order book to encode external events and calendar regularities, further enriching the feature space that our machine learning models can use to hunt for contrarian opportunities.

5.3 Event-Driven & Seasonal Features

Price- and microstructure-based features, developed in the previous sections, rely entirely on the internal dynamics of the tape: how prices, spreads, and order flow evolve in time. In real markets, however, many large moves are triggered by *discrete external events* (earnings, macro releases, news) or by highly predictable *calendar patterns* (day-of-week effects, turn-of-the-month, scheduled announcements).

If we ignore these time markers, our contrarian models risk mixing together two qualitatively different situations:

- A large move with no obvious news, which may be a genuine inefficiency and often mean-reverts.
- A large move right after major news, which may reflect a genuine information update and may *not* revert quickly (or may even continue).

The goal of this section is to show how to encode events and calendar structure into *learnable features* so that models can disentangle these cases. Specifically, we want features that:

- Represent events and seasonal patterns in a numeric form suitable for statistical and machine learning models.
- Capture known post-event and seasonal anomalies, including overreaction and drift.
- Are robust across time, avoiding look-ahead and minimizing structural breaks.

We proceed in four steps: defining and timestamping events, encoding event-related features, constructing seasonal and calendar features, and finally integrating these with our existing price and microstructure predictors.

What Counts as an "Event"?

In the context of equity (or broader asset) trading, an event is a discrete, time-stamped piece of information that can plausibly affect the asset's value or risk. Common examples include:

- **Firm-level events**: earnings announcements, guidance revisions, dividend announcements, mergers and acquisitions, management changes, major product launches.
- **Macro events**: central bank decisions (e.g., FOMC), inflation and employment releases, GDP data, major policy announcements.
- **News and sentiment events**: major newswire headlines, analyst rating changes, credit rating actions, large insider transactions, aggregated news sentiment scores.

The first step in feature engineering is to create a clean, time-stamped *event database*. For each event e, you want at least:

- A timestamp t_e (or intraday time-of-day for high-frequency work).
- An identifier of the affected asset(s) or universe (e.g., ticker or macro category).
- Basic categorical labels (earnings vs. dividends vs. M&A, etc.).
- If available, a numerical *magnitude* or *surprise* measure (earnings surprise, macro surprise, sentiment score).

This database becomes an input into your time-series panel of returns and microstructure variables; the event fields are then transformed into features observed at or before each prediction time.

Encoding Earnings and Other Discrete Announcements

Earnings announcements are a canonical example because they are regular, relatively well-structured, and associated with both overreaction and drift anomalies.

Event Indicators and Age Features

Let t denote your prediction time (e.g., just before the close of a given day). For each asset i and each type of event (say, earnings), we can define:

- A binary *recent-event indicator*:

  $$\text{EarningsRecent}_{i,t} = \mathbb{1}\{\text{asset } i \text{ had an earnings event in the last } K \text{ days}\}.$$

- An *event age* feature: the time since the last event in trading days,

  $$\text{EarningsAge}_{i,t} = t - t_i^{lastEarnings},$$

  where $t_i^{lastEarnings}$ is the most recent earnings event time at or before t; if none exists within a certain lookback, you may cap or set this to a special value.

These simple features already allow a model to learn that, for example, post-earnings drift in one direction may dominate in the first few days after the announcement and decays as $\text{EarningsAge}_{i,t}$ increases.

Surprise Magnitude and Direction

A crucial element is the *surprise*: the difference between what was announced and what the market expected. For earnings, a common version is the standardized earnings surprise:

$$\text{SUE}_{i,t_e} = \frac{\text{ActualEPS}_{i,t_e} - \text{ExpectedEPS}_{i,t_e}}{\widehat{\sigma}_i^{(EPS)}},$$

where $\widehat{\sigma}_i^{(EPS)}$ is an estimate of the historical variation in EPS forecast errors for firm i.

We then propagate this event-only number into the time series as a feature that decays with time since the event. For any day $t \geq t_e$,

$$\text{EarningsSurprise}_{i,t} = \text{SUE}_{i,t_e},$$

possibly multiplied by a decaying function of $\text{EarningsAge}_{i,t}$ such as $\exp(-\lambda\,\text{EarningsAge}_{i,t})$.

Interpreting this feature:

- Large positive $\text{EarningsSurprise}_{i,t}$ indicates a strong positive shock that might have been initially over- or under-reacted to.
- Large negative values indicate negative surprises.

By combining $\text{EarningsSurprise}_{i,t}$ with post-event returns and price-based overextension measures, the model can learn patterns such as: *after extremely positive surprises, the first-day move is often an over-reaction that modestly mean-reverts over the next week.*

Event-Time Windows and Averaged Patterns

A useful way to think about event effects is in *event time* rather than calendar time. For each event, define day 0 as the event date (or bar), day $+1$ as the next trading day, and so on. If we average returns across many earnings events binned by surprise deciles, we frequently see:

- A large day-0 move aligned with surprise.
- Some continuation or drift for a few subsequent days.
- Occasional reversal if the initial move overshoots.

We do not need to hard-code this pattern; instead, we create features such as:

$$\text{EventDay}_{i,t} = t - t_e \quad \text{(capped at some max horizon)},$$

and categorical flags for "in event window" (e.g., $\mathbb{1}\{\text{EventDay}_{i,t} \in [0, 5]\}$), which allow the model to infer average behavior conditional on being in certain post-event windows.

News and Sentiment Encodings

Not all events are nicely scheduled or numerical. News headlines and text are more diffuse but highly relevant to short-term mispricing and reversals. A typical workflow is:

- Use a separate pipeline (e.g., natural language processing) to transform raw news or social media into:

  - Asset-level *sentiment scores* at time stamps, such as $\text{SentimentScore}_{i,t_e} \in [-1, 1]$.
  - Possibly separate indicators of news volume or attention intensity.

- Aggregate these into time-bucketed features for trading:

$$\text{SentimentAgg}_{i,t,\Delta t} = f\left(\{\text{SentimentScore}_{i,u} : u \in [t - \Delta t, t)\}\right),$$

  where f might be a sum, mean, or volatility of scores.

To capture overreaction and reversal after news, we can form:

- *Recent sentiment level*: smoothed or exponentially weighted sentiment over the last day or few hours.
- *Sentiment surprise*: deviation of current sentiment from a long-term baseline.
- *Attention flags*: indicators that sentiment magnitude or news volume is extreme.

Models that see both sentiment and price-based z-scores can learn, for example, that sharp price jumps occurring alongside strong positive sentiment are more likely to partially reverse once attention fades, while those with weak or conflicting sentiment patterns behave differently.

Calendar and Seasonal Features

Beyond discrete news, markets exhibit regular patterns tied to the calendar. These *seasonal* effects are often modest at the individual-asset level but systematic across large universes and long histories. Properly encoded, they help models distinguish between "just a Friday pattern" and a genuine anomaly.

Day-of-Week and Month-of-Year Effects

Two of the simplest and most common seasonal encodings are:

- **Day-of-week** indicators: for each trading day t, define

$$\text{DowMon}_t = \mathbb{1}\{\text{day-of-week}(t) = \text{Monday}\},$$

and similarly for Tuesday through Friday. One of the days is typically omitted to avoid perfect collinearity. In intraday settings, you can combine day-of-week with time-of-day buckets.

- **Month-of-year** indicators: for monthly or longer-horizon strategies, encode January through December as one-hot features (again omitting one as baseline).

These categorical features let the model learn small but persistent regularities, such as:

- Slightly different volatility or drift profiles on Mondays versus Fridays.
- Month-end or quarter-end flows creating predictable pressure on certain days.

Turn-of-the-Month and Holiday Effects

Empirical studies often find higher average returns around the turn of the month and idiosyncratic patterns around major holidays. We can reflect this in features:

- *Turn-of-the-month flag*:

$$\text{TOM}_t = \mathbb{1}\{\text{trading day } t \text{ is within } k \text{ days of the month change}\},$$

with k typically between 1 and 3.

- *Pre-/post-holiday flags*: for each known market holiday H, we can tag the last trading day before H and the first trading day after H with special indicators.

These flags help the model capture patterns such as pre-holiday rallies or post-holiday reversals, without forcing us to impose any fixed strategy rule a priori.

Intraday Seasonality

At intraday frequencies, volume and volatility follow highly regular patterns across the trading day (e.g., high at open and close, low at midday). For each intraday interval indexed by (d, τ), where d is date and τ is a time-of-day bucket, we can define:

- A *time-of-day index* τ (e.g., 1 for first 5 minutes, 2 for second 5 minutes, etc.).
- One-hot encodings or cyclic encodings (e.g., sin and cos of $2\pi\tau/T$) so models can represent intraday cycles.

Separately, we can normalize volume and volatility by their typical values at that time-of-day to produce more stationary features. For example, if $\widehat{V}_\tau$ is typical (e.g., median) volume for bucket τ over a recent history,

$$\widetilde{\text{Vol}}_{d,\tau} = \frac{\text{Volume}_{d,\tau}}{\widehat{V}_\tau}$$

is a relative volume measure indicating whether current trading activity is above or below normal for that time-of-day. Similar normalization can be applied to realized volatility.

These relative metrics are particularly important when interpreting price and OFI signals; a large move accompanied by unusually high relative volume carries a different message from the same move on very thin trading.

Design Principles for Stable Event and Seasonal Features

Event- and calendar-based features create powerful context, but they are also a common source of subtle look-ahead bias and instability. Several design principles help mitigate these risks.

Causality and Announcement Timing

For scheduled events (earnings, macro, FOMC), exact announcement times matter. To preserve causality:

- Only use an event's information *after* the actual release time t_e. If you trade at the open and earnings are reported after the close, the open of the next day can use the earnings surprise; the close of the same day cannot.

- For intraday models, timestamp features at the appropriate bar or tick following the event. If your bars are 5 minutes long, an event at 14:02 belongs to the bar $[14{:}00, 14{:}05)$, not earlier bars.

For macro and news sentiment features, ensure that any transformations (e.g., computing an aggregate sentiment for the last hour) use only headlines and scores up to the prediction time.

Relative and Rank-Based Encodings

The scale and distribution of surprises and sentiment scores can change over time as coverage and methodologies evolve. To increase robustness:

- Use *standardized surprises*, such as dividing by historical volatility of the same measure for the same firm or macro series.

- Use *rank-based encodings*, for example:

$$\text{SurpriseRank}_{i,t} = \frac{\text{rank of SUE among contemporaneous events}}{\text{number of events at } t_e},$$

  so that the model learns patterns based on being in the top or bottom decile rather than on raw magnitudes, which may drift.

Similarly, day-of-week and time-of-day effects can be encoded as categorical variables rather than assuming fixed numeric effects.

Interacting Events with Price and Microstructure Features

Events and calendar flags are most informative when interpreted together with price and microstructure context:

- A large negative return on day 0 of an earnings announcement with a strongly negative surprise is very different from a large negative return on a random day with no events.

- A spread spike and OFI burst on FOMC day at 14:00 is qualitatively different from the same pattern at 11:00 on a normal day.

In linear models, you can explicitly include interaction terms, e.g., EventFlag $\times$ ReturnZScore. In more flexible machine learning models (trees, neural networks), these interactions are often learned implicitly. The key is to ensure that both components (events and prices) are present and cleanly encoded.

A Practical Feature Set for Events and Seasonality

Combining the ideas above, a practical feature block for event-driven and seasonal information, ready to be merged with your existing price and microstructure features, might include:

- **Event proximity and type**
  - Indicators for being within K days (or bars) of the most recent earnings, major macro release, or other key event.
  - Event age features (time since last event) and possibly time until next scheduled event.
  - One-hot encodings for event type (earnings, dividend, M&A, rating change, macro category).
- **Event magnitude and sentiment**
  - Standardized surprise metrics (e.g., SUE) and their ranks.
  - Recent aggregated news/sentiment scores, normalized relative to historical levels.
  - Flags for extreme sentiment or surprise (e.g., top/bottom deciles).
- **Seasonal and calendar flags**
  - Day-of-week and month-of-year one-hot features.
  - Turn-of-the-month and holiday proximity indicators.
  - Time-of-day encodings for intraday strategies, plus normalized (relative) volume and volatility.

- **Regime-awareness**
  - Optional tags for high-impact days (e.g., FOMC, major macro) that often have distinct return and order-flow patterns.
  - Combining regime tags with volatility state from previous chapters (e.g., high vs. low volatility regime).

All of these features are computed in a strictly causal manner and are relatively stable over time when defined in standardized or rank-based terms. They allow a machine learning model to learn nuanced patterns such as:

- *On non-event days*, extreme negative returns with little sentiment and normal spreads tend to mean-revert quickly.
- *Immediately after large positive earnings surprises*, positive drifts may continue for a few days, even if the initial move was sizable.
- *On Fridays before holidays*, intraday moves may be less informative due to low participation and abnormal seasonal patterns.

In combination with the price-based and microstructure features from earlier sections, these event-driven and seasonal encodings complete a richer, context-aware feature space. This, in turn, gives our contrarian models a better chance of distinguishing between genuine inefficiencies and rational, news-driven repricings—a distinction that lies at the heart of robust anomaly hunting.

5.4 Pairwise & Spread Features

So far, our feature engineering has focused on the behavior of a *single* asset: its own prices, order flow, and event calendar. Many profitable contrarian strategies, however, are inherently *relative-value*: they trade mispricings between two (or more) related assets rather than outright direction. Examples include:

- Two share classes of the same firm.
- A stock and its futures contract or ETF.
- Two banks in the same country.
- A sector ETF and a basket of its constituents.

In these settings, the basic unit of analysis is not a single price but a *spread*—a weighted combination of prices that we expect to be roughly stationary. When this spread deviates far from its "normal" range, we anticipate mean reversion, and we trade accordingly.

This section develops a toolkit for turning raw pair prices into cointegration-aware spreads, dynamic hedge ratios, and spread-based features that make relative-value mispricings explicit and learnable.

Correlation vs. Cointegration: Why Spreads Can Revert

It is tempting to pick pairs simply because their returns are highly correlated. However, high correlation does *not* guarantee that the price difference will be mean-reverting.

Correlation: Co-Movement, Not an Anchor

Two assets X and Y can have highly correlated returns because they react similarly to common factors (e.g., the market), yet their *price levels* can drift apart over time. A simple example is:

$$P_t^X = 100 + \sum_{s=1}^{t} \epsilon_s, \qquad P_t^Y = 100 + \sum_{s=1}^{t} \epsilon_s + 0.1s,$$

where ϵ_s are common shocks. Returns are highly correlated, but the price difference

$$P_t^Y - P_t^X = 0.1t$$

drifts linearly: there is no tendency to revert.

Correlation is therefore not enough for pair trading. We need a stronger condition.

Cointegration: A Stable Long-Run Relationship

Intuitively, a pair is suitable for mean-reverting spreads if there exists a *stable equilibrium relationship* between the prices. This is captured by the notion of *cointegration*.

Let P_t^X and P_t^Y be two nonstationary price processes (e.g., unit root processes). They are cointegrated if there exists a constant β and an intercept α such that the linear combination

$$S_t = P_t^Y - \beta P_t^X - \alpha$$

is stationary (or at least much more stable than either price alone). In economic terms, S_t measures the deviation from a long-run equilibrium; if S_t wanders too far, economic forces (arbitrage, substitution, common fundamentals) tend to pull it back.

From a feature-engineering perspective, S_t is our raw *spread series*. We then normalize and transform S_t to estimate how extreme the current deviation is and how likely it is to mean-revert.

Estimating Hedge Ratios and Constructing Spreads

To compute a spread S_t, we need an estimate of the hedge ratio β and, optionally, an intercept α. There are several practical approaches, each with pros and cons.

Static Regression-Based Hedge Ratio

A simple and widely used method is to run a linear regression over a historical window:

$$P_t^Y = \alpha + \beta P_t^X + \varepsilon_t.$$

We can estimate α and β via ordinary least squares (OLS) over a training period (e.g., the past year of daily prices). The estimated coefficients $(\widehat{\alpha}, \widehat{\beta})$ are then used to define the spread:

$$S_t = P_t^Y - \widehat{\beta} P_t^X - \widehat{\alpha}.$$

- $\widehat{\beta}$ is the *hedge ratio*: the number of units of X to short (if $\widehat{\beta} > 0$) for each unit of Y that we go long, to create a market-neutral position.

- S_t is the resulting "residual" that represents relative mispricing.

If the residuals ε_t appear stationary (mean-reverting), then S_t is a promising candidate for a contrarian signal.

Rolling and Dynamic Hedge Ratios

Static hedge ratios assume that the relationship between X and Y is fixed. In practice, fundamentals and volatility can change, so we often estimate β over a rolling window:

- Choose a window length N (e.g., 60 or 120 trading days).
- For each time $t \geq N$, run OLS on $\{(P^X_{t-N+1}, P^Y_{t-N+1}), \ldots, (P^X_t, P^Y_t)\}$ to obtain $\widehat{\beta}_t$ and $\widehat{\alpha}_t$.
- Define the time-varying spread:
$$S_t = P^Y_t - \widehat{\beta}_t P^X_t - \widehat{\alpha}_t.$$

This rolling procedure produces dynamic hedge ratios that can adapt to gradual regime shifts. However, shorter windows yield more responsive but noisier estimates; longer windows produce more stable but slower-to-adjust ratios. Regularization (e.g., shrinkage of $\widehat{\beta}_t$ toward a prior) can help stabilize estimates.

Cointegration Tests and Pair Selection

When dealing with many potential pairs, we typically:

- Use economic intuition and sector classifications to limit candidates to plausibly related names.
- For each candidate pair (X, Y), estimate a hedge ratio and test whether the residual series S_t appears stationary (e.g., via an augmented Dickey–Fuller test on ε_t).
- Select pairs with stronger evidence of cointegration and reasonable spread properties (variance, liquidity, etc.).

This step—selecting pairs and verifying stationarity—helps control multiple-testing risk and ensures that our spread features are grounded in genuine long-run relationships rather than incidental co-movement.

Normalizing Spreads: Z-Scores and Reversion Diagnostics

Once we have a spread series S_t, we treat it much like the single-asset price deviations from earlier sections: we measure how "stretched" S_t is relative to its recent behavior.

Spread Z-Score

Compute the rolling mean and standard deviation of the spread over a window of length N:

$$\overline{S}_t(N) = \frac{1}{N}\sum_{i=0}^{N-1} S_{t-i}, \qquad \widehat{\sigma}_t^{(S)}(N) = \sqrt{\frac{1}{N-1}\sum_{i=0}^{N-1}\left(S_{t-i} - \overline{S}_t(N)\right)^2}.$$

The *spread z-score* is then

$$Z_t^{(S)} = \frac{S_t - \overline{S}_t(N)}{\widehat{\sigma}_t^{(S)}(N)}.$$

Interpretation:

- $Z_t^{(S)} \approx 0$ means the spread is near its rolling mean; no obvious mispricing.
- $Z_t^{(S)} \gg 0$ means Y is relatively rich vs. X (given the hedge ratio); contrarian traders may short the spread (short Y, long X).
- $Z_t^{(S)} \ll 0$ means Y is relatively cheap vs. X; we might go long the spread (long Y, short X).

In many pairs strategies, entry and exit rules are defined in terms of $Z_t^{(S)}$ crossing thresholds (e.g., enter at $|Z_t^{(S)}| > 2$, exit when $|Z_t^{(S)}| < 0.5$). For our purposes, we think of $Z_t^{(S)}$ and related quantities as *features* that a model can use to *learn* such behaviors.

Reversion Speed and Half-Life

To understand the strength of mean reversion, we can model the spread as an autoregressive process of order 1:

$$S_t = \phi S_{t-1} + \eta_t,$$

with $|\phi| < 1$ and η_t a noise term. The closer ϕ is to zero, the faster the spread reverts; the closer to one, the slower.

A convenient summary is the *half-life* of shocks:

$$\text{HalfLife} = \frac{\ln(0.5)}{\ln|\phi|}.$$

This is the expected time it takes for the impact of a shock to be cut in half. We can estimate ϕ over a rolling window and use HalfLife_t as a feature: pairs with faster reversion may support shorter-horizon trading; those with slower reversion require longer holding periods and different risk management.

Visualizing Spreads and Trading Regions

The following figure illustrates a synthetic example: two asset prices, their implied hedge ratio, and the derived spread z-score. Highlighted regions mark entry and exit points based on extreme deviations and subsequent reversion.

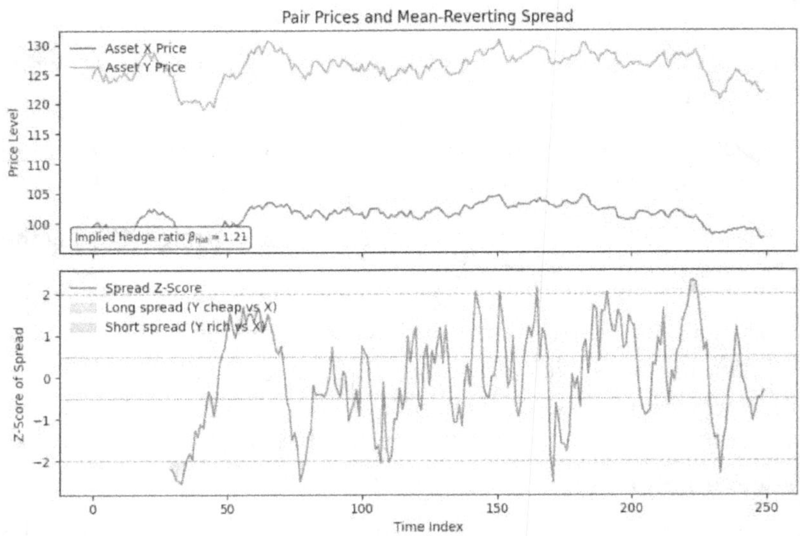

In practice, we would not hard-code entry and exit rules based on these thresholds. Instead, we supply $Z_t^{(S)}$ and related features to a model, which can learn which regions of spread overextension and which contexts (volatility, events, liquidity) are most predictive of profitable reversion.

Additional Spread Dynamics as Features

Beyond the raw spread and its z-score, many informative properties of the spread can be converted into features.

Asymmetry in Up vs. Down Moves

Some spreads may revert symmetrically: positive and negative deviations behave similarly. Others may exhibit *asymmetry*: perhaps rich states revert faster than cheap states, or vice versa.

We can encode such behavior through:

- Separate indicators for positive and negative z-scores (e.g., $\mathbb{1}\{Z_t^{(S)} > 0\}$ and $\mathbb{1}\{Z_t^{(S)} < 0\}$).
- Nonlinear transforms such as $(Z_t^{(S)})_+ = \max(Z_t^{(S)}, 0)$ and $(Z_t^{(S)})_- = -\min(Z_t^{(S)}, 0)$ as separate features.

These allow the model to learn state-dependent behavior instead of assuming symmetry.

Co-Movement with Market and Sector Factors

Spreads are not fully insulated from the wider market. If both X and Y are exposed to a common factor (e.g., a sector ETF), then shifts in that factor can induce short-term distortions in the spread.

We can model the spread residual relative to common factors:

$$S_t = \gamma_0 + \gamma_1 F_t^{mkt} + \gamma_2 F_t^{sec} - u_t,$$

and examine the residual u_t as a more refined mispricing measure. Practical implementations often:

- Include factor returns (market, sector, style) as features alongside $Z_t^{(S)}$.

- Compute spread z-scores *after* regressing out factor effects; the resulting factor-neutral spread may exhibit cleaner mean reversion.

Cross-Sectional Spread Ranks

When trading many pairs, it is useful to know not only how stretched a given spread is relative to its own history, but also where it stands in the cross-section *today*. You can define:

$$\text{SpreadRank}_t^{(i)} = \frac{\text{rank of } |Z_t^{(S,i)}| \text{ among all pairs at } t}{\text{number of pairs at } t},$$

where i indexes the pair. High $\text{SpreadRank}_t^{(i)}$ indicates that pair i is among the most mispriced spreads at that time, which may be especially attractive for contrarian bets (subject to risk and turnover constraints).

Implementation Considerations and Regime Breaks

Pairwise and spread features are powerful but fragile: if the underlying economic relationship breaks (e.g., a merger, a business model shift), then the spread may cease to be mean-reverting.

Detecting and Handling Regime Breaks

Several diagnostics help flag potential regime changes:

- A persistent drift in S_t or a sudden change in its mean or variance.
- A sharp shift in the estimated hedge ratio $\widehat{\beta}_t$ over a short period.
- Degradation of cointegration test statistics over recent data.

When such signals appear, we might:

- Temporarily disable trading in the affected pair (set a regime flag feature and let the model learn to assign low weight).

- Re-estimate long-run relationships on a reset window.
- Tighten risk limits or cap position sizes when regime uncertainty is high.

Encoding a simple *regime flag* or *pair health score* as a feature can allow models to systematically de-emphasize fragile relationships.

Look-Ahead Control and Rolling Estimation

As with earlier sections, we must avoid look-ahead bias when estimating hedge ratios and spread statistics:

- At prediction time t, $\widehat{\beta}_t$ and $\widehat{\alpha}_t$ must be estimated using only data up to t.
- Rolling means, standard deviations, and AR(1) coefficients must be computed over historical windows that end at t.
- Cross-sectional rankings (e.g., $\text{SpreadRank}_t^{(i)}$) must use only contemporaneous data at t, not future outcomes.

A typical workflow for each day t (or intraday bar) is:

- Update rolling OLS for each pair to obtain $\widehat{\beta}_t$, $\widehat{\alpha}_t$.
- Compute S_t, $\overline{S}_t(N)$, $\widehat{\sigma}_t^{(S)}(N)$, $Z_t^{(S)}$.
- Update AR(1) estimates and derived half-life features.
- Compute cross-sectional ranks and regime flags.
- Feed all these features, along with price, microstructure, and event-seasonal features, into the prediction model for the next-horizon spread return.

A Template for Spread-Based Alpha Features

To close, we summarize a coherent set of pairwise and spread features suitable for contrarian, market-neutral strategies:

- **Core spread construction**
  - Dynamic hedge ratio $\widehat{\beta}_t$ (and possibly $\widehat{\alpha}_t$) estimated via rolling regression.
  - Raw spread $S_t = P_t^Y - \widehat{\beta}_t P_t^X - \widehat{\alpha}_t$.
- **Spread normalization**
  - Rolling mean $\overline{S}_t(N)$ and volatility $\widehat{\sigma}_t^{(S)}(N)$.
  - Spread z-score $Z_t^{(S)}$ and its lags (e.g., $Z_{t-1}^{(S)}, Z_{t-2}^{(S)}$).
  - Nonlinear transforms $(Z_t^{(S)})_+$, $(Z_t^{(S)})_-$ to capture asymmetry.
- **Reversion diagnostics**
  - Rolling AR(1) coefficient $\widehat{\phi}_t$ for the spread.
  - Derived half-life HalfLife_t.
  - Volatility of spread changes over short horizons (realized volatility of S_t).
- **Context and cross-section**
  - Cross-sectional rank of $|Z_t^{(S)}|$ across pairs.
  - Factor exposures or residualized spreads (after removing market/sector effects).
  - Regime flags or health scores indicating potential structural breaks.

Together, these features convert raw cointegrated price relationships into a structured, stationary input space where machine learning models can systematically hunt for relative-value mean-reversion signals. Integrated with the single-asset, microstructure, and event-seasonal features from earlier sections, they complete our feature-engineering toolkit for contrarian anomaly detection across both directional and market-neutral strategies.

Chapter 6

Backtesting, Evaluation & Robustness

Most quant strategies die not because the idea is bad, but because the evidence was fragile. This chapter turns your contrarian signals into court-grade exhibits: we will replay the market exactly as it was seen at the time, subtract realistic frictions, dissect where every dollar of PnL came from, and then stress-test your backtests for hidden data-mining. By the end, you will know not just how much your strategy made on paper, but how much of that you can trust with real capital.

6.1 Backtesting Architecture & Point-in-Time Simulation

In the previous chapter we treated anomaly signals largely in the abstract: you learned how to design contrarian predictors, engineer features, and think statistically about return distributions. Those ideas are useless, however, unless you can test them in a laboratory that faithfully replays market history as it actually unfolded. This section is about building that laboratory.

There is a large gap between a *spreadsheet backtest*—"if I buy on days when the signal is > 0, my average return is X"—and a true *simulation environment* that processes an evolving information set, places orders, experiences fills, and updates positions and P&L through time. Naive backtests often:

- implicitly assume you know future index membership or delisting events (survivorship bias),
- use accounting data on its publication date rather than when the market could first have known it (look-ahead bias),
- ignore intraday price paths and assume frictionless execution at the close or at VWAP, and
- shortcut details of orders, fills, and cash flows.

A serious backtesting system for contrarian, anomaly-driven trading must instead behave like a miniature exchange plus portfolio manager, operating on information that was genuinely available at each decision point. Conceptually, we want a *research and execution sandbox* that can be dropped into the live environment with minimal changes.

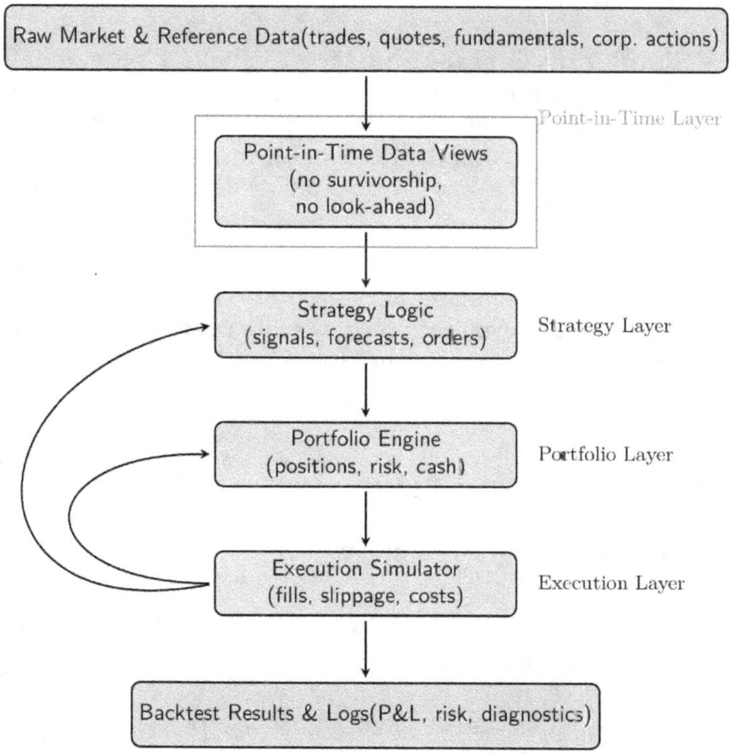

From Toy Backtests to a Simulation Engine

A useful way to think about backtesting is as a constrained software engineering problem: you want to answer a statistical question ("does this signal have edge, net of costs, under realistic constraints?") while obeying strict rules about information flow and market mechanics.

We will contrast two mindsets:

- **Event-study mindset.** You assemble historical returns, sort them by some signal, average the outcomes, and infer an "effect". This is quick, often insightful, and acceptable for early hypothesis screening. But it ignores portfolio interactions, position sizing, execution, and path-dependence.

- **Simulation engine mindset.** You build a system that steps through time, updating state (positions, cash, risk exposures), consuming only the information available at that time, and emitting actions (orders) that feed an execution model. This is more work, but it is the only way to evaluate a strategy you might actually trade.

Our goal is not to eliminate quick-and-dirty analysis; rather, it is to ensure that anything you would show to an investment committee is produced by a simulation engine that respects market structure and information constraints.

Core Architectural Principles

A robust backtesting architecture rests on several design principles:

- **Point-in-time information sets.** At any decision time t, the strategy sees only features derived from data with timestamps $\leq t$ as they were known then. Corporate actions, restatements, index reconstitutions, and delistings must be represented correctly.

- **Explicit modeling of orders and fills.** Orders carry side, size, price limits, and persistence through time. They are filled by an execution simulator that respects liquidity, spreads, and slippage.

- **Separation of concerns.** The system separates:

  - the *data layer* (storage, point-in-time views),
  - the *strategy layer* (signals, rules mapping signals to orders),
  - the *portfolio layer* (positions, risk, constraints), and
  - the *execution layer* (fills and costs).

  This modularity makes the system testable and reusable.

- **Determinism and reproducibility.** Given the same code, configuration, and random seeds, a backtest must produce identical results. Determinism is your friend when debugging and defending results to risk and governance teams.

- **Performance and scalability.** Contrarian strategies often operate at high turnover, with large universes and intraday data. The architecture must be efficient enough to re-run experiments frequently.

We now unpack these principles, starting with the heart of the system: point-in-time data structures.

Point-in-Time Data Structures

The Information Set Concept

In time-series terms, a strategy's decision at time t must be a function of the *filtration* $\mathcal{F}_t$: all information that has arrived up to and including t. In practice, this means:

- You can use prices up to t, but not $t + 1$.

- You can use a company's earnings report only after its official release time (e.g., after market close on the announcement date).

- You cannot condition on knowledge of future index membership, corporate events, or delistings.

Any violation of this principle introduces *look-ahead bias* or *data leakage*. A point-in-time (PIT) data structure enforces this by design.

Prices, Universes, and Survivorship Bias

Price histories are the easiest to imagine in PIT form: a time series of quotes or bars keyed by symbol and timestamp. The subtler issues arise with the *universe* of tradable instruments:

- A survivorship-biased universe uses today's list of symbols (e.g., current S&P 500 members) and projects it backward in time, implicitly assuming delisted or bankrupt firms never existed.
- A point-in-time universe stores, for each date t, the set of symbols that were actually active and tradable at that time, including those later delisted or removed.

To eliminate survivorship bias, your data layer must maintain:

- symbol-level metadata with start and end dates of trading,
- mappings for ticker changes, mergers, and spin-offs, and
- historical index membership tables with effective-from and effective-to dates.

When the backtester asks "what is my eligible universe on 2014-06-30?", the PIT layer answers from those historical records, not from today's snapshots.

Fundamentals and Publication Lags

Fundamental data (earnings, book value, analyst forecasts) is particularly prone to look-ahead bias because many databases report the *period end date* but not the *publication date*. For example, a company's Q4 results might have:

- period end: 31 December 2024,
- earnings release: 15 February 2025.

A naive backtest that aligns all accounting variables by period end will happily allow you to use Q4 earnings on 2 January 2025, which is impossible in reality. A PIT store instead stamps the record with the first date on which the market could reasonably have known it (the release time, plus a conservative delay if necessary).

When you compute a valuation feature such as price-to-book, the PIT layer should ensure that on 10 January 2025, the latest book value used is from Q3 2024, not Q4 2024. Only after 15 February 2025 does the Q4 figure become available.

Labels and Features Without Leakage

In machine-learning terms, the backtester uses:

- *features* X_t (constructed from PIT data up to t), and
- *labels* $Y_{t+\tau}$ (future outcomes over horizon τ) for training and evaluation.

The training pipeline must enforce that X_t uses only information from $\mathcal{F}_t$. Common leakage sources include:

- using future volatility or traded volume when constructing signals,
- normalizing features with statistics computed over the full sample (e.g., z-scoring using future data),
- encoding future corporate events (e.g., using restated earnings data without versioning).

A clean architecture isolates *offline* preprocessing (e.g., computing rolling means using only past data) in the PIT layer and exposes finalized, leak-free features to the strategy logic. For ML, the same PIT features must be usable both in training and in backtest simulation, so that the model sees identical inputs.

The Backtesting Pipeline: Data, Strategy, Portfolio, Execution

Given a PIT data layer, the rest of the system resembles a small trading firm in miniature. At a high level, you run:

- a simulation clock (driving time forward),
- a strategy engine (deciding what to do given the current state),
- a portfolio engine (tracking positions and constraints), and
- an execution simulator (turning orders into trades and costs).

Simulation Clock and Event Loop

There are two main designs:

- **Bar-driven engines.** Time advances in fixed increments (e.g., daily, 5-minute bars). At each bar close, the engine collects all relevant events (new data, orders, fills) and processes them. This is often sufficient for daily contrarian strategies.
- **Event-driven engines.** Time advances to the next *event*: a new quote, trade, order, or fill. This allows fine-grained intraday strategies and more precise modeling of execution, at the cost of complexity and performance.

Both approaches share the same conceptual flow. At each step:

- The PIT layer updates the current observations (prices, features, corporate actions).
- The strategy logic consumes these and generates orders.
- The execution simulator processes orders against the market model to produce fills.
- The portfolio engine updates positions, cash, and risk metrics.

Strategy Logic: From Signals to Orders

The strategy layer focuses on *what* to trade and *why*. It:

- reads PIT features and model forecasts (e.g., expected return, risk, or ranking scores),
- applies decision rules or optimization (e.g., mean–variance, risk-parity, or heuristic allocation),
- generates target positions or explicit orders (e.g., buy 100 shares of stock A at market, sell 50 shares of stock B with a limit).

Crucially, the strategy layer does not:

- know anything about fill prices, intraday slippage, or venue selection,
- hard-code position accounting or portfolio constraints.

Those responsibilities live downstream, making it easier to plug the same strategy into both backtest and live trading environments.

Portfolio Engine: Positions, Risk, and Constraints

The portfolio engine maintains the state variables:

- current positions (by symbol),
- cash and margin balances,
- realized and unrealized P&L,
- risk exposures (factor loadings, sector weights, leverage, liquidity).

Given target positions or orders from the strategy layer, the portfolio engine can:

- check constraint violations (e.g., leverage < 2, sector exposures bounded),
- compute required trades to move from the current portfolio to the target (order generation can live here instead of the strategy),
- pass these trades to the execution simulator.

For contrarian strategies, the portfolio engine must be able to handle:

- high turnover and frequent rebalancing,
- short-selling (including borrow availability and costs, if modeled),
- cash drag when fully hedged or waiting for opportunities.

Execution Simulator: Orders, Fills, and Costs

The execution simulator is where we approximate the microstructure of trading. It:

- takes incoming orders (with side, size, type, and limits),
- uses market data (quotes, depth, volume) to determine if and how they fill,
- applies transaction costs (commissions, fees) and *implicit* costs (spreads, slippage, market impact).

Even a simple daily bar backtest should at least:

- prevent execution at prices outside the bar's high/low,
- approximate fill prices using open/close/VWAP depending on assumed execution schedule,
- charge a spread cost proportional to the bid–ask spread on that day.

Later in the chapter we will refine this into richer cost and impact models, but the architecture must already be capable of swapping execution models in and out without changing strategy code.

Eliminating Common Data and Modeling Leaks

With the overall architecture in mind, we can be more concrete about typical failure modes and their fixes.

Survivorship Bias in Security Universes

- **Leak.** Using today's active ticker list as your historical universe.
- **Symptom.** Backtests show artificially high Sharpe ratios, especially for long-only strategies, because failed firms are missing.

- **Fix.** Maintain historical security master data with start and end dates. In the PIT layer, derive the universe at time t from those records. For index-based universes, store full reconstitution histories and rules.

Look-Ahead in Accounting and Alternative Data

- **Leak.** Aligning accounting data by period end or by fiscal year, ignoring publication dates and lags. Doing the same with alternative data (e.g., analyst recommendations) that are backfilled in the database.

- **Symptom.** Fundamental or alternative-data signals appear unrealistically predictive; anomalies look too good to be true.

- **Fix.** Store, for each record, both the economic period and the first-available timestamp. Construct features using only records with first-available times $\leq t$. For ML labels, ensure that training and validation splits respect temporal order.

Feature Engineering and Normalization Leakage

- **Leak.** Computing cross-sectional z-scores using the full dataset, or normalizing by a mean and variance estimated from the entire sample before splitting into train and test.

- **Symptom.** Model performance collapses out-of-sample, especially when market regimes change.

- **Fix.** Treat feature engineering as part of the PIT layer. For time-series transformations (e.g., rolling means, volatilities), use only past data. For scaling, either:

  - recompute cross-sectional scaling at each date using only the current cross-section, or
  - fit scalers on training data only, then apply to subsequent periods.

Event-Driven vs. Bar-Driven Engines

The choice between event-driven and bar-driven engines hinges on the temporal granularity of your strategy and the realism required.

Bar-Driven Engines

For many daily contrarian anomalies (e.g., buying stocks after large one-day drops), a bar-driven engine is sufficient:

- Time advances in daily steps.
- At each close (or open), you:
  - read PIT features based on end-of-day data,
  - compute target positions,
  - simulate trades at next day's open or close with a spread/slippage model,
  - update portfolio state.

Bar-driven engines are simpler to implement and faster to run. They are excellent for research where execution details are not central.

Event-Driven Engines

If you trade intraday reversals, liquidity imbalances, or order-book anomalies, bar-level aggregation can be misleading. An event-driven engine:

- consumes a stream of events (quotes, trades, order book updates, order submissions, fills),
- updates state at each event,
- allows timing-sensitive logic (e.g., "cancel if not filled in 30 seconds").

Event-driven engines add complexity:

- They require high-quality intraday data with microsecond or millisecond timestamps.
- They demand careful performance engineering (vectorization, batching, or compiled components) to remain tractable.

However, the architectural separation we have described (data, strategy, portfolio, execution) carries over: only the simulation clock and event loop differ. This is why investing in a modular architecture pays off.

Walk-Forward and Nested Validation as First-Class Citizens

An anomaly-hunting research program rarely runs a single backtest. You will repeatedly:

- tune hyperparameters (lookback windows, thresholds, regularization strengths),
- adjust universes, constraints, and cost models,
- try different model classes (linear, tree-based, neural).

If you do this naively on a single in-sample period, you will overfit. To defend against this, your backtesting architecture must make *out-of-sample* evaluation first-class, not an afterthought.

Walk-Forward Testing

Walk-forward testing partitions time into sequential windows:

- Train your model on $[t_0, t_1]$, test on $[t_1, t_2]$.
- Then roll forward: train on $[t_0, t_2]$, test on $[t_2, t_3]$.
- Continue until you cover the full sample.

Your engine should:

- automate this process (given a configuration of window sizes and step lengths),
- ensure that for each test window, features are still PIT and no training data leaks into the future,
- collect performance metrics across all test windows into a coherent report.

Nested Cross-Validation for Hyperparameter Tuning

For machine learning models, you often need an inner loop for hyperparameter selection and an outer loop for unbiased performance estimation. In time series, this becomes *nested walk-forward* rather than random-fold cross-validation.

Architecturally, this implies:

- a configuration layer that describes hyperparameter grids and search strategies,
- an experiment runner that orchestrates:
  - inner-loop backtests on training subwindows for each hyperparameter setting,
  - selection of the best settings based on inner-loop metrics,
  - outer-loop backtests on unseen test windows using the chosen settings,
- persistent logging of all runs, settings, and results for later analysis.

Embedding walk-forward and nested validation into the backtesting architecture (rather than scripting them ad hoc around it) greatly reduces the chance of subtle leakage mistakes and enhances reproducibility.

Determinism, Logging, and Reproducibility

Finally, a robust backtesting environment must support institutional-grade *research hygiene*:

- **Deterministic runs.** All sources of randomness (e.g., stochastic execution models, random initializations in ML) should be controlled via explicit seeds. Simulation results should be reproducible on demand.
- **Configuration as code.** Strategy parameters, universe definitions, cost models, and evaluation settings should be captured in configuration files or code modules, version-controlled alongside the strategy.
- **Structured logging.** Each backtest should produce machine-readable logs:
  - inputs: data versions, code revisions, configuration hashes,
  - outputs: P&L time series, risk metrics, diagnostics,
  - run metadata: runtime, hardware, errors or warnings.

  This enables post-hoc analysis and auditability.
- **Experiment registries.** For teams, maintaining an experiment registry (even a simple database or table) that records each run, its configuration, and key results is invaluable. It prevents duplicated work, makes meta-analysis easier (e.g., deflated Sharpe adjustments later in the chapter), and enforces discipline.

In sum, a backtesting architecture for contrarian, anomaly-driven trading is more than a P&L calculator. It is a carefully designed simulation environment that mirrors the live trading stack, enforces point-in-time information flow, supports realistic portfolio and execution modeling, and makes rigorous validation workflows easy rather than painful. In the next sections we will build on this foundation to introduce transaction cost and market impact modeling, richer performance metrics, and tools to adjust for the many tests you inevitably run when hunting anomalies.

6.2 Transaction Cost & Market Impact Modeling

In the previous section we built a backtesting architecture that replays history using point-in-time data and realistic order and portfolio mechanics. That architecture gives you a clean laboratory. The next question is: *what laboratory conditions do you assume about trading frictions?*

For contrarian strategies, this is not a side issue. Many anomaly signals look attractive *before* costs and disintegrate once you include even modest frictions. High turnover, trading into stress, and trading against the tape—all hallmarks of contrarian trading—tend to push you into the most expensive parts of the market's cost curve.

This section formalizes trading costs as a first-class component of the simulation. We will:

- decompose costs into explicit and implicit components;
- explain how bid–ask spreads, slippage, and market impact arise from basic microstructure;
- introduce static and dynamic cost models suitable for backtesting;
- link cost models to *capacity*: how much capital the strategy can realistically deploy; and
- show how to integrate cost and impact modules into the backtesting engine so that all performance is measured net of costs.

Throughout, the emphasis is on models that are simple enough to implement but realistic enough to prevent self-deception.

Why Cost Modeling Matters More for Contrarian Strategies

Consider two stylized strategies:

- A slow-moving value strategy that rebalances quarterly, altering positions by a few percent of ADV (average daily volume).
- A short-horizon contrarian strategy that buys sharp drops and sells sharp rallies, turning over its book every few days and sometimes trading 10–20% of ADV in stressed names.

If both have a *gross* annualized Sharpe ratio of 1.0 before costs, they are not equally attractive:

- The value strategy trades infrequently in relatively calm conditions, often at low participation rates. Realistic frictions might subtract, say, 0.5%–1% per year.
- The contrarian strategy trades often, in the direction of mean reversion, at precisely the times when spreads are wide and liquidity is thin. Frictions can easily consume several percent per year or more.

Ignoring this difference in a backtest confuses *signal quality* with *implementation feasibility*. A robust research process therefore treats cost modeling as seriously as signal design.

Decomposing Transaction Costs

It is useful to decompose trading costs into two broad categories:

- **Explicit costs:** directly observable line items on your brokerage or exchange statement.
- **Implicit costs:** the slippage and price impact you suffer while getting a trade done.

Explicit Costs

Common explicit cost components include:

- *Commissions:* fees paid to brokers for executing trades. These may be per-share (e.g., $0.005 per share) or ad valorem (e.g., 1 bp of notional).
- *Exchange and regulatory fees:* charges levied by exchanges and regulators per share or per trade.
- *Taxes and stamp duties:* in some markets, taxes on certain types of trades (e.g., UK stamp duty on some equity purchases).
- *Borrow fees for shorts:* stock loan fees or rebates when holding short positions.

These costs are typically additive and scale linearly with traded volume or notional. In backtests, they can often be applied via simple formulas such as a fixed number of basis points (bps) per unit of turnover.

Implicit Costs

Implicit costs are more subtle. They arise because the market is not a single price you can transact at arbitrarily large size, but rather an order book with finite depth and other participants reacting to your trades.

Key components are:

- **Bid–ask spread.** If you cross the spread by buying at the ask or selling at the bid, you pay roughly half the spread (in expectation) relative to the mid-price. This is the baseline cost of immediacy.
- **Slippage.** The difference between a reference price (often the mid or last price when you decided to trade) and the actual execution price. Slippage includes crossing the spread *plus* additional drift in the price while you are executing.
- **Market impact.** Your trades themselves move the price. Large, aggressive orders, especially in illiquid names, can push prices against you: buying drives prices up, selling drives them down. Impact has both:

  - a *temporary* component (the price impact decays after you finish trading), and
  - a *permanent* component (information the market infers from your trade).

From a backtesting perspective, slippage and market impact are tightly intertwined. Many practical models roll them into a single "effective cost" function of your trading rate relative to market liquidity.

From Microstructure Intuition to Simple Models

We do not need a full microstructure theory to build useful cost models, but some intuition helps.

Spread as the Cost of Immediacy

Think of the best bid and ask as a small "toll" around the mid-price:

- If you are willing to wait and post a limit order at the mid or inside the spread, you might earn part of that toll (as a market maker).
- If you demand immediate execution, you pay the toll by crossing the spread.

For many backtests, especially at daily frequency, a simple and robust assumption is:

$$\text{spread cost} \approx \frac{1}{2} \times \text{quoted spread} \times \text{signed trade size},$$

expressed in basis points (bps) of notional traded. Here, the "half spread" is the average disadvantage relative to an ideal mid-price execution.

Impact Growing Nonlinearly with Trade Size

Empirically, executing a larger fraction of ADV is disproportionately expensive. A common stylized fact is that impact grows as a concave power law in participation rate:

$$\text{impact cost} \propto \left(\frac{\text{trade volume}}{\text{ADV}}\right)^{\gamma}, \quad 0.5 \lesssim \gamma \lesssim 1.$$

Intuitively:

- Trading 1% of ADV is usually cheap; there is ample liquidity.
- Trading 10% of ADV already consumes a significant portion of the day's natural flow.
- Trading 30% of ADV can dominate the order book and severely move prices.

This suggests modeling cost per unit traded as an increasing function of the *participation rate*

$$\rho = \frac{Q}{\text{ADV}},$$

where Q is your traded volume.

Static Cost Models: First-Order Approximations

As a starting point, many practitioners use *static* cost models: approximate, time-invariant formulas that map turnover into cost. These are crude but vastly better than ignoring costs.

Linear Cost in Turnover

The simplest model is:

$$\text{cost in bps} = c_{bps} \times \text{turnover},$$

where turnover is the fraction of portfolio traded (e.g., 100% if you fully rotate the book) and c_{bps} is a constant per-unit cost estimate.

For example, you might assume 10 bps round-trip cost (both sides) in developed equities. Then:

- A strategy with 100% annual turnover pays about 10 bps per year in costs.
- A strategy with 1000% annual turnover pays about 100 bps per year.

This model collapses all nuances (spread differences, liquidity regimes, market stress) into a single constant. It is acceptable for rough capacity analysis or when detailed data is unavailable, but should not be the final word for high-turnover contrarian strategies.

Half-Spread Penalties

A somewhat more refined static model is to charge a half-spread on each trade:

$$\text{cost in bps} = \frac{1}{2} \times \text{spread in bps} \times \frac{|Q|}{\text{portfolio notional}}.$$

If you have historical spreads per instrument and date, you can apply this daily. If you only have approximate average spreads by asset class or capitalization bucket, you can use representative values (e.g., 3 bps for large-cap equities, 10–20 bps for small caps, more for illiquids).

For contrarian strategies that systematically trade in wider-spread situations (after large moves, in stressed names), using historical spreads rather than a global constant is already a major improvement.

Dynamic Cost and Impact Models

To better capture the interaction between your trades and market liquidity, we move to *dynamic* models that depend on:

- participation rate $\rho = Q/\text{ADV}$,
- volatility σ,
- current spreads and depth,
- execution schedule (how long you take to complete the trade).

A Simple Parametric Impact Curve

A widely used structure is:

$$\text{total cost (bps)} = c_{fixed} + c_{spread} \times s + c_{impact} \times \rho^{\gamma},$$

where:

- c_{fixed} captures explicit per-trade fees and minimal slippage,
- s is the normalized spread (e.g., in bps),
- c_{spread} turns spread into cost (approximately half the spread for market orders),
- c_{impact} and γ control how strongly cost grows with participation rate.

Typical behaviors:

- For small ρ (e.g., $< 1\%$ of ADV), the cost is dominated by spread and fixed terms.
- As ρ increases, the ρ^{γ} term becomes dominant, reflecting growing impact.

You can calibrate $(c_{fixed}, c_{spread}, c_{impact}, \gamma)$ using historical trade and quote data or, lacking that, use industry heuristics and stress-test across plausible ranges.

Interaction with Execution Schedules

How you schedule a large order over time matters. Suppose you want to trade a quantity Q over a time horizon T:

- An *aggressive* schedule (front-loaded) executes quickly, capturing current prices but causing higher temporary impact.

- A *patient* schedule (TWAP/VWAP-style over T) spreads the trading over many small slices, reducing instantaneous impact but exposing you to price drift risk while you wait.

A simple way to model this in backtesting is:

- Split Q into n child orders q_i, each with its own participation rate $\rho_i = q_i/\text{ADV}_i$ for the bar or interval.
- Apply the impact curve to each q_i separately, summing total cost.

In a daily bar backtest, you might approximate execution at the day's VWAP with participation rate given by your *daily* trading volume relative to ADV. In more granular intraday backtests, you can tie q_i and ρ_i to intraday volume profiles.

Volatility-Dependent Costs

Spreads and impact tend to widen with volatility. A simple enhancement is to scale cost coefficients with volatility:

$$c_{impact,eff} = c_{impact} \times f(\sigma),$$

where $f(\sigma)$ is an increasing function, for example proportional to recent realized volatility. This captures the intuition that trading during crises is more expensive.

Calibrating Cost Models

Calibration is where models meet data. The best case is when you have access to:

- your own historical order and execution records;
- corresponding trade and quote (TAQ) data or similar;
- reference benchmarks (e.g., VWAP, mid-price paths) for the same intervals.

Measuring Realized Slippage

For each historical order, you can compute realized slippage:

$$\text{slippage} = \text{signed}(\text{fill price} - \text{benchmark price}),$$

expressed in bps. The benchmark price might be:

- the decision price (mid or last at order creation),
- the venue VWAP over the execution window,
- or another appropriate reference.

You then regress or otherwise model slippage as a function of:

- participation rate ρ,
- spread s,
- volatility σ,
- order type (market, limit, passive, aggressive),
- time of day, venue, and instrument class.

This produces empirical estimates of your effective cost curve, which can then be simplified into a parametric form for backtesting.

Using Public or Broker-Provided Curves

If you lack your own detailed history, brokers often provide generic cost models or tools (e.g., pre-trade cost estimators) for different regions, instruments, and participation rates. While not tailored to your exact flow, they are far better than arbitrary guesses.

In research, you can use those curves to parameterize your backtest cost model and then *stress-test*:

- run backtests with base, optimistic, and conservative cost assumptions;

- examine whether the strategy remains attractive across this range.

If a strategy's viability hinges on unrealistically low costs, you should treat it as unproven.

Capacity and the Cost–Turnover Trade-Off

Transaction costs do more than reduce returns; they impose *capacity limits*. A strategy that looks compelling at $10 million may be untradeable at $1 billion because cost and impact grow with size.

Defining Capacity

One practical definition of capacity is the largest capital level C^* for which the strategy's *net* expected performance satisfies some minimum threshold, e.g.:

$$\text{expected net Sharpe}(C^*) \geq S_{min}$$

or

$$\text{expected net return}(C^*) \geq R_{min},$$

where net means after applying the cost and impact model appropriate for trading at capital C^*.

Scaling Experiments in Backtests

To estimate capacity within your backtest:

- Choose a grid of capital levels $C_1 < C_2 < \cdots < C_K$.
- For each C_k, re-run the backtest with:
  - position sizes, order quantities, and participation rates scaled to reflect trading with capital C_k;
  - the same signal and decision rules.

- Measure net performance metrics (return, Sharpe, drawdown) as functions of C_k.

Because participation rates ρ increase with capital, the cost model will impose stronger drag at higher C_k. Visualizing net performance versus C_k makes the notion of capacity concrete.

For contrarian strategies, you will often see a sharp deterioration beyond a certain size, especially in smaller or stressed names. This is a feature, not a bug: it tells you that the anomaly is *real but small.*

Integrating Costs into the Backtesting Engine

A cost model is only as useful as its integration into your simulation environment. From the architectural perspective laid out in the previous section, you want:

- a dedicated *cost and impact module* in the execution simulator;
- clear interfaces so you can swap cost models without changing strategy logic;
- backtest outputs that always report *net-of-cost* performance alongside gross metrics.

Execution Simulator Workflow with Costs

For each order:

- The execution simulator determines a fill schedule and provisional execution prices based on the chosen execution model (e.g., VWAP, market-on-open).
- For each fill slice q_i:
  - compute relevant state: ρ_i, s_i, σ_i, etc.;
  - apply the cost model to get cost per unit and total cost;
  - adjust the effective execution price to include slippage and impact.

- Aggregate explicit and implicit costs; update realized P&L and cash.

The key is that from the strategy's perspective, it only observes fills and effective prices. It does not see the details of cost modeling, which encourages cleaner separation of concerns.

Reporting Net Performance and Cost Diagnostics

Every backtest report should, by default, answer:

- What is the gross performance (ignoring costs)?
- What is the net performance (after costs)?
- How much of the signal's edge is consumed by:
  - explicit costs,
  - spread and slippage,
  - market impact?
- How do costs break down by:
  - instrument, sector, or region;
  - trade direction (long vs. short, entry vs. exit);
  - time period or market regime?

A simple but informative diagnostic is a table or plot of average cost per trade and per unit turnover by bucket (e.g., participation rate buckets). If you see that most of your P&L comes from trades executed at high participation rates with high impact, you may want to redesign the strategy or its execution.

Putting It All Together

By this point, you should view cost and impact modeling as an inseparable part of anomaly research, not an afterthought. The workflow is:

- Design your signal and strategy logic using the point-in-time architecture from the previous section.
- Choose a cost and impact model appropriate to your asset class, data, and turnover profile.
- Calibrate or at least sensibly parameterize the model using historical executions, TAQ data, or broker curves.
- Integrate the model into the execution simulator so that all backtests yield net-of-cost results.
- Run scaling experiments to understand capacity and robustness to cost assumptions.

In the forthcoming section on performance metrics and attribution, we will build on this foundation to decompose net performance into components: how much comes from signal quality, how much is lost to costs, and how these relationships vary across time and market regimes. Only with that full picture can you judge whether a contrarian anomaly strategy is not just statistically intriguing, but genuinely tradeable.

6.3 Performance Metrics & Attribution

By this point, you have a backtesting engine that respects point-in-time information and incorporates realistic transaction cost and impact models. The next question is deceptively simple:

Given a backtest output—an equity curve, positions, trades, and costs—how do we decide whether the strategy is any good, and why?

An equity curve alone is not enough. Two strategies with identical final wealth can differ radically in risk, path profile, reliance on specific anomalies, and sensitivity to costs. In this section we build a disciplined language for describing what a strategy is doing and where its performance comes from.

We will proceed in three steps:

1. Define core performance and risk metrics for a single backtest.

2. Show how to relate strategy returns to simple factors, so that you do not mistake beta for alpha.
3. Introduce performance attribution: decomposing P&L by signal, sector, and time, including cost attribution.

Throughout, we assume you have a time series of portfolio returns (both gross and net of costs), as produced by the architecture in earlier sections.

Core Risk-Adjusted Performance Metrics

Let $\{r_t\}_{t=1}^{T}$ be the strategy's periodic (e.g., daily) net returns, and let $r_{f,t}$ be the corresponding risk-free rate (which may be close to zero at daily frequencies). Let $\bar{r}$ denote the average of $\{r_t\}$, and σ_r their standard deviation.

Sharpe Ratio

The Sharpe ratio is the workhorse of performance measurement. For excess returns $x_t = r_t - r_{f,t}$,

$$\text{Sharpe} = \frac{\mathbb{E}[x_t]}{\sqrt{\text{Var}(x_t)}} \approx \frac{\bar{x}}{\sigma_x},$$

with annualization by multiplying numerator and denominator according to the number of periods per year.

- **Interpretation.** Average excess return per unit of total volatility.
- **Strengths.** Simple, scale-invariant: if you double leverage, both mean and volatility double and Sharpe is unchanged.
- **Limitations.** Assumes volatility is an adequate risk proxy. It implicitly treats upside and downside volatility symmetrically and can be misleading for skewed or fat-tailed return distributions—which contrarian strategies often exhibit.

In practice, you should always compute Sharpe but never stop there.

Information Ratio

When comparing a strategy to a benchmark (e.g., a market index or style factor), the information ratio (IR) focuses on *active* returns:

$$a_t = r_t - b_t, \quad \mathrm{IR} = \frac{\mathbb{E}[a_t]}{\sqrt{\mathrm{Var}(a_t)}} \approx \frac{\bar{a}}{\sigma_a},$$

where b_t is the benchmark return at t.

- **Interpretation.** Average excess return per unit of tracking error relative to the benchmark.
- **Use for anomalies.** Many anomaly strategies are "long-short" or hedged. The IR against an appropriate benchmark (e.g., hedge fund index, factor portfolio) helps you see if you add value beyond simply taking certain factor bets.

Sortino Ratio and Downside Focus

The Sortino ratio replaces total volatility with *downside* volatility:

$$\mathrm{Sortino} = \frac{\mathbb{E}[x_t]}{\sqrt{\mathbb{E}[(\min(x_t, 0))^2]}},$$

so that only negative deviations from zero (or from a target rate) contribute to risk.

For contrarian strategies that experience occasional sharp losses but frequent small gains, Sortino can help distinguish strategies with similar Sharpe but very different downside profiles.

Drawdowns and Path-Dependent Risk

Investors experience drawdowns, not variances. Given a cumulative wealth process W_t (starting at $W_0 = 1$),

$$\mathrm{DD}_t = 1 - \frac{W_t}{\max_{s \le t} W_s}$$

is the drawdown at time t; the *maximum drawdown* is:

$$\text{MDD} = \max_t \text{DD}_t.$$

Related to this is *time under water*: the total duration the strategy spends below its previous peak.

- **Why path matters.** Two strategies with the same Sharpe may differ in MDD and time under water. A contrarian strategy that occasionally falls 30% and takes three years to recover may be uninvestable for many institutions, even if its Sharpe is decent.
- **Backtest reporting.** Always include a drawdown chart along-side the equity curve and summarize metrics like MDD and median time under water.

Skewness, Tail Risk, and Payoff Profile

Contrarian strategies often earn small, regular profits by leaning against price moves, punctuated by large losses when trends persist. This generates:

- *Negative skewness:* the left tail of the return distribution is heavier than the right.
- *High kurtosis:* more extreme events than a normal distribution would predict.

While formal skew and kurtosis statistics are easy to compute, a more intuitive diagnostic is the *hit rate* and *payoff ratio.*

Hit Rate and Payoff Ratio

Define:

- Hit rate: proportion of periods with positive returns:

$$H = \frac{\#\{t : r_t > 0\}}{T}.$$

- Payoff ratio: average gain on winning periods divided by average loss on losing periods:

$$P = \frac{\mathbb{E}[r_t \mid r_t > 0]}{|\mathbb{E}[r_t \mid r_t < 0]|}.$$

Many successful contrarian strategies exhibit:

- $H > 0.5$ (win more often than they lose),
- but $P < 1$ (when they lose, they tend to lose more per event).

Trend-following strategies often show the opposite: lower hit rate but higher payoff ratio. Seeing (H, P) helps you internalize whether the strategy is "picking up nickels" or "riding big winners", and whether that pattern aligns with your risk appetite.

Turnover and Cost Drag

Given the emphasis on realistic cost modeling in the previous section, turnover becomes a key descriptive metric:

$$\text{turnover}_t = \frac{\sum_i |q_{i,t}|}{\text{portfolio notional at } t},$$

where $q_{i,t}$ is the traded notional (buy or sell) for instrument i at time t. You can report:

- average turnover per period,
- annualized turnover,
- and turnover distributions (e.g., how often do we trade more than 20% of the portfolio in a day?).

In addition, you should measure:

- *average cost per unit turnover (bps)*, and

- *fraction of gross alpha consumed by costs.*

For high-turnover contrarian strategies, this cost drag is often the main constraint on viability and capacity.

Avoiding Beta Masquerading as Alpha

Once you understand standalone performance, the next step is to ask: *What is driving these returns?* A strategy might appear to exploit an anomaly when, in fact, it is mostly a disguised bet on market direction or simple style factors.

Factor-Based Decomposition

Let r_t be your strategy's excess return, and let $f_{1,t}, \ldots, f_{K,t}$ be returns of K risk factors: e.g., market, size, value, momentum, quality, low-volatility. A simple linear model is:

$$r_t = \alpha + \sum_{k=1}^{K} \beta_k f_{k,t} + \varepsilon_t.$$

Here:

- β_k is the exposure to factor k,
- α is the intercept (residual return unexplained by the factors),
- ε_t are residuals.

Interpretation:

- If most of the strategy's average return comes from $\sum_k \beta_k \mathbb{E}[f_{k,t}]$ and α is small or insignificant, your "anomaly" may simply be a combination of known factors.
- If α remains meaningful after controlling for salient factors, you have stronger evidence of genuine residual alpha.

Time-Varying Exposures

Contrarian strategies may dynamically change factor exposures over time (e.g., becoming long value and short momentum in certain regimes). To understand this:

- estimate factor loadings in rolling windows (e.g., 1–3 years), and
- plot the evolution of $\beta_k(t)$ alongside strategy performance.

This helps answer questions such as:

- Does the strategy accidentally become a large market beta trade during crises?
- Are we consistently short momentum when it underperforms, amplifying drawdowns?

Such insights feed back into both risk management and signal design.

Attribution by Signal, Sector, and Time

So far we have treated the strategy as a monolith. In practice, anomaly strategies are portfolios of signals and exposures, often across many instruments. To manage and improve them, you need to know:

- Which signals are actually contributing?
- Which sectors or regions drive P&L?
- Are returns concentrated in a specific period or regime?

This is the role of performance attribution.

Signal-Level Attribution

Suppose your strategy combines M signals or "alphas"—for example, a short-term reversal signal, a medium-term momentum signal (perhaps used as a filter), and a value signal. You convert those into target positions or trades each day.

A practical signal attribution framework typically proceeds as follows:

1. For each instrument i at time t, record:
   - its position $w_{i,t}$ (weight or notional),
   - its realized return $r_{i,t}$,
   - the contribution of each signal m to that position or trade (e.g., via the signal's score or its share in the combined forecast).
2. Define an allocation rule that attributes each instrument's P&L to signals. For example, if the combined forecast is a weighted sum of normalized signals,

$$F_{i,t} = \sum_{m=1}^{M} \lambda_m S_{i,t}^{(m)},$$

   you can allocate the instrument's P&L in proportion to $\lambda_m S_{i,t}^{(m)}$ (after some normalization to avoid sign issues).
3. Aggregate over instruments and time to obtain per-signal P&L:

$$\text{PnL}^{(m)} = \sum_t \sum_i \text{PnL}_{i,t} \cdot w_{i,t}^{(m)},$$

   where $w_{i,t}^{(m)}$ is the fraction of forecast influence from signal m.

Even a coarse approximation—for example, attributing by whichever signal has the strongest absolute score for each trade—is valuable. It can reveal that a seemingly "multi-signal" strategy is actually dominated by one component, or that a particular signal generates P&L but at the cost of large drawdowns.

Sector and Region Attribution

Sector and region attribution provide a more classical view. For each sector s and time t:

- compute sector P&L

$$\mathrm{PnL}_{s,t} = \sum_{i \in s} w_{i,t-1} r_{i,t} \cdot \text{portfolio notional},$$

- accumulate over time to obtain sector-level equity curves.

You can then answer:

- Do certain sectors systematically contribute more alpha or more risk?
- Is the strategy unintentionally concentrated in specific industries?
- How do costs and turnover vary by sector?

For contrarian strategies, it is common to see particularly strong (and risky) contributions from volatile sectors such as financials or small-cap technology. Attribution makes this explicit.

Time and Regime Attribution

Performance can be highly regime-dependent. To understand this, segment the backtest into time buckets:

- calendar periods (e.g., years, quarters),
- volatility regimes (e.g., high vs. low VIX),
- market states (e.g., bull vs. bear markets).

For each segment, compute:

- average return, volatility, Sharpe,
- drawdown statistics,
- turnover and costs.

You may discover, for instance, that:

- the strategy performs well in calm or moderately volatile markets,
- but experiences outsized losses in sharp, trending sell-offs,
- and that trading costs spike exactly in those stressed regimes.

This informs both risk limits (e.g., scaling down exposure when volatility exceeds a threshold) and the credibility of the anomaly (is it robust across decades and different macro conditions, or does it rely on a single episode?).

Cost Attribution

Building on the previous section's cost modeling, you should attribute not only *returns* but also *costs*. For each trade or fill, your execution simulator already computes:

- explicit costs (commissions, fees),
- spread/slippage components,
- impact components.

You can aggregate these by:

- signal,
- sector/region,
- trade direction (long vs. short, opening vs. closing),
- regime (e.g., volatility bucket).

This allows you to answer nuanced questions:

- Does a particular signal generate gross alpha but lose most of it to impact?

- Are our short trades consistently more expensive than our long trades?
- In which sectors or regimes are we "overpaying" for our edge?

Often, you will find that a small subset of trades accounts for a large fraction of costs. This can motivate targeted rule changes (e.g., avoid trading in the last minutes of the day in very illiquid names, or cap participation rates in certain sectors).

A Minimal but Complete Backtest Report

To synthesize these ideas into something you can consistently produce and interpret, it is helpful to specify what a "minimal but complete" backtest report contains. At a minimum, for each strategy and configuration, you should compile:

1. **Overview.**
   - Equity curve and drawdown plot.
   - Key summary statistics: annualized return, volatility, Sharpe, Sortino, MDD, time under water.
   - Hit rate and payoff ratio.
2. **Risk and factor exposure.**
   - Basic beta estimates to major asset classes.
   - Factor regression results (alpha, betas, R^2).
   - If relevant, rolling factor exposures.
3. **Turnover and costs.**
   - Turnover statistics (average, distribution).
   - Average cost per unit turnover, total cost drag (in bps and as a fraction of gross alpha).
4. **Attribution.**
   - P&L by signal (where applicable).

- P&L and costs by sector/region.
- Performance by time period or regime.

With such a report, an investment committee (or your future self) can quickly address three central questions:

1. *What is the expected risk-adjusted return?* (Sharpe/IR, Sortino, drawdowns, tail risk.)
2. *Where does it come from?* (Signals, sectors, factors.)
3. *How fragile is it?* (Dependence on specific regimes, sensitivity to costs, reliance on particular exposures.)

Connecting Metrics and Attribution to Research Decisions

Performance metrics and attribution are not just reporting tools; they are feedback mechanisms for the research loop:

- If signal-level attribution shows one alpha consistently underperforming and consuming costs, you may retire or redesign it.
- If factor decomposition reveals large unintended exposures, you may adjust portfolio construction to neutralize those factors.
- If regime attribution shows vulnerability to certain environments, you may incorporate regime indicators into your risk or sizing rules.
- If cost attribution highlights specific sectors or trading styles as particularly expensive, you may refine execution or apply caps and filters.

In later sections, when we discuss multiple-testing defenses like deflated Sharpe, you will see how these same metrics play a role in quantifying statistical evidence after accounting for the number of strategies you have tried. For now, the key takeaway is that robust anomaly research does not end when an equity curve looks good. It ends when you can explain, in a structured and quantitative way, *how* those returns arise, *what risks and costs* they entail, and *how stable* they are across dimensions that matter to real capital.

6.4 Multiple Hypothesis Defense & Deflated Sharpe

So far in this chapter you have learned how to run realistic backtests, account for costs and impact, and interpret performance using a rich set of metrics and attribution tools. All of that infrastructure solves one half of the problem: *if* a strategy is real, you can measure it properly.

The other half is more subtle: in a modern research process you will try *many* ideas, tweak *many* hyperparameters, and backtest *many* variations. Even if markets were pure noise, some of those trials would look surprisingly good just by chance.

This section is about defending yourself against that illusion. We will:

- Make the notion of "research degrees of freedom" and multiple testing concrete.
- Introduce the *deflated Sharpe ratio* as a way to discount apparent performance for these effects.
- Explain Probability of Backtest Overfitting (PBO) and Superior Predictive Ability (SPA) tests as complementary tools.
- Show how these diagnostics fit into a sane anomaly-hunting workflow.

The Multiple Testing Problem in Anomaly Hunting

In classical statistics, multiple testing is often explained in terms of p-values: if you run N independent tests at 5% significance, you should expect about $0.05N$ "significant" results just by luck. The same logic applies, more informally, to Sharpe ratios and backtests.

Implicit vs. Explicit Hypotheses

When you read a paper, it may present a single clean hypothesis: say, "stocks with high short-term reversals earn abnormal returns." In your research environment, you rarely work so cleanly. You may:

- try several lookback windows (1, 2, 5 days);
- test different universes (large-cap only, all stocks, ex-financials);
- adjust holding periods and exit rules;
- add filters (e.g., volatility screens, volume screens);
- swap model classes or regularization hyperparameters.

Each combination is, in effect, a separate hypothesis. Even if you never formalize them as such, they count. If you run 200 such variants and pick the best Sharpe, that best Sharpe is *overstated* relative to the true underlying edge.

Why This Matters More for Machine Learning

Machine learning amplifies this problem because:

- Model classes have many degrees of freedom (trees, networks, ensembles).
- Hyperparameter space is large.
- Feature engineering can spawn hundreds of correlated predictors.

You will almost inevitably spend considerable time tuning such systems. Without explicit defenses, you will end up with an impressive-looking backtest whose Sharpe owes more to search intensity than to true anomaly structure.

Deflated Sharpe Ratio: Intuition

The *deflated Sharpe ratio* (DSR) is an attempt to answer a simple practical question:

> Given that I tried many strategies and selected the one with the highest observed Sharpe, how much of that Sharpe could plausibly be due to luck alone, taking into account non-normal returns and finite sample noise?

The DSR is not a new metric you report instead of Sharpe. It is an *adjusted* Sharpe-like quantity that tries to strip away the part of the Sharpe that can be explained by:

- non-normality (skew, kurtosis),
- finite sample length,
- and the number of strategies or trials effectively run.

You can think of it as: "If I account for these effects, the Sharpe I can credibly report is not S_{obs} but $S_{deflated}$, which is smaller and more conservative."

Components of the Adjustment

The DSR framework (in its common formulations) typically involves:

- Estimating the distribution of the Sharpe ratio under the null hypothesis of no true alpha, using:
  - sample length T,
  - sample skewness and kurtosis of returns.
- Considering the fact that you did not pick a random Sharpe from this distribution, but the *maximum* of N such draws (for the N strategies or variants you tested).

- Computing a critical Sharpe level $S^\star$ such that, under the null and after multiple-testing adjustment, only a small fraction (e.g. 5%) of strategies would exceed $S^\star$ by luck.

The deflated Sharpe is then, informally, your observed Sharpe S_{obs} *measured against* this elevated threshold, often expressed as a z-score or significance level.

You do not need to memorize the formula. What matters is the behavior:

- For long samples and mild non-normality with few trials, $S_{deflated} \approx S_{obs}$.
- As you increase the number of trials N or encounter more skewed, fat-tailed returns, $S^\star$ rises and the deflated Sharpe shrinks.
- At some point, you may find that an observed Sharpe of 1.5 is no longer compelling once you account for the fact that you effectively ran a hundred mildly correlated experiments.

Interpreting Deflated Sharpe in Practice

Suppose you have:

- $N = 50$ reasonably distinct strategy variants,
- each tested over $T = 8$ years of daily data,
- and the best observed annualized Sharpe among them is $S_{max} = 1.8$.

A DSR calculation may tell you:

- Under the null of no alpha, the distribution of Sharpe ratios from these 50 experiments has a maximum that often reaches 1.2–1.4 just due to noise.

- After adjusting for this and for non-normality, the deflated Sharpe corresponding to 1.8 is equivalent, say, to an "effective" Sharpe of around 1.1 or a p-value that is barely below conventional thresholds.

The exact numbers will depend on the details, but the message is clear: that flashy 1.8 is not as special as it looks.

You can use this in at least three ways:

- **Evidence thresholding.** Require that DSR exceeds some conservative benchmark (e.g., corresponding to a one-sided 5% or 1% test) before promoting a strategy.
- **Model comparison.** When choosing between several candidates, compare their deflated Sharpes rather than only their raw Sharpes.
- **Research documentation.** Report both S_{obs} and the DSR, along with your estimate of N (how many trials or degrees of freedom were effectively used).

Immediately after introducing DSR, it is helpful to visualize what is going on.

In this schematic:

- The blue histogram represents observed Sharpes from many strategies or tries.
- The dashed red line is a deflated Sharpe cutoff: a threshold that few strategies exceed once multiple testing is considered.
- Strategies whose Sharpes lie between zero and the cutoff may look attractive in isolation, but collectively are what you *should* expect from noise.

Probability of Backtest Overfitting (PBO)

While DSR adjusts a single observed Sharpe for multiple trials, Probability of Backtest Overfitting (PBO) addresses a slightly different question:

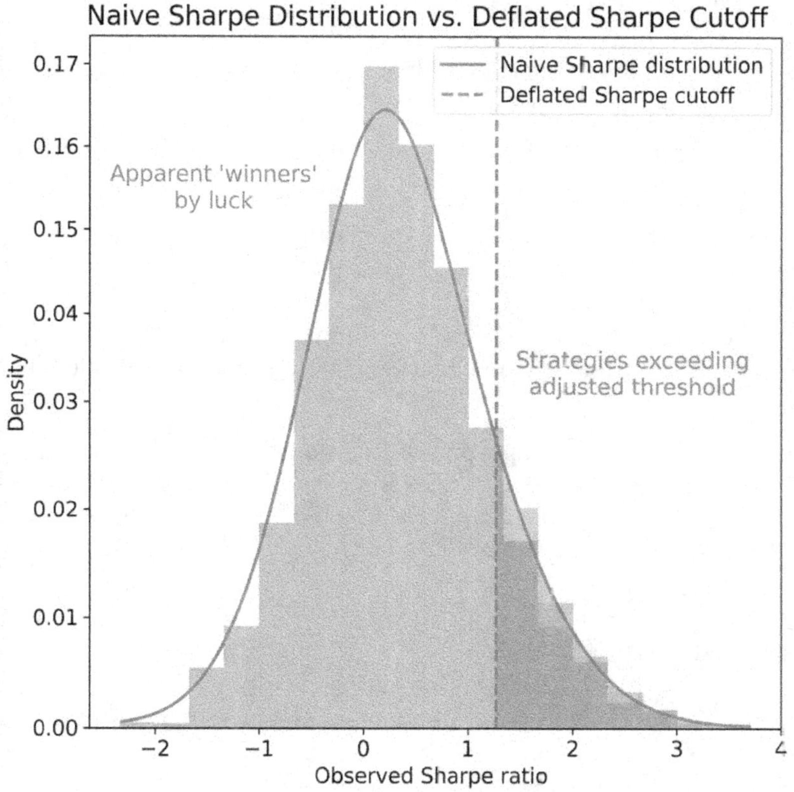

If I select the strategy that looks best in sample, what fraction of the time should I expect it to *underperform* out of sample compared to the rest of the candidate strategies?

Basic PBO Idea

PBO is usually implemented via a repeated resampling scheme over time:

- Split the full backtest period into several contiguous subperiods (e.g., 8 or 10 blocks).

- For each resampling iteration:
  - randomly select some blocks as "in-sample" and the rest as "out-of-sample";
  - for each candidate strategy, compute its in-sample and out-of-sample performance (e.g., Sharpe or mean return);
  - identify the in-sample winner (highest Sharpe) and record its rank out-of-sample relative to peers.
- Repeat many times to build an empirical distribution of how often the in-sample winner ends up in various out-of-sample ranks.

The PBO is then the proportion of iterations in which the in-sample winner ranks below median (or below some other threshold) out-of-sample. A high PBO means that the process of "picking the best backtest" is likely to select an overfit strategy.

Interpreting PBO

- If PBO is close to 50%, then picking the in-sample winner is no worse than randomly picking among the candidates; you may have limited evidence for any strong preference.
- If PBO is much higher (say 70–90%), your selection procedure is likely overfitting: the best in-sample strategy tends to disappoint out-of-sample.
- A low PBO (significantly below 50%) suggests that genuine skill or signal structure is helping you select strategies that also do well out-of-sample.

PBO is especially useful when you have a family of related strategies (e.g., many hyperparameter settings of a contrarian ML model). It quantifies how dangerous it is to trust the top of the in-sample leaderboard.

Superior Predictive Ability (SPA) Tests

The Superior Predictive Ability (SPA) test is a formal statistical procedure designed to answer yet another kind of question:

> Among a set of candidate strategies, is there *any* strategy whose predictive performance is significantly better than that of a benchmark, after accounting for data-snooping over the whole set?

Unlike DSR, which adjusts *one* Sharpe, or PBO, which looks at rank stability, SPA tests consider the full collection of candidate strategies and control the data-snooping bias collectively.

Conceptual Outline

Very roughly, an SPA test proceeds as follows:

- For each strategy $j = 1, \ldots, M$, compute a performance differential $d_{j,t}$ at each time t relative to a benchmark (e.g., strategy return minus benchmark return).
- Compute some summary statistic D_j of performance for each strategy (e.g., mean of $d_{j,t}$).
- Let $D_{max} = \max_j D_j$ be the best observed performance across all strategies.
- Use bootstrap methods (that respect time-series dependence) to approximate the distribution of D_{max} under the null hypothesis that no strategy beats the benchmark.
- Compare the actual D_{max} to this null distribution to obtain a p-value.

Interpretation: A small SPA p-value indicates that it is unlikely all strategies are equally bad as the benchmark; at least one has superior predictive ability. A large p-value suggests that the apparent winners could easily have arisen by chance given the number of strategies and their dependence structure.

How These Tools Fit Together

DSR, PBO, and SPA are not mutually exclusive; they look at the problem from complementary angles:

- **DSR** focuses on the *magnitude* of evidence for a single strategy, given multiple trials and return properties.
- **PBO** focuses on the *selection process* and how often the in-sample winner fails out-of-sample.
- **SPA** focuses on the *family* of strategies and whether any of them truly outperforms a benchmark, adjusting for data-mining across the family.

In a robust anomaly research workflow, you might:

- Generate a family of candidate strategies using your backtesting engine (with proper cost modeling and point-in-time data).
- Use SPA-like logic to see whether the family as a whole contains any credible winners relative to a benchmark.
- For leading candidates:
  - compute DSR to adjust their Sharpe for multiple trials;
  - estimate PBO to understand the risk that choosing the best backtest is overfitting;
  - cross-check performance across regimes and out-of-sample periods.

The outcome is rarely a binary "yes or no" verdict. More often, you arrive at nuanced statements such as:

> "We tested about 80 reasonable strategy variants. SPA suggests that at least one is better than the benchmark at the 5% level. Our preferred variant has an observed Sharpe of 1.6, but its deflated Sharpe is closer to 1.1 when accounting for multiple testing. PBO indicates that, historically, picking the in-sample winner would underperform in roughly

40% of resampling splits—so there is a non-trivial risk of overfitting, but not overwhelming. Combined with economic intuition and robustness checks, we judge the evidence as moderately strong, but size the strategy conservatively."

Practical Workflow and Governance Implications

From a practical and governance perspective, these tools help you formalize standards for "enough evidence." Some suggestions:

- **Predeclare candidate sets.** When feasible, specify in advance the grid of hyperparameters or model variants you plan to test. This makes it easier to define N or M for DSR and SPA.
- **Log all experiments.** Tie backtests and their configurations into an experiment registry (as discussed later in the chapter). This prevents silent inflation of research degrees of freedom.
- **Set evidence thresholds.** For example, require:
  - DSR exceeding a chosen z-score (e.g., equivalent to one-sided 5%),
  - SPA p-value below some threshold,
  - PBO not excessively high.

  These thresholds need not be rigid, but they create a default standard.
- **Communicate uncertainty.** When presenting to risk or investment committees, show both naive and adjusted metrics. For instance, include a small table:

	Observed	Adjusted / Deflated	Interpretation
Sharpe	1.8	1.2	After accounting for trials
PBO	–	35%	Moderate overfitting risk
SPA p-value	–	3%	Some evidence vs. benchmark

- **Align with model risk policies.** In institutional settings, model risk teams and regulators are increasingly concerned with backtest overfitting, especially for ML-based strategies. Using tools like DSR, PBO, and SPA—and documenting their results—helps demonstrate that you are managing this risk deliberately.

Linking Back to Anomaly Hunting

Anomaly hunting lives at the intersection of statistics, economics, and engineering. The temptation is always to keep searching until you find an attractive pattern; with modern compute and flexible models, you almost always will.

The defenses in this section do not eliminate that temptation, but they give you:

- a quantitative way to discount performance inflated by search,
- a yardstick for how often backtest winners might fail out-of-sample,
- and a formal test of whether any member of a large candidate set truly adds predictive value.

Combined with the backtesting architecture, transaction cost modeling, and attribution tools from earlier sections, they help you move from "this backtest looks good" to "this anomaly appears robust enough to risk capital, and here is the quantified evidence to support that judgment."

6.5 Research Hygiene, Reproducibility & Explainability

By now you have seen how easy it is to produce seductive backtests, and how much work is required to make them realistic: point-in-time data, cost and impact modeling, robust performance metrics, and multiple-testing defenses. The final step is to ensure that your research process itself is *trustworthy*.

Trustworthiness has three pillars:

- **Research hygiene:** clear organization, naming, and logging so that any result can be traced back to specific data, code, and parameters.
- **Reproducibility:** the ability to rerun an experiment and obtain the same result, even months later and even on different machines.
- **Explainability:** for machine learning models in particular, the ability to say *why* the model behaves as it does, without leaking future information.

This section codifies concrete practices that turn your backtesting environment into a robust research platform and, for institutional readers, lay the foundation for satisfying model risk and governance requirements.

What Is Research Hygiene and Why Does It Matter?

Research hygiene is the set of practices that prevent your research lab from devolving into a pile of unlabeled notebooks, ad hoc scripts, and half-remembered parameter tweaks.

In a small personal project, you might get away with this. In a serious anomaly-hunting program, poor hygiene leads to:

- **Irreproducible results:** you cannot reproduce a promising backtest because the data snapshot or random seed changed.
- **Subtle bugs:** unnoticed data leakage due to a local hack that never made it into the main codebase.
- **Wasted effort:** different researchers unknowingly rerun similar experiments because no one can see what has already been tried.
- **Governance risk:** you cannot explain to risk or compliance how a live strategy was derived, or what evidence supported its deployment.

Research hygiene is not glamorous, but it is what makes a sophisticated research stack usable and defensible.

Versioning Data and Models

The first principle of reproducibility is simple:

> *Every backtest must know exactly which data and which model it used.*

That requires explicit **versioning**.

Versioned Datasets

Data evolve over time:

- Vendors correct errors, restate histories, and backfill fields.
- You may add new coverage (e.g., new markets or asset classes).
- You might change preprocessing (e.g., different outlier handling).

If you simply point your code at "the current database," your results will drift as the underlying data change. To prevent this:

- Assign a *version identifier* to each logical dataset snapshot, e.g., `prices_v2025-01-15` or a git commit hash if data transformations are code-defined.
- Store metadata alongside the dataset:
  - data source and extraction date,
  - preprocessing steps and code versions,
  - coverage details (time range, universe).
- Ensure that backtest configurations reference dataset versions, not just paths. For example:

```
data:
  prices: prices_v2025-01-15
  fundamentals: fundamentals_v2024-12-01
  corporate_actions: ca_v2025-01-10
```

This way, rerunning a backtest in the future means using *the same* data snapshot, even if the live research environment has moved on.

Model Versioning

Machine learning models introduce a second axis of change: the model itself. You need to track:

- **Architecture:** model type and structure (e.g., gradient boosting with specific depth and learning rate; neural network with certain layers).
- **Hyperparameters:** regularization strengths, learning rates, number of trees, etc.
- **Training data and labels:** which samples and time periods were used, and with what preprocessing.
- **Randomness:** initialization seeds, data shuffling order, and any stochastic components.

For each trained model, assign a unique model identifier, plus:

- store the model artifact (e.g., serialized object),
- record its training configuration and data versions,
- record evaluation metrics on both training and validation periods.

This is analogous to code version control but at the model level. It allows you to answer questions like:

> "Which model is currently driving the live strategy? When and how was it trained? What backtested evidence supported this version over the previous one?"

Deterministic Pipelines and Controlled Randomness

Many backtests—especially those involving ML—use randomness in:

- splitting data into train and validation folds,
- initializing model weights,
- sampling hyperparameters in random searches,
- simulating order execution with stochastic components.

Randomness is not inherently bad. But uncontrolled randomness destroys reproducibility: rerunning the same experiment gives slightly (or very) different results, and debugging becomes guesswork.

Determinism as a Default

Aim for *deterministic* pipelines:

- Use fixed random seeds passed through all libraries (e.g., NumPy, PyTorch, TensorFlow, scikit-learn).
- Ensure your backtesting engine processes events in a deterministic order (e.g., sorted by timestamp, then by a stable secondary key).
- Avoid hidden sources of nondeterminism, such as:
  - parallelism without controlled seeds,
  - non-associative floating-point reductions that depend on thread scheduling.

If a particular component *must* be stochastic (e.g., a Monte Carlo execution model), treat that randomness as an explicit input:

- log the seed(s),
- allow rerunning with the same seeds for exact reproduction,
- or run multiple seeds and report distributions of outcomes, so that performance estimates are robust to randomness.

Configuration, Logging, and Experiment Registries

Having versioned data and deterministic code is necessary but not sufficient. You still need to know:

> *Which combination of data, code, parameters, and random seeds produced this particular backtest result?*

This is where configuration management, logging, and experiment registries come in.

Configuration as Code

Rather than scattering parameters throughout scripts or notebooks, capture them in structured configuration files (YAML, JSON, LaTeX tables, etc.) under version control. A typical backtest config might specify:

- universes and filters,
- data versions,
- signal definitions and hyperparameters,
- portfolio construction rules,
- cost and impact model settings,
- evaluation horizons and walk-forward scheme.

Then your backtest runner can take a single configuration object as input and:

- produce results,
- save the configuration alongside outputs for later inspection.

Structured Logging

Each backtest run should emit machine-readable logs. At minimum, log:

- **Run metadata:** timestamp, user, machine, environment (library versions, OS).
- **Inputs:** data versions, model versions (if pre-trained), configuration hash or ID, random seeds.
- **Outputs:**
  - summary performance metrics (Sharpe, drawdowns, costs),
  - factor exposures,
  - attribution results (by signal, sector, etc.),
  - locations of detailed time-series outputs (equity curves, per-trade logs).
- **Status:** success/failure, warnings, unexpected events (e.g., illiquid trades rejected).

This information can be held in files, a database, or specialized experiment tracking tools. The key is that each run is identifiable and auditable.

Experiment Registries

An *experiment registry* is a central catalog of backtests and model training runs. It allows you to:

- quickly see which configurations have already been tried,
- search for experiments by tag (e.g., "reversal_strategy_v3", "EM universe"),
- compare metrics across runs systematically,
- generate meta-analyses (e.g., for deflated Sharpe calculations, you know how many distinct strategies were tried).

Even a simple table with columns like

ID	Date	Config ID	Data Versions	Key Metrics
exp_0012	2025-02-15	rev_v3_cfg7	prices_v2025-01	Sharpe=1.1, MDD=12%
exp_0013	2025-02-16	rev_v3_cfg8	prices_v2025-01	Sharpe=0.7, MDD=8%

is a large improvement over digging through ad hoc logs or notebook cells.

Audit Trails and Governance

For institutions, research hygiene must support not only the researchers but also:

- risk committees,
- compliance and model risk groups,
- regulators or external auditors.

They will want to know:

> *What evidence supported the strategy at deployment? How has it evolved since? Were changes controlled and documented?*

Audit Trails for Strategy Lifecycle

A robust audit trail links:

- **Initial hypothesis and design.** A concise description of:
  - economic intuition (why might this anomaly exist?),
  - intended data and universe,
  - planned validation structure (walk-forward, out-of-sample periods).
- **Research runs.** References to the experiments and models that informed decisions, with their configurations and results.

- **Approval and deployment.** Dates, committees, and any constraints imposed (e.g., caps on leverage or capacity).
- **Post-deployment changes.** Version history of:
  - signal definitions,
  - model retrainings,
  - parameter adjustments,
  - code refactors affecting production.

Importantly, *live* changes to strategies should follow a process similar to software releases: review, test, approval, deployment, and documentation. This prevents silent drift in models and signals that cannot be justified later.

Explainability for Machine Learning Signals

The final piece is explainability: making sense of the behavior of ML-driven strategies. For contrarian trading, explainability serves several purposes:

- **Sanity checks.** Does the model act in ways that align with economic intuition, or is it exploiting artifacts?
- **Leakage detection.** Feature importance patterns can sometimes reveal that a feature is encoding future information.
- **Stakeholder communication.** Risk managers and investors are more comfortable with models they can understand at least at a high level.

Feature Importance Tools (e.g., SHAP)

Many modern ML models (gradient boosting, random forests, neural nets) use complex nonlinear relationships between inputs and outputs. Global feature importance measures and local explanation methods help unpack this.

One widely used family of tools is based on *Shapley values* from cooperative game theory, commonly implemented as SHAP (SHapley Additive exPlanations):

- For each prediction (e.g., a forecasted return for stock i at time t), SHAP attributes the prediction to individual input features.
- Aggregating over many predictions yields a global picture of which features tend to increase or decrease the forecast, and by how much.

Example usage in a contrarian context:

- You train a model using:
  - short-term returns,
  - volatility indicators,
  - liquidity measures,
  - fundamental valuation ratios,
  - sentiment or news scores.
- SHAP analysis reveals that:
  - extreme short-term negative returns contribute strongly to positive forecasts (consistent with mean reversion),
  - high liquidity and moderate volatility amplify the forecast (safer to trade),
  - extreme valuation levels play a secondary role.

This pattern aligns with a plausible story: the model is essentially a refined contrarian signal that prefers liquid, moderately volatile names. If instead SHAP indicated that some obscure technical variable with suspect timing dominates the forecast, you would investigate possible data leakage.

Partial Dependence and Accumulated Local Effects

Partial dependence plots (PDPs) and related tools like *accumulated local effects* (ALE) help understand how changing one feature, holding others roughly fixed, affects model predictions.

For example, you can:

- plot the model's average forecast as a function of recent return, to see the shape of its contrarian response;
- examine how the model's behavior changes with volatility or liquidity.

Again, this provides an intuitive check: if the model's response to a feature is wildly non-monotonic or spiky, you may be overfitting noise.

Avoiding Explainability-Induced Leakage

Explainability tools themselves operate on data, and careless usage can introduce leakage. To avoid this:

- Fit explanation models (e.g., SHAP) using only training and validation data, not future periods reserved as true out-of-sample.
- Ensure that features used for explanations are the same leak-free point-in-time features used in training and backtesting.
- Avoid deriving new features from future realizations during the explanation process.

Explainability must sit *inside* the same point-in-time and multiple-testing discipline as the rest of your research.

A Blueprint for a Robust Research Workflow

We conclude by assembling these elements into a coherent workflow for anomaly research and deployment:

- **Hypothesis logging.** When starting a project, record:
  - the economic idea,
  - the intended data and feature set,
  - pre-specified tests or criteria where possible.
- **Data preparation with PIT constraints.** Build features using the point-in-time architecture; version the resulting datasets.
- **Model training and backtesting.** Use deterministic pipelines and walk-forward or nested validation; log every run into an experiment registry with full configuration and metrics.
- **Cost-aware evaluation.** Always evaluate net-of-cost performance with calibrated transaction cost and impact models.
- **Multiple-testing adjustment.** For families of strategies or hyperparameters, compute deflated Sharpe, PBO, and (where appropriate) SPA statistics to adjust evidence for trial-and-error.
- **Attribution and explainability.** Perform signal- and sector-level attribution; apply SHAP/PDP-style tools to understand model behavior, while guarding against leakage.
- **Governance and audit.** For candidates approaching deployment, assemble:
  - a concise narrative (intuition, design, limitations),
  - a standardized backtest report (metrics, attribution, costs),
  - multiple-testing diagnostics,
  - explainability summaries,
  - and links to all underlying experiments and data/model versions.
- **Production monitoring.** After deployment:
  - monitor live performance versus backtested expectations,
  - track feature distributions and model outputs for drift,
  - periodically re-run explainability analyses to ensure behavior remains aligned with intent.

This may sound elaborate, but each step builds directly on machinery you already have: the backtesting engine, cost models, experiment registry, and explainability tools. The payoff is not only cleaner research but also the ability to defend your anomaly strategies to sophisticated stakeholders—and to yourself—with clarity and confidence.

Chapter 7

Portfolio Construction, Execution & Adaptive Deployment

Signals don't pay the bills until they survive contact with the real market. In this chapter we turn abstract alpha scores into live, scalable portfolios that can withstand drawdowns, hostile liquidity, and changing regimes-while staying compliant and observable enough that you actually sleep at night.

7.1 Risk Measures & Drawdown Control

In the previous chapter we focused on how to extract contrarian signals and translate them into hypothetical returns: we learned how to test whether the signals carry genuine edge and how to avoid backtest pathologies. In this section we assume that step is complete: you have a reasonably robust contrarian signal that produces a stream of daily (or intraday) P&L.

The new question is not "how much can I make?" but rather "how bad can it get along the way, and can I survive it?" For contrarian strategies this question is especially acute. By construction, you are leaning against recent price moves, buying what has just gone down and selling what has just gone up. In many regimes, that is precisely what hurts the most in the short term.

Our goal is therefore twofold:

- Quantify risk in ways that reflect both tail behavior and the *path* of losses.
- Design simple, rule-based overlays that cap drawdowns and keep the strategy liveable for real investors.

We proceed in three steps: traditional risk measures, path-dependent drawdown concepts, and then practical drawdown control mechanisms.

Core Risk Measures: Volatility, Downside Risk, VaR and ES

We start with the familiar building blocks, but keep in mind their limitations for contrarian books.

Volatility as a First Approximation

Let r_t denote the strategy return over period t (e.g., daily). The most common risk measure is the standard deviation (volatility)

$$\sigma = \sqrt{\mathrm{Var}(r_t)} \approx \sqrt{\frac{1}{T-1}\sum_{t=1}^{T}(r_t - \bar{r})^2},$$

where $\bar{r}$ is the sample mean.

Volatility is useful because:

- It is easy to estimate and widely understood.
- Under Gaussian assumptions, many other risk measures can be expressed as multiples of σ.

- It scales nicely with time under those same assumptions ($\sigma_{annual} \approx \sigma_{daily}\sqrt{252}$).

However, contrarian strategies often display:

- *Fat tails*: extreme losses larger and more frequent than Gaussian.
- *Skewness*: occasional large negative moves when trends extend and the strategy keeps leaning against them.
- *Volatility clustering*: calm periods punctuated by bursts of turmoil.

Volatility alone does not distinguish between upside and downside fluctuations, and it is insensitive to the shape of the tails. We therefore refine it.

Downside Deviation and Semi-Variance

Investors are usually more concerned about returns below some target (often zero) than about symmetric fluctuations. Downside deviation focuses only on bad outcomes:

$$\sigma^- = \sqrt{\mathbb{E}\left[\min(r_t - r^*, 0)^2\right]},$$

where r^* is a target return (e.g., 0 or the risk-free rate). In sample form,

$$\sigma^- \approx \sqrt{\frac{1}{T^-} \sum_{t:r_t<r^*} (r_t - r^*)^2},$$

where T^- is the number of periods with $r_t < r^*$.

For contrarian strategies, r^* is typically set to 0, and you can interpret σ^- as "how rough the downside is". This already aligns better with an investor's pain than plain volatility.

Value at Risk (VaR)

Value at Risk (VaR) asks: for a chosen horizon h and confidence level α (e.g., $h = 1$ day, $\alpha = 95\%$), what is the loss L such that

$$\mathbb{P}(\text{Loss over } h \leq L) = \alpha?$$

Equivalently, the VaR_α is the α-quantile of the loss distribution:

$$\text{VaR}_\alpha = \inf\{x : \mathbb{P}(\text{Loss} \leq x) \geq \alpha\}.$$

A daily 95% VaR of 2% means: on 95% of days, you expect to lose no more than 2%. Importantly, it *does not* tell you how bad the remaining 5% of days might be.

There are three broad ways to estimate VaR:

- **Parametric VaR**: assume returns follow some distribution (often Gaussian or Student-t) and compute quantiles analytically using estimated μ and σ.
- **Historical VaR**: take the empirical α-quantile of past returns.
- **Monte Carlo VaR**: simulate future returns (e.g., from a fitted GARCH or factor model) and compute the quantile of simulated losses.

For contrarian portfolios, historical and Monte Carlo approaches are usually preferable: parametric Gaussian VaR will dangerously understate tail risk in the presence of fat left tails.

Expected Shortfall (ES) / Conditional VaR

Expected Shortfall (ES), also called Conditional VaR, answers the complementary question: if we are in the bad $(1-\alpha)$ tail, what is the *average* loss? Formally,

$$\text{ES}_\alpha = \mathbb{E}[\text{Loss} \mid \text{Loss} > \text{VaR}_\alpha].$$

Where VaR looks at the cliff's edge, ES looks at the average height of the drop once you have gone over. ES is especially relevant for contrarian strategies because trend extensions often cause sequences of losses that are individually bad but, in aggregate, worse than you might infer from a single-period VaR.

In practice, you can estimate ES historically by averaging the worst $(1-\alpha)\%$ of losses in your return history.

Estimation Choices: Windows, Robustness, and Concentration

The quality of your risk estimates matters as much as the choice of metric.

Overlapping vs. Non-Overlapping Windows

Risk parameters (σ, VaR, ES) are typically estimated over rolling windows. Using *overlapping* windows (e.g., 252-day rolling estimates) each day shares most of its data with the previous day. This produces smooth risk estimates but introduces statistical dependence across estimates.

Using *non-overlapping* windows (e.g., recomputing risk every month using the last 1 year of data) yields more statistically independent estimates but less smoothness. For live risk management, overlapping windows are standard; just remember that smoothness is not the same as precision.

Robust Estimators for Fat Tails

Contrarian return distributions can be distorted by a few very large events. In small samples, these can either dominate your risk metrics or be absent entirely, giving a false sense of safety.

Practical remedies include:

- **Robust volatility**: use median absolute deviation (MAD) or winsorized standard deviation (capping extreme returns) as cross-checks.
- **Tail-focused checks**: explicitly compute maximum loss, ES, and the number of tail events observed.
- **Stress scenarios**: superimpose historical crisis patterns or hypothetical shocks (e.g., a 5-sigma market move) onto your strategy to see how it would have behaved.

Position Concentration and Leverage

Risk is not only about the distribution of portfolio returns, but also about how those returns are generated:

- **Concentration**: If a few positions or sectors dominate your risk, the portfolio is exposed to idiosyncratic shocks, which may be correlated with the conditions that trigger contrarian trades (e.g., sector-specific crashes).
- **Leverage**: Borrowing magnifies both volatility and drawdowns. A seemingly low-volatility mean-reversion signal can become fragile when levered aggressively.

In practice, it is helpful to compute *component VaR* and *marginal VaR*: how much each position contributes to portfolio VaR, and how VaR would change if you slightly increased a given position. This ties risk back to position sizing, which we will revisit in the next section of the chapter.

Path-Dependent Risk: Drawdowns, Underwater Curves, and Time to Recovery

Traditional risk measures compress the entire return history into one number. They mostly ignore the *order* of returns. For investor psychology and mandate constraints, the order is often decisive. Losing 20% in a single week feels very different from losing it slowly over two years, even if the total loss is the same.

This motivates path-dependent measures.

Maximum Drawdown

Let V_t denote the portfolio value (or cumulative P&L) at time t, with V_0 normalized to 1. The running peak up to time t is

$$M_t = \max_{s \le t} V_s.$$

The drawdown at time t is then

$$D_t = \frac{V_t - M_t}{M_t},$$

a negative number or zero. The *maximum drawdown* (MDD) over a horizon $[0, T]$ is

$$\text{MDD} = \min_{0 \le t \le T} D_t,$$

i.e., the worst percentage drop from any prior peak.

Maximum drawdown captures the worst cumulative pain experienced by an investor who joined at the best possible time (the previous peak). For contrarian strategies, which may endure protracted periods of being "early" against strong trends, MDD can be substantially larger than what volatility or VaR would suggest.

Underwater Curves

An *underwater curve* is simply the time series of drawdowns $\{D_t\}$. Plotting D_t below the equity curve provides a powerful visualization:

- How often does the strategy make new highs?
- How deep and how long are the typical underwater episodes?
- Are large drawdowns isolated or do they cluster?

For contrarian portfolios, you often see long, shallow drawdowns punctuated by occasional deeper events when trends become very strong. This pattern must be acceptable to the investors funding the strategy.

Time to Recovery and Underwater Duration

The time to recovery from a drawdown starting at a peak time t^* is the smallest $\tau \geq 0$ such that $V_{t^*+\tau} \geq M_{t^*}$. We can compute:

- The **maximum time to recovery**: the longest underwater spell.
- The **average time to recovery**: how long investors typically wait to get back to even.

These metrics are critical for contrarian systems: a 15% drawdown that recovers in 2 weeks may be tolerable; the same 15% that takes 2 years to recover is far more dangerous to your business, even if pure Sharpe ratios are identical.

Drawdown Overlays: Turning Risk Measures Into Survival Rules

Risk measurement without risk *control* is only half the job. We now translate the concepts above into practical overlays that sit *on top of* your signal and portfolio construction. The signal may say "buy more", but the overlay can reply "not at this leverage".

Volatility Targeting

Volatility targeting adjusts exposure so that realized volatility stays near a pre-specified target σ_{target}.

Let $\hat{\sigma}_t$ be your current estimate of portfolio volatility (e.g., from a rolling 60-day window). Given an unconstrained target position vector $\mathbf{w}_t^{raw}$, you scale it by a factor

$$k_t = \frac{\sigma_{target}}{\hat{\sigma}_t},$$

subject to leverage limits, to obtain

$$\mathbf{w}_t = \min\{k_t, k_{max}\}\,\mathbf{w}_t^{raw}.$$

When markets become turbulent and $\hat{\sigma}_t$ spikes, k_t shrinks and the portfolio naturally de-levers. In calm conditions, k_t can expand, but you cap it at k_{max} to avoid excessive leverage.

This mechanism helps contrarian strategies that otherwise might lean too heavily into violent reversals during stress episodes.

Risk Budgeting Across Signals

In a multi-signal setup, you can think of each signal or sub-portfolio as consuming a portion of a total risk budget. For example, you might stipulate that no single signal can contribute more than 30% of total portfolio VaR.

If $\text{VaR}^{(i)}$ is the VaR contribution of signal i and VaR^{tot} is total VaR, you enforce

$$\frac{\text{VaR}^{(i)}}{\text{VaR}^{tot}} \leq b_i,$$

where b_i is a pre-assigned budget (e.g., 0.3). If a signal's risk contribution exceeds its budget, you scale down its positions.

For contrarian strategies this prevents a single particularly noisy anomaly—for example, a small-cap mean reversion sleeve with high idiosyncratic risk—from dominating portfolio tail risk.

Stop-Losses vs. Stop-Outs and Capital Throttles

A naive approach is to impose *position-level stop-losses*: if a trade loses more than $x\%$, you liquidate it. For contrarian strategies this can be counterproductive, because:

- The whole idea is to buy into weakness; many successful trades look awful just before they rebound.
- Position-level stops can force you to crystallize losses at precisely the worst time, creating pro-cyclical liquidation.

Instead, we recommend *portfolio-level* rules that respond to aggregate pain, not individual wobbles.

Equity-based stop-out. Define a maximum tolerated drawdown D_{max} (e.g., -15%). If the running drawdown D_t breaches D_{max}, you trigger a "stop-out": reduce gross exposure to some defensively low level (say 20–30% of normal), or even go flat.

Capital throttle. Rather than an all-or-nothing stop-out, you can map drawdown to a continuous exposure multiplier $c(D_t)$, for example:

$$c(D_t) = \begin{cases} 1, & D_t \geq -5\%, \\ 0.5, & -10\% \leq D_t < -5\%, \\ 0.2, & -15\% \leq D_t < -10\%, \\ 0, & D_t < -15\%. \end{cases}$$

You then set

$$\mathbf{w}_t = c(D_t)\,\mathbf{w}_t^{target},$$

where $\mathbf{w}_t^{target}$ comes from your portfolio construction engine. This throttle shrinks risk as pain accumulates, without forcing instant liquidation at any particular price point.

Designing Non-Procyclical Rules

The key challenge is to avoid overlays that mechanically *buy high and sell low*. Some practical design principles:

- Use **slow-moving** risk metrics (e.g., 20–60 day realized volatility, drawdown measured over weeks or months) rather than intraday noise.
- Let overlays **control leverage**, not the directional sign of trades. For a contrarian book, you typically want to remain contrarian, just at lower size when pain is high.
- Set thresholds using **out-of-sample backtests** and **stress scenarios**, not hand-waving. For each candidate rule, ask: how often would it have triggered historically, and did it help or hurt long-term Sharpe and maximum drawdown?

Integrating Drawdown Control into Backtests and Live Systems

Drawdown overlays are only useful if they are part of the entire workflow, from backtest to production.

Backtest Integration

When you evaluate a contrarian strategy in backtest, you should:

- Simulate the *raw* strategy returns based purely on the signal.
- Layer on the volatility targeting and drawdown overlays, recomputing positions and returns as if those rules had been in place.
- Compare key metrics (Sharpe, maximum drawdown, time to recovery, tail risk) across the raw and risk-controlled versions.

Often, you will find that mild throttling—for example, halving exposure after a 10% drawdown—has modest impact on long-run return but significantly improves survivability metrics. That is the kind of trade-off institutional investors appreciate.

Monitoring and Automated De-Risking

In live trading, an automated risk engine should:

- Compute rolling volatility, VaR/ES, equity curve, and drawdown at a suitable frequency (daily for end-of-day strategies, intraday for high frequency).

- Evaluate drawdown and volatility against pre-defined thresholds.

- Automatically update exposure multipliers (vol targeting and capital throttle factors) and generate new target positions when thresholds are crossed.

- Log all changes and breaches for auditability and post-mortem analysis.

Human oversight remains essential. Portfolio managers should periodically review whether the overlays are firing as expected, or whether they are either too sensitive (choking the strategy) or too lax (allowing unacceptable drawdowns).

Illustrative Example: Equity, Drawdown, and Risk Overlays

To tie the concepts together, Figure illustrates a stylized contrarian strategy. The top panel shows the equity curve V_t, the middle panel the underwater curve D_t, and the bottom panel a rolling volatility/-VaR estimate. Vertical markers indicate times when drawdown or risk metrics trigger exposure cuts.

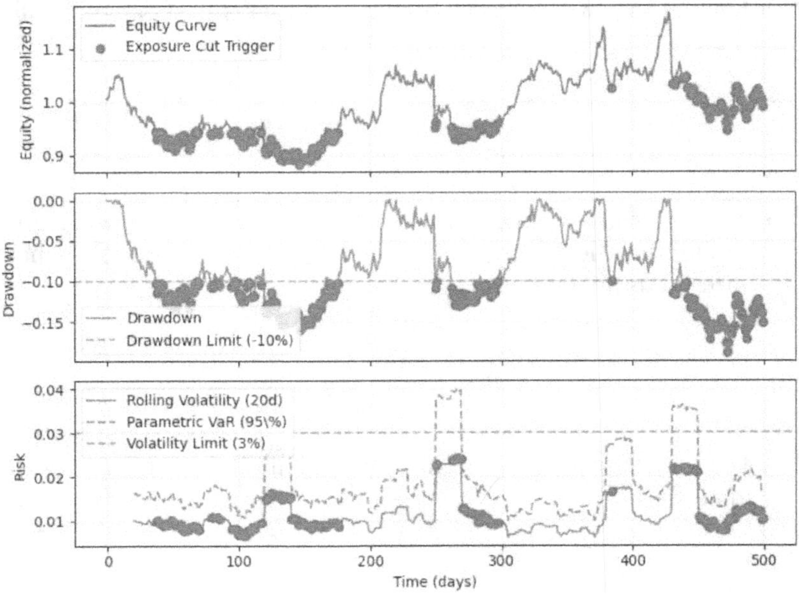

Figure 7.1: Illustrative equity curve, underwater (drawdown) profile, and rolling volatility/VaR for a stylized contrarian strategy. Red markers indicate points where drawdown or risk limits would trigger exposure cuts.

In your own research, you should produce an analogous figure for each candidate strategy and each proposed overlay configuration. This immediately reveals whether your risk controls are appropriately calibrated or are either too timid or too aggressive.

Documenting and Defending Risk Limits

Finally, robust risk management for contrarian strategies requires not only good design but also clear communication. For each strategy you should be able to articulate:

- The primary risk measures you monitor (volatility, downside deviation, VaR/ES, maximum drawdown, time to recovery).

- The precise numerical limits (e.g., annualized volatility target, maximum permissible drawdown, risk budgets by sleeve).
- The overlays in place (volatility targeting, capital throttle, portfolio-level stop-out) and the logic by which they adjust exposure.
- Historical evidence (backtests and stress tests) showing that these rules would have contained losses during past crises without destroying the strategy's long-run edge.

This documentation is essential when discussing the strategy with investment committees, risk teams, and regulators. More importantly, it is a commitment device for you: when the next prolonged trend move hits and your contrarian engine starts to hurt, having pre-agreed, quantitatively justified drawdown rules helps you act systematically rather than emotionally.

In the next section we will build on this foundation and show how to incorporate these risk constraints directly into portfolio construction and position sizing, so that contrarian signals are expressed in a way that is not only profitable in backtests, but also robust and survivable in live trading.

7.2 Portfolio Construction & Position Sizing

In the previous section we treated risk as a first-class object: we defined volatility, downside deviation, VaR and ES, and we focused on path-dependent quantities such as drawdowns and time-to-recovery. We also introduced overlays such as volatility targeting and capital throttles that keep a contrarian strategy survivable in live trading.

We now assume that work is done: you have a validated contrarian signal that emits scores $s_{i,t}$ for asset i at time t, and you have risk limits that describe how much total risk and drawdown you are willing to tolerate. The practical question is:

How do we turn these scores into an actual portfolio of

positions, sized and hedged so that they respect our risk constraints and exploit the signal efficiently?

We will proceed in four stages:

1. Clarify the design space: long-only vs. long–short, neutrality choices, and mandate constraints.
2. Map raw model scores into *cleaned* scores and preliminary weights.
3. Embed risk, turnover, and factor constraints through simple optimization.
4. Use Kelly-style ideas to control overall leverage and position sizing, and apply factor-neutral hedging.

Throughout, we keep the focus on contrarian strategies, where the signals are often noisy and capacity constraints matter.

From Scores to Portfolio Design: Choosing the Book Structure

Before manipulating scores, you must decide the broad shape of the portfolio. This is driven by investor mandate, capital structure, and implementation platform.

Long-Only vs. Long–Short

- **Long-only**: You can only buy assets (e.g., a long-only equity fund). A contrarian signal here typically overweights temporarily depressed names and underweights temporarily frothy ones, but all weights remain non-negative.
- **Long–short**: You can hold both long and short positions. This is the natural habitat for many contrarian anomalies (e.g., residual mean reversion, pairs trading), because you can directly sell what looks rich and buy what looks cheap.

Long–short books allow you to isolate the anomaly more cleanly by hedging out broad factors, but they introduce short-borrow, margin, and financing constraints.

Neutrality: Dollar, Beta, Sector, Factor

A contrarian strategy can ride on top of, or attempt to neutralize, broad market and style risks. Common choices:

- **Dollar-neutral**: Total long market value equals total short market value, so net exposure is close to zero.
- **Beta-neutral**: The portfolio's sensitivity to the market factor is near zero (e.g., $\beta \approx 0$ vs. a broad index), even if dollar exposure is not exactly neutral.
- **Sector- or industry-neutral**: Within each sector or industry, longs and shorts roughly balance. This stops the contrarian book from unintentionally becoming, say, a big sector-rotation trade.
- **Factor-neutral**: Exposure to standard risk factors (market, size, value, quality, momentum, etc.) is constrained to be small. The target is to earn returns primarily from the contrarian signal, not from incidental factor bets.

You rarely achieve all of these perfectly; instead, you decide which ones are critical for your mandate. For example, a market-neutral equity contrarian strategy will typically impose dollar- or beta-neutrality and tight factor constraints, while a long-only strategy may only control sector weights and overall tracking error versus a benchmark.

Cleaning Scores: From Raw Signals to Usable Inputs

Model outputs are rarely ready to be turned directly into positions. Scores may be noisy, unbounded, or have outliers due to data glitches. The cleaning stage conditions the scores so they behave well in portfolio construction.

Standardization and Monotone Transforms

Let $s_{i,t}$ be the raw score (e.g., predicted next-period residual return, or z-scored mispricing). In a cross-sectional strategy, we usually normalize scores across the asset universe at each time t:

$$\tilde{s}_{i,t} = \frac{s_{i,t} - \mu_t}{\sigma_t},$$

where μ_t and σ_t are the cross-sectional mean and standard deviation of scores on date t. This yields scores with mean zero and unit variance across assets, making them comparable over time and across universes.

Sometimes, we apply a monotone non-linear transform $f(\cdot)$ to reduce the influence of extreme scores without changing the ranking:

$$\hat{s}_{i,t} = f(\tilde{s}_{i,t}),$$

with examples including:

- Hyperbolic tangent: $f(x) = \tanh(x)$, which squashes large positive/negative values towards ± 1.
- Clipping: $f(x) = \min(\max(x, -k), k)$ for some k (e.g., $k = 3$).
- Logistic: $f(x) = \frac{1}{1+e^{-x}} - 0.5$, mapping scores into $(-0.5, 0.5)$.

These transforms improve robustness: a single extreme score caused by a data error should not dominate portfolio weights.

Winsorization and Outlier Control

Even after normalization, occasional outliers can persist. A standard technique is *winsorization*: replacing extreme values with a percentile threshold. For instance, at each date t:

$$\hat{s}_{i,t} = \begin{cases} q_{t,\alpha} & \text{if } \tilde{s}_{i,t} < q_{t,\alpha}, \\ \tilde{s}_{i,t} & \text{if } q_{t,\alpha} \leq \tilde{s}_{i,t} \leq q_{t,1-\alpha}, \\ q_{t,1-\alpha} & \text{if } \tilde{s}_{i,t} > q_{t,1-\alpha}, \end{cases}$$

where $q_{t,\alpha}$ is the α-quantile of $\tilde{s}_{i,t}$ across assets (e.g., $\alpha = 1\%$).

This preserves most of the cross-sectional structure while protecting against rare but harmful score spikes.

From Cleaned Scores to Preliminary Weights

Once scores are cleaned, we construct a simple mapping from scores to preliminary portfolio weights. This stage deliberately ignores many constraints; it is a first approximation that will then feed into a more rigorous optimization.

Linear Score-to-Weight Mapping

For a cross-sectional long–short contrarian equity strategy with N assets at time t, a commonly used mapping is:

$$w_{i,t}^{\text{pre}} = \frac{\hat{s}_{i,t}}{\sum_{j=1}^{N} |\hat{s}_{j,t}|},$$

followed by scaling to achieve a desired gross exposure G:

$$w_{i,t}^{\text{pre}} \leftarrow G \cdot w_{i,t}^{\text{pre}}.$$

Here:

- If $\hat{s}_{i,t} > 0$ the asset is long; if $\hat{s}_{i,t} < 0$ it is short.
- The denominator normalizes the absolute weights so that $\sum_i |w_{i,t}^{\text{pre}}| = G$.

This construction ensures the portfolio is dollar-neutral (net exposure near zero) by symmetry.

Controlling Concentration via Cross-Sectional Scaling

The raw mapping above might still yield overly concentrated weights if a few assets have large scores (even after cleaning). To avoid this, we can impose explicit concentration caps, e.g.:

$$|w_{i,t}^{\text{pre}}| \leq w_{\max},$$

for some small $w_{\max}$ (e.g., 1% of NAV per name). A simple way is to:

1. Compute unconstrained w^{pre} from scores.
2. Clip w^{pre} to $[-w_{\text{max}}, w_{\text{max}}]$.
3. Renormalize to restore the desired gross exposure G.

For long-only portfolios, weights are non-negative and usually constructed relative to a benchmark:

$$w_{i,t}^{\text{pre}} = w_{i,t}^{\text{bench}} + k \cdot \hat{s}_{i,t},$$

with subsequent re-scaling to satisfy $\sum_i w_{i,t}^{\text{pre}} = 1$ and any sector or issuer caps.

Process Diagram: From Scores to Target Positions

Before we move into formal optimization, it is helpful to visualize the full flow from scores to implementable positions. Figure shows a block diagram of the process.

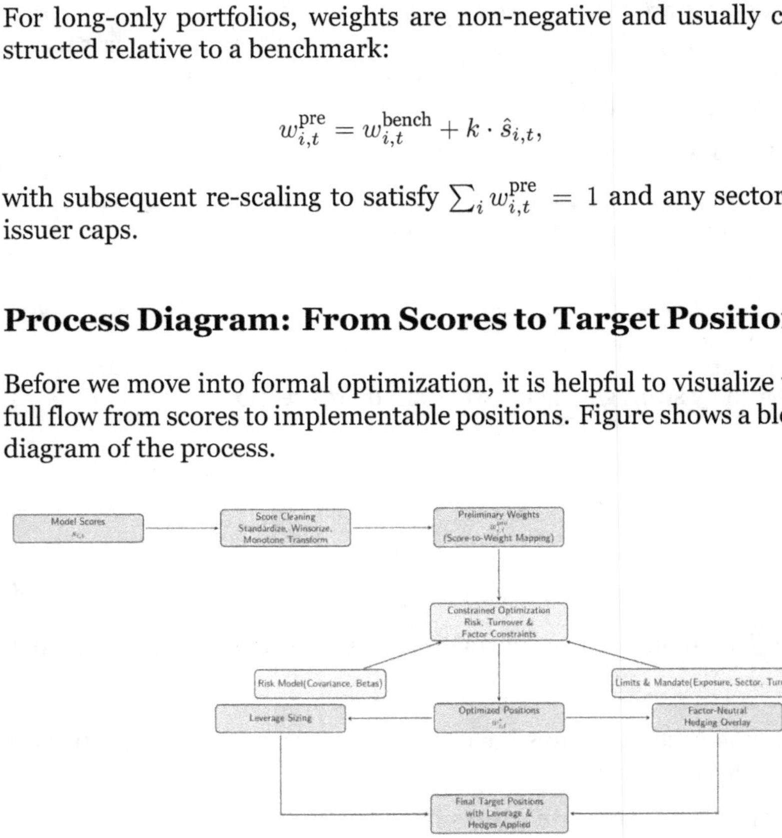

Constrained Optimization: Embedding Risk and Turnover

The preliminary weights provide a good starting point, but they do not yet incorporate many critical real-world constraints: sector caps, factor exposure limits, maximum leverage, turnover control, etc. We now introduce a simple constrained optimization framework that treats these jointly.

Mean–Variance with a Reference Portfolio

Suppose we have:

- A vector of expected alphas α_t, often proportional to the cleaned scores $\hat{s}_{i,t}$.
- A risk model with covariance matrix Σ_t for asset returns.
- A reference portfolio $\mathbf{w}_t^{\text{ref}}$ (e.g., yesterday's portfolio or a benchmark).

A common objective is to choose new weights $\mathbf{w}_t$ that balance alpha against risk and turnover:

$$\max_{\mathbf{w}_t} \quad \alpha_t^\top \mathbf{w}_t - \frac{\lambda}{2} \mathbf{w}_t^\top \Sigma_t \mathbf{w}_t - \gamma \|\mathbf{w}_t - \mathbf{w}_t^{\text{ref}}\|_1,$$

subject to constraints on exposure, leverage, and factor risks. Here:

- λ controls risk aversion.
- γ penalizes turnover via the ℓ_1 norm (absolute changes in weights), approximating transaction costs.

In practice, you may approximate the ℓ_1 or use quadratic penalties for tractability, depending on your optimizer.

Exposure and Leverage Constraints

Typical linear constraints include:

$$\begin{aligned}
\sum_i w_{i,t} &= 0 && \text{(dollar-neutral)} \\
\mathbf{1}^\top |\mathbf{w}_t| &\le G_{\max} && \text{(gross exposure limit)} \\
w_{i,t}^{\min} \le w_{i,t} &\le w_{i,t}^{\max} && \text{(name-level bounds)} \\
\mathbf{B}^\top \mathbf{w}_t &\approx 0 && \text{(factor/beta neutrality)}
\end{aligned}$$

where **B** is a matrix of factor loadings (e.g., market beta, size, value, momentum). For sector caps, you treat sector exposures as factors with upper/lower bounds.

Turnover Constraints

Beyond adding a penalty, you can impose explicit turnover bounds:

$$\sum_i |w_{i,t} - w_{i,t-1}| \leq \tau_{\text{max}},$$

where τ_{max} is the maximum fraction of NAV you are willing to trade in one period.

This is particularly important for contrarian signals with short half-lives: you want to exploit quick mean reversion, but if you trade too aggressively your transaction costs and market impact may consume all the edge.

Kelly-Style Sizing: How Much Risk to Take

So far, we have focused on *relative* weights: which assets to overweight or underweight. We now connect portfolio *scale* to the estimated edge and risk.

Single-Bet Kelly Intuition

Consider a simple gamble with expected excess return μ and variance σ^2 per dollar bet. The Kelly fraction for maximizing long-term log-wealth is:

$$f^* = \frac{\mu}{\sigma^2}.$$

If you bet a fraction f of capital each period, then:

- If $f < f^*$, you grow more slowly but more safely.
- If $f > f^*$, you risk ruin; overbetting is fatal.

For a portfolio, this idea generalizes but the key intuition remains: *optimal size is proportional to signal strength and inversely proportional to risk.*

Portfolio-Level Kelly Fraction

Suppose your optimized contrarian portfolio $\mathbf{w}_t$ (with unit gross exposure) has:

- Expected excess return μ_{port} (per period).
- Variance $\sigma^2_{\text{port}} = \mathbf{w}_t^\top \Sigma_t \mathbf{w}_t$.

Then a Kelly-style total leverage L^* might be:

$$L^* = \frac{\mu_{\text{port}}}{\sigma^2_{\text{port}}}.$$

In practice, both μ_{port} and σ^2_{port} are estimated with noise; moreover, investors are risk-averse and capital is finite. Therefore, you almost never run full Kelly. Instead, you choose a fractional Kelly level $c \in (0, 1)$:

$$L = c \cdot L^*.$$

Values like $c \in [0.2, 0.5]$ are common in practice. This fractional Kelly leverage L then scales your portfolio weights:

$$\mathbf{w}_t^{\text{final}} = L \cdot \mathbf{w}_t^*,$$

subject to overall leverage and drawdown overlays from the previous section. If volatility targeting and drawdown throttles are also in place, you use the minimum leverage implied by all risk controls.

Factor Exposures and Hedging

Even when you impose factor constraints in optimization, residual exposures can arise due to estimation error, discrete lot sizes, or soft rather than hard constraints. It is good practice to explicitly diagnose and, if necessary, hedge factor exposures.

Diagnosing Factor Tilts

Given factor loadings matrix **B** (assets × factors) and portfolio weights **w**, the portfolio's factor exposures are:

$$\mathbf{f} = \mathbf{B}^\top \mathbf{w}.$$

For a contrarian strategy that aims to be market-neutral and momentum-neutral, for example, you might monitor:

$$f_{\text{MKT}}, \quad f_{\text{MOM}},$$

and compare them against allowed bands (e.g., $|f_{\text{MKT}}| \leq 0.05$, $|f_{\text{MOM}}| \leq 0.02$). If exposures breach limits, you adjust.

Overlay Hedges

One simple way to correct residual factor exposures is to use overlay hedges in liquid instruments. For example:

- If $f_{\text{MKT}} > 0$ (long market beta), short index futures or ETFs to bring β back towards zero.
- If $f_{\text{MOM}} < 0$ (short momentum), potentially add a momentum ETF or futures overlay to cap the exposure, depending on mandate.

These overlays are particularly useful when individual stock positions are already at name-level or sector-level bounds: instead of distorting many positions to fix one factor exposure, you can use a small number of index-like instruments.

The key is to remember that overlays consume part of your risk and leverage budget. In the risk engine, the hedges must be accounted for together with the core contrarian positions.

Putting It All Together: A Step-by-Step Recipe

To summarize, a practical workflow for turning contrarian scores into robust portfolios is:

1. **Input:** Model scores $s_{i,t}$, risk model Σ_t, factor loadings $\mathbf{B}$, last-period weights $\mathbf{w}_{t-1}$, and mandate limits.

2. **Score cleaning:** Standardize, apply monotone transformations, and winsorize scores to obtain $\hat{s}_{i,t}$.

3. **Preliminary weights:** Map $\hat{s}_{i,t}$ to $w_{i,t}^{\text{pre}}$ via linear score-to-weight rules, subject to basic concentration bounds.

4. **Constrained optimization:** Solve a mean–variance-type problem with alpha proportional to $\hat{s}_{i,t}$, penalizing risk and turnover, and imposing exposure, leverage, and factor constraints to get optimized raw positions $\mathbf{w}_t^*$.

5. **Kelly-style sizing:** Estimate the expected return and variance of $\mathbf{w}_t^*$, compute a conservative fractional Kelly leverage, and apply overall risk overlays (volatility targeting, capital throttles).

6. **Factor hedging:** Compute factor exposures of the leveraged portfolio, and apply overlay hedges in index or factor instruments to keep exposures within agreed bands.

7. **Output:** Final target positions $\mathbf{w}_t^{\text{final}}$ that the execution system will attempt to reach, subject to transaction cost models and trading constraints.

Each step should be backtested jointly, not in isolation. The final test of a portfolio construction pipeline is whether it transforms a noisy contrarian signal into a set of trades that are:

- **Consistent** with the intended anomaly.
- **Risk-controlled** in terms of volatility, drawdown, and factor exposures.
- **Implementable** given liquidity, turnover, and leverage constraints.

In the next section, we connect these target portfolios to the realities of trading by examining execution algorithms and smart order routing, and by quantifying how much of the theoretical alpha survives once the trades hit the market.

7.3 Execution & Smart Order Routing

In the previous sections we learned how to turn contrarian scores into risk-aware portfolios, and how to size those portfolios within volatility and drawdown limits. Conceptually, we now know *what* we want to hold: a target vector of positions $\mathbf{w}_t^{final}$ for each rebalancing time t.

This section addresses the last, crucial step: turning *target positions* into *actual fills* in real markets. The portfolio engine might say, "buy 50,000 shares of stock A and sell 40,000 of stock B," but markets are not frictionless pipes. Prices move, order books are finite, other traders react, and your own orders can move the market.

For contrarian strategies, execution is especially delicate:

- You frequently trade *against* the prevailing short-term flow: buying what is falling and selling what is rising.
- Your alpha is often short-lived; waiting too long can let the edge decay.
- Your trades can be informative: a large contrarian buyer during a sell-off may be noticed and front-run or faded by others.

Our goal is to design an execution and routing framework that:

- Respects microstructure realities: spreads, depth, volatility, and venue differences.
- Minimizes implementation shortfall (slippage and costs) relative to the theoretical portfolio P&L.
- Controls information leakage and market impact so that our contrarian trades do not become self-defeating.

We proceed gradually: from basic microstructure concepts, to execution cost and slippage measurement, to algorithmic execution styles and smart order routing, and finally to feedback loops from execution back into portfolio construction.

Microstructure Basics for Portfolio Quants

A contrarian portfolio manager does not need to be a full-time market microstructure researcher, but must understand a few core concepts that directly affect execution quality.

Limit Order Books, Spreads, and Depth

Most modern electronic markets are organized as limit order books:

- **Bid**: the highest price at which some participant is currently willing to buy a given quantity.
- **Ask (offer)**: the lowest price at which someone is willing to sell.
- **Bid–ask spread**: ask – bid; the immediate round-trip cost for a small trade.
- **Depth**: the available quantity at each price level on both sides.

A simple stylized picture:

```
Price    Bid Size   |   Ask Size   Price
--------------------------------------------
100.00     200      |     0        ------
 99.99     500      |    150       100.01
 99.98     800      |    400       100.02
```

Crossing the spread—submitting a marketable order to buy at the ask or sell at the bid—guarantees an immediate fill up to the available depth, but you pay the spread and possibly move the price if your order overwhelms the available quantity at the best price.

Intraday Volume and Volatility Patterns

Liquidity is not constant throughout the day:

- Near the open and close, volumes and volatility tend to be higher; spreads may start wide at the open and narrow later.
- Midday often sees thinner books and lower volume, but sometimes also tighter spreads.

Execution algorithms exploit these patterns by timing large trades to coincide with more liquid intervals, or by smoothing trading across the day to match average conditions.

For contrarian strategies, the timing problem is intertwined with alpha half-life:

- If the expected mean reversion occurs mostly overnight or in the first hour, you may need to execute aggressively soon after signal generation.
- If the signal decays over several days, you can afford more patient, liquidity-seeking execution.

From Ideal P&L to Realized P&L: Implementation Shortfall

Once target trades are known, the most important performance measure for the execution layer is *implementation shortfall*. This quantifies how much P&L you lose between the theoretical, frictionless portfolio and what you actually realize in the market.

Defining Implementation Shortfall

Suppose your portfolio engine computes target weights at time t based on a reference price P_t^{ref} (e.g., the mid-quote at decision time). Without costs and impact, your hypothetical P&L from t to horizon T would be based on trading exactly at P_t^{ref}.

In reality, your execution system trades at a series of prices $\{P_{t,k}^{exec}\}$ as child orders fill over time. Implementation shortfall is:

$$\text{IS} = (\text{Theoretical P\&L using } P_t^{ref}) - (\text{Actual P\&L using } P_{t,k}^{exec}),$$

aggregated across all assets and trades.

Breaking it down:

- **Spread cost**: Half the spread paid when you cross the market (buy at ask, sell at bid).

- **Impact cost**: Adverse price movement caused by your own trading pressure.
- **Timing cost**: Random, exogenous price movement that happens while your order is executing.
- **Fees and taxes**: Explicit commissions, exchange fees, and any transaction taxes.

For contrarian portfolios, *impact cost* is often the most relevant: your orders may push prices further away from where you want them (e.g., buying into a falling market might slow the decline but also cause a temporary bounce against you).

Measuring Slippage in Practice

To control implementation shortfall, you must measure it systematically:

- For each parent order (e.g., "buy 10,000 shares of XYZ"), record:
  - The decision price P^{ref}.
  - The schedule of executions: times and sizes of each fill and their prices.
- Compute the volume-weighted average price (VWAP) of your fills:

$$P^{VWAP} = \frac{\sum_k q_k P_k^{exec}}{\sum_k q_k}.$$

- Define slippage: for a buy order,

$$\text{Slippage} = \frac{P^{VWAP} - P^{ref}}{P^{ref}};$$

  for a sell order, the sign is reversed.

Aggregating slippage statistics over time and across names helps you diagnose whether your algos are too aggressive (large, consistent adverse slippage) or leaving alpha on the table (extremely small slippage, but slow completion and missed opportunity).

Execution Algorithm Families

Modern execution relies heavily on algorithmic trading. Instead of sending one large order, you hand a *parent order* to an execution engine, which slices it into many *child orders* that adapt to market conditions.

The main algo families can be understood in terms of *speed* (how fast they try to complete the order) and *visibility* (how much they expose in the displayed order book).

TWAP: Time-Weighted Average Price

A TWAP (Time-Weighted Average Price) algo slices a parent order evenly over a specified period. For example, to buy 60,000 shares over one hour, a TWAP might send 1,000-share child orders once per minute.

- **Pros**: Simple, predictable, and relatively insensitive to volume patterns.
- **Cons**: Can be too aggressive in illiquid periods and too timid in liquid bursts; may reveal a regular pattern that others exploit.

TWAP can be reasonable when:

- Your order is small relative to typical volume.
- You do not have strong beliefs about intraday volume profiles.

VWAP: Volume-Weighted Average Price

A VWAP algo targets trading in proportion to expected intraday market volume. If 10% of daily volume typically trades in the first half hour, a VWAP schedule tries to execute roughly 10% of your order in that window, and so on.

- **Pros**: Aligns trading with periods of higher natural liquidity, reducing impact.
- **Cons**: Requires a reliable volume profile; if everyone uses VWAP, crowding may occur at peak volume times.

Contrarian strategies often benefit from VWAP-like schedules when the alpha horizon is longer than a day and urgency is moderate.

POV: Participation-of-Volume

A POV (participation-of-volume) algo trades a fixed fraction ρ of the *realized* market volume in real time. For example, with $\rho = 5\%$, for every 10,000 shares that trade in the market during a short interval, your algo aims to trade about 500.

- **Pros**: Self-adjusting to current liquidity; avoids becoming more than a certain fraction of flow.
- **Cons**: Completion time is uncertain; if volume dries up, your order may remain partially filled.

POV is natural for contrarian books that must avoid pushing the market around too much but can tolerate uncertain completion, particularly in smaller or less liquid names.

Liquidity-Seeking and Impact-Minimizing Algos

These algorithms adapt more dynamically, scanning multiple venues for hidden or lightly displayed liquidity, deciding when to post passive limit orders vs. crossing the spread, and altering aggression based on real-time metrics such as:

- Spread width and recent changes.
- Order book imbalance (more depth on bid vs. ask).
- Short-term volatility.
- Recent trade sizes and directions.

They may:

- Start passively, posting inside the spread if possible.
- Become aggressive (crossing the spread) if too little is filling or if urgency is high.

- Route opportunistically to dark pools or off-exchange venues when large opposing orders are detected.

For contrarian strategies with short alpha half-lives, well-calibrated liquidity-seeking algos can be powerful, but they must be constrained to avoid "chasing" prices when markets move abruptly.

Choosing Execution Styles for Contrarian Trades

Given a target order and knowledge of the signal's time scale and risk constraints, how do you choose an appropriate execution style?

Alpha Half-Life and Urgency

A simple mental model:

- **Fast-decaying alpha** (minutes to hours): execution must be correspondingly fast. You may choose:
  - Aggressive liquidity-seeking algos.
  - High participation rates in POV (e.g., 10-20% of volume).
- **Medium horizon alpha** (days): you can spread execution over a trading session or two:
  - VWAP with modest aggressiveness.
  - POV with lower participation (1-5%), with caps on daily volume to respect capacity.
- **Slow alpha** (weeks): execution can be patient and opportunistic:
  - Passive posting near the best bid/ask or inside the spread.
  - TWAP or VWAP with strong preference for liquidity-providing orders.

For contrarian portfolios, a common pattern is:

- *Initial entry* is somewhat urgent (you want to exploit the mispricing) but not at all costs.

- *Rebalancing* and *exit* can often be slower and more cost-sensitive, since the edge has typically decayed or reversed.

Risk Constraints and Aggression Levels

Execution cannot ignore risk constraints defined earlier:

- If volatility spikes and drawdown overlays have cut leverage, execution may prioritize rapid de-risking (e.g., quickly reducing positions in stressed names), even at the cost of higher impact.
- If risk is well within limits and the signal will remain valid, the execution engine can privilege lower-impact, more passive styles.

A simple approach is to codify *execution profiles*, parameter sets that tune aggression:

- Profile A: high urgency, high participation, more marketable orders.
- Profile B: medium urgency, balanced passive/aggressive.
- Profile C: low urgency, mostly passive, strict volume caps.

The portfolio system chooses a profile per order based on:

- Signal decay (alpha half-life).
- Current risk state (drawdown, volatility).
- Order size relative to average daily volume (ADV).

Smart Order Routing Across Venues

Most instruments now trade across multiple venues (exchanges, dark pools, alternative trading systems). Smart Order Routing (SOR) decides where and how to send each child order.

Venue Differences

Venues differ on several axes:

- **Fees and rebates**: maker/taker pricing, exchange fees, and rebates for providing liquidity.
- **Displayed vs. hidden liquidity**: some venues display full order books; others allow dark or partially hidden orders.
- **Latency and fill probabilities**: how quickly orders are acknowledged and filled; how often pegged or midpoint orders get executed.
- **Regulatory and routing rules**: best execution obligations, internalization rules, and venue-specific constraints.

A good SOR engine continuously learns which venues are best for each symbol and order type, given current market conditions.

Balancing Cost, Fill Probability, and Information Leakage

SOR logic seeks a balance among three competing goals:

- **Low explicit cost**: choose venues and order types with lower fees and better rebates, all else equal.
- **High fill probability**: route to venues with real, executable liquidity; avoid chasing phantom quotes.
- **Controlled information leakage**: avoid blasting large, aggressive orders across many lit venues at once, which can signal your intentions.

For contrarian strategies, leakage is particularly dangerous: if others infer that you are aggressively buying a falling stock, they may front-run or fade your activity, undermining mean reversion.

Practical SOR designs include:

- Routing small, probing orders to multiple venues to sample depth, then concentrating larger orders where fills occur at low cost.
- Using dark pools and midpoint crossing for a fraction of the order when spread is wide and lit liquidity is thin.
- Limiting the number of simultaneously active child orders visible at the top of different books to reduce footprint.

Safeguards: Kill Switches, Volume Caps, and Stress Behavior

Execution algorithms, left entirely on their own, can behave badly in stressed markets. Examples include:

- Continuing to consume liquidity in a flash crash, exacerbating drawdowns.
- Crossing increasingly wide spreads as volatility spikes, leading to enormous slippage.

To prevent this, robust execution frameworks incorporate safeguards:

Kill Switches and Circuit Breakers

Global kill switches allow the firm to:

- Cancel all outstanding orders immediately.
- Stop new child orders from being sent, either across all strategies or for specific books.

Triggers can be:

- Portfolio-level: drawdown beyond a critical threshold during the day.
- Execution-level: slippage beyond a multiple of expected cost; spreads or volatility breaching pre-set bounds.

These should be pre-defined and backtested so that they are rarely triggered in normal conditions but act decisively in truly abnormal ones.

Per-Name and Per-Order Volume Caps

You can cap:

- Maximum participation in ADV for a name (e.g., not more than 10–20% per day).

- Maximum participation in intraday volume over a short horizon (e.g., not more than 30% of any 5-minute bucket).

These caps prevent your contrarian strategy from morphing into the market in that name, which not only increases impact but also reveals your presence.

Spread- and Volatility-Aware Throttling

Execution logic should react to sudden widening of spreads or jumps in short-term volatility:

- When spreads widen sharply, switch to more passive posting or pause crossing the book.
- When volatility spikes, re-evaluate urgency profiles: you may wish to de-risk quickly in some cases, but not at any price.

Because we already track volatility and drawdowns in the risk engine, it is natural to feed those metrics into the execution engine as well.

Learning from Execution: Feedback into Portfolio Construction

Execution is not a one-way street. The realized costs and slippage patterns you observe should influence how you construct portfolios and size orders going forward.

Updating Transaction Cost Models

Portfolio optimization relies on transaction cost models to penalize excessive turnover and large trades. These models often assume cost functions of the form:

$$\text{Cost} \approx c_1 \cdot |q| + c_2 \cdot \frac{q^2}{ADV},$$

where q is the trade size. Execution data let you estimate c_1 and c_2 by regressing realized slippage on order size and relative volume.

Regular updates help you:

- Adjust turnover penalties in the optimizer.
- Reduce target sizes in names where execution is consistently expensive.

Capacity and Alpha Decay

If your execution logs show that:

- Slippage grows sharply as order sizes increase.
- P&L per unit risk declines as AUM grows.

Then your contrarian strategy may be hitting capacity limits. You can respond by:

- Limiting gross exposure or AUM allocated to that strategy.
- Focusing on more liquid universes or down-weighting illiquid names in the score-to-weight mapping.

Similarly, by comparing the timing of trades and subsequent returns, you can empirically estimate how quickly alpha decays. If you find that most contrarian edge materializes within a few hours, you may need to upgrade your execution urgency and microstructure models.

Execution-Aware Portfolio Design

Eventually, portfolio construction and execution should be designed together:

- The optimizer uses empirically calibrated cost models so that target orders are "execution-friendly" from the outset.
- The execution engine provides real-time and historical metrics that refine these models and alert when past assumptions break.

For contrarian trading, this joint design is vital: the whole point is to harvest small, noisy edges by trading against short-term flows. If execution costs and impact are not tightly controlled, those edges vanish long before reaching the investor.

In the next section, we will step back from the intraday details and focus on how contrarian strategies adapt to changing market regimes: detecting when anomalies weaken or invert, and adjusting models and portfolios so that the entire signal-construction-portfolio-execution chain remains robust over time.

7.4 Regime Detection & Model Adaptation

Up to this point in the chapter, we have assumed a relatively stable world. We built risk measures and drawdown controls under the idea that the distribution of returns is stationary enough to be summarized by volatility, VaR, and drawdowns. We then converted contrarian scores into portfolios and discussed how to execute those portfolios with minimal slippage.

Reality is less kind. The statistical properties of returns, correlations, and liquidity change over time. A contrarian edge that works well in one environment can fade, invert, or disappear in another. If your models and portfolio rules assume that yesterday's behavior will continue forever, you are implicitly betting on *no structural change*—a bet history repeatedly falsifies.

In this section we focus on making contrarian strategies *adaptive rather than brittle*. We will:

1. Clarify what we mean by regimes and structural breaks.
2. Review practical tools for detecting regime shifts using your strategy's own data.
3. Describe adaptation mechanisms: retraining, reweighting, and decay.
4. Show how to combine fast- and slow-reacting components to avoid overfitting noise.
5. Emphasize logging, precommitted rules, and backtesting of adaptation itself.

The goal is not to perfectly forecast every regime shift, but to make sure that when the world changes in a sustained way, your contrarian engine does not keep fighting the last war.

What is a Regime?

Informally, a regime is a span of time over which the data-generating process is "similar enough" that a fixed model does a reasonable job. Regimes can differ along multiple dimensions:

- **Volatility**: calm vs. stormy markets.
- **Correlation structure**: diversified vs. highly correlated assets.
- **Liquidity**: tight spreads and deep books vs. wide spreads and fragile depth.
- **Behavior of target anomalies**: some anomalies may strengthen, weaken, reverse sign, or vanish.

A *structural break* is a regime change large enough that the old model's assumptions are materially violated. For example:

- A persistent rise in cross-sectional correlation that makes stock-picking contrarian signals much noisier.
- A shift in microstructure (e.g., tick size changes, new trading rules) that alters intraday mean-reversion patterns.
- Regulatory or macro events that permanently change liquidity or risk premia in certain assets.

As portfolio quants, we do not need to explain *why* each break occurs. Our task is to detect that a regime has changed in a way that matters for our strategies, and then to adapt in a disciplined manner.

Practical Regime Detection Tools

Regime detection is inherently noisy: any finite sample of returns can look anomalous simply by chance. We therefore favor simple, robust tools that focus on stability of key metrics, rather than trying to "name" every possible regime.

Rolling Performance and Stability Checks

The most direct view of regime behavior comes from your strategy's own P&L and hit rate.

Let r_t^{strat} be the strategy return at time t. Consider rolling windows of length W (e.g., 3 months, 6 months):

- Rolling mean:
$$\hat{\mu}_t = \frac{1}{W} \sum_{k=0}^{W-1} r_{t-k}^{\text{strat}},$$
- Rolling volatility:
$$\hat{\sigma}_t = \sqrt{\frac{1}{W-1} \sum_{k=0}^{W-1} (r_{t-k}^{\text{strat}} - \hat{\mu}_t)^2},$$
- Rolling Sharpe:
$$\widehat{\text{Sharpe}}_t = \frac{\hat{\mu}_t}{\hat{\sigma}_t},$$
- Rolling hit rate (fraction of positive-return periods).

Plotting these over time immediately shows whether the strategy's edge is roughly stable or deteriorating. For a healthy contrarian strategy, you expect:

- Some fluctuations in rolling Sharpe, but no prolonged periods of negative Sharpe beyond what you modeled in backtests.
- Hit rate staying above a modest threshold (e.g., $> 50\%$ for many mean-reversion systems), adjusting for your design.

To formalize this, you can apply *stability tests*:

- Compare performance in early vs. recent subperiods (e.g., pre- and post-event windows) using t-tests or non-parametric tests.
- Conduct a simple CUSUM (cumulative sum) test on residuals to detect shifts in mean.

These tests do not prove a structural break but provide statistical evidence that "things are no longer as they were."

Change-Point Detection in Returns and Residuals

More formal change-point detection methods model returns as coming from different distributions before and after an unknown break time τ. A basic approach:

- Assume returns are piecewise stationary:

  $$r_t^{\text{strat}} \sim \mathcal{D}_1 \quad \text{for } t \leq \tau, \quad r_t^{\text{strat}} \sim \mathcal{D}_2 \quad \text{for } t > \tau,$$

  with possibly different means and variances.
- Use likelihood-based or non-parametric algorithms to estimate τ and test whether $\mathcal{D}_1$ and $\mathcal{D}_2$ differ materially.

In practice, it is often more informative to work with *residuals* rather than raw returns. If your contrarian model predicts a return $\hat{r}_t$ and you observe r_t, define residuals $\varepsilon_t = r_t - \hat{r}_t$. You then monitor whether the distribution of ε_t (mean, variance, autocorrelation) remains stable. A drift in residual mean, or a change from roughly white noise to autocorrelated residuals, suggests the model is mis-specified for the new regime.

Hidden Markov Models and State-Switching Models

For more advanced setups, you can use Hidden Markov Models (HMMs) or state-switching models to infer *latent regimes* from returns or volatility:

- Assume there are K latent states (e.g., low-vol, high-vol) with transition probabilities p_{ij} from state i to j.
- In each state, returns follow a different distribution (e.g., different mean and variance).
- Use expectation–maximization (EM) or Bayesian methods to infer state sequences and parameters from historical data.

The value of such models is less in precise identification of each state and more in producing a *smoothed indicator* of market regime, such as:

$$\mathbb{P}(\text{High-vol regime at time } t).$$

Your contrarian engine can then condition leverage, turnover, or signal weightings on these probabilities.

However, HMMs and similar models can be sensitive to misspecification and overfitting. They should supplement—not replace—simpler rolling diagnostics.

Model Adaptation: Retraining, Reweighting, and Decay

Once you detect that the regime has changed in a meaningful way, the next step is adjusting your models and portfolios. We distinguish three main adaptation levers:

1. Retraining models on updated data windows.
2. Reweighting models or signals in ensembles.
3. Applying decay to old data, models, and signals.

These levers can be combined and should be governed by pre-specified policies.

Retraining Policies: Rolling and Expanding Windows

Machine learning models for contrarian trading are trained on historical data: features X_t and labels (future returns) y_t. In a stable regime, you might be comfortable training on a long expanding window from inception to present. But when regimes shift, older data may become less relevant.

Two standard approaches:

Rolling windows. Train on a fixed-length trailing window, e.g., the last T_{train} months:

$$\mathcal{D}_{\text{train}}(t) = \{(X_s, y_s) : t - T_{\text{train}} \leq s < t\}.$$

This makes the model more sensitive to recent behavior and naturally forgets ancient data.

Expanding with decay. Use all past data but downweight older observations via a decay factor $\delta \in (0, 1)$:

$$w_s = \delta^{t-s},$$

where w_s is the weight of observation s when training at time t. Older observations influence the model less, but are not discarded entirely.

In deciding between these, consider:

- If regimes change abruptly and often, rolling windows with moderate length can be more robust.
- If changes are gradual, an expanding window with decay may better exploit the full history while still adapting.

Crucially, *retraining frequency* should be aligned with both data frequency and regime stability. Daily retraining of complex models may be unnecessary and risky unless supported by strong evidence and infrastructure.

Signal and Model Reweighting

Most serious trading systems already use ensembles: combinations of models, signals, or sub-strategies. Regime adaptation can be implemented by changing the weights assigned to these components rather than constantly redefining each model.

Let $\alpha_t^{(k)}$ be the signal from component k at time t. The overall signal is:

$$\alpha_t = \sum_{k=1}^{K} w_t^{(k)} \alpha_t^{(k)},$$

where $w_t^{(k)}$ are model weights.

Regime diagnostics—such as recent performance of each component, or their behavior under particular volatility states—inform how you update $w_t^{(k)}$:

- Downweight components whose recent risk-adjusted performance has significantly deteriorated beyond what was seen in backtests.
- Upweight components that continue to perform in the current regime.

To avoid chasing noise, weight updates should be:

- **Smoothed**: e.g., exponential moving average updates rather than abrupt changes.
- **Constrained**: limit how much weight can move in a single step and enforce diversity of components so the portfolio is not dominated by one signal.

An example update rule for weights might be:

$$w_{t+1}^{(k)} \propto w_t^{(k)} \cdot \exp\left(\eta \cdot \widehat{\text{Sharpe}}_{t,\text{recent}}^{(k)}\right),$$

with normalization to sum to one, where η controls sensitivity and $\widehat{\text{Sharpe}}_{t,\text{recent}}^{(k)}$ is recent performance of component k.

Decay of Features and Models

Features themselves may lose predictive power over time, especially in the face of changing market microstructure or investor behavior. You can:

- Monitor feature importance over time (for tree-based models) or coefficient stability (for linear models).
- Apply explicit decay to feature groups associated with fragile patterns (e.g., very short-horizon microstructure signals).
- Retire features whose contribution consistently drops below a threshold, after thorough backtesting.

Similarly, *model versions* should have life cycles. When you roll out a new model, you do not necessarily delete the old one; you may:

- Keep it as a low-weighted ensemble member, decaying its weight unless future performance justifies revival.
- Use it as a fallback in case the new model exhibits anomalous behavior.

This creates a controlled evolution of the model set, rather than an abrupt, untested switch.

Fast vs. Slow Reactivity: Avoiding Overfitting to Noise

Adaptation carries its own risks. Reacting too quickly to every run of bad luck can destroy a valid strategy; reacting too slowly means carrying a dead or inverted anomaly for too long.

A useful conceptual tool is to separate:

- **Fast-reacting components**: designed to pick up short-term changes in volatility, liquidity, or microstructure (e.g., volatility targeting, intraday execution aggressiveness).
- **Slow-reacting components**: designed to respond only to sustained degradation or structural shifts in anomaly behavior (e.g., retraining windows, model weights).

You can think of two overlay layers:

1. A *risk and exposure layer* that reacts relatively quickly, cutting leverage and tightening exposures when drawdowns or volatility spike (as in earlier sections).
2. A *model adaptation layer* that changes signals and model parameters only after accumulative evidence of regime change.

In practice, this means:

- Use daily or weekly volatility and drawdown metrics to adjust leverage and trade urgency.
- Use multi-month rolling performance and residual stability to trigger model retraining or reweighting.

This separation helps prevent the common mistake of rewriting or discarding a model simply because it experienced a few bad weeks in a turbulent but statistically unremarkable period.

Regime-Aware Portfolio Adjustments

So far we have discussed adapting models and signals. Regimes also directly affect the *expression* of those signals in portfolio construction.

Exposure Scaling by Regime

Suppose your regime indicator z_t takes values in {*Calm*, *Stressed*}, whether derived from a simple volatility threshold or an HMM. You can predefine regime-dependent exposure multipliers $c(z_t)$:

$$c(\text{Calm}) = 1, \qquad c(\text{Stressed}) = c_{\text{low}} < 1.$$

Your target portfolio weights become:

$$\mathbf{w}_t^{\text{regime}} = c(z_t) \cdot \mathbf{w}_t^{\text{base}},$$

where $\mathbf{w}_t^{\text{base}}$ comes from the standard portfolio construction pipeline.

This is a form of regime-aware volatility targeting. It complements, but does not replace, the drawdown and volatility overlays developed earlier.

Regime-Conditioned Constraints

You may also change portfolio constraints by regime, for example:

- Tighter gross and net exposure limits in stressed regimes.
- Lower sector or factor caps when correlations spike.
- Stricter turnover limits when liquidity deteriorates and execution costs rise.

These adjustments are encoded as alternative parameter sets for the optimizer, selected based on regime indicators. Again, the key is that these rules are defined *ex ante* and backtested, not improvised during crisis.

Logging, Governance, and Backtesting Adaptation Itself

Adapting models and portfolios in response to regime changes introduces a new source of potential bias: hindsight. After a bad period, it is tempting to say, "we would have reduced exposure here, reweighted components there, and avoided the pain." Without discipline, such stories become unfalsifiable.

To avoid this, treat adaptation rules as first-class citizens in your research process.

Explicit Playbooks

A regime playbook is a document (or code configuration) that codifies:

- The metrics you monitor (rolling Sharpe, hit rate, residual diagnostics, volatility, correlations).
- Thresholds or statistical tests that trigger specific actions (e.g., retrain model, downweight signal, change regime state).
- The magnitude and speed of each action (how much leverage reduction, how quickly model weights can move).

You then:

- Backtest the combined strategy + adaptation logic as one system.
- Log all regime changes and adaptation events in live trading: what triggered them, what actions were taken.

Versioning and Rollbacks

Each substantial model or parameter change should be versioned:

- Model version IDs linked to code snapshots, training data specifications, and training parameters.
- Clear records of when each version was active and why it was promoted or demoted.

This supports both regulatory requirements and internal learning. If a new model underperforms substantially, you can:

- Roll back to a previous, safer version according to predefined rules.
- Analyze post-mortem whether the adaptation logic was too sensitive, not sensitive enough, or mis-specified.

Stress-Testing Adaptation

Finally, test how your adaptation rules behave under extreme but plausible scenarios:

- Simulate long periods of low performance followed by recovery, and vice versa.
- Check that the system does not thrash: repeatedly turning models on and off or moving weights wildly in response to random fluctuations.
- Ensure that in true regime breaks (e.g., sign inversion of a key anomaly), the system does eventually reduce or remove capital from the failing component.

In doing so, you are not just stress-testing the strategy *within* a regime, but the resilience of the *model life cycle* itself.

In summary, regime detection and model adaptation are about humility and discipline. Humility, because we acknowledge that our contrarian models will not work forever without modification. Discipline, because all adaptations must be governed by clear rules, tested in backtests, and executed with proper logging and governance. In the final section of this chapter, we turn to the operational layer that makes such discipline possible in production: live monitoring, compliance, and governance frameworks that keep adaptive contrarian strategies both effective and safe.

7.5 Live Monitoring, Compliance & Governance

In the previous sections we built a complete pipeline: we turned contrarian signals into risk-aware portfolios, executed those portfolios intelligently across venues, and added regime-detection logic so models and exposures can adapt as markets evolve. We now assume all of that machinery is in place and ask a different question:

> *How do we operate this system safely, day after day, in the real world?*

This is the domain of live monitoring, compliance, and governance. It is where quantitative elegance meets operational reality: data feeds drop, exchanges misbehave, models drift, and regulations constrain what you may or may not trade.

For contrarian strategies, the stakes are high. These books intentionally lean into short-term pain and often run with leverage or short exposure. Left unattended, they can spiral into large losses or operational failures quickly. A robust operational layer must therefore:

1. Monitor the health of portfolios, models, and infrastructure in near real time.
2. Detect statistical drift and decay in signals and data distributions.
3. Enforce compliance and ethical constraints, especially around short selling and corporate events.
4. Provide governance processes and decision rights so that human oversight is structured, not ad hoc.

We cover each of these in turn.

Live Monitoring: Seeing the Strategy in Motion

Monitoring is about turning raw logs and data streams into a concise but comprehensive view of whether the strategy is behaving as intended.

Core Portfolio and Risk Metrics

At a minimum, a monitoring dashboard for a live contrarian book should display, at appropriate frequencies (intraday and daily):

- **P&L**: intraday and cumulative P&L, both in absolute terms and relative to risk (e.g., realized intraday Sharpe).

- **Risk exposures**:
  - Current and projected volatility.
  - VaR/ES versus limits.
  - Maximum and current drawdown.
- **Exposures by dimension**:
  - Gross and net exposure.
  - Sector, country, and asset-class breakdowns.
  - Factor exposures (market beta, size, value, momentum, etc.).
- **Turnover and trading activity**:
  - Daily and intraday turnover.
  - Realized slippage versus cost model predictions.
  - Volume participation (share of ADV per name).

For each metric, you should show not only the current value but also its position relative to pre-defined bands or limits. For instance, daily VaR at 1-day 99% should be visually flagged when it approaches a risk limit.

Data and Model Health Checks

Operational failures often start in mundane places: a feed goes stale, a column is misaligned, or a model server crashes. Live monitoring therefore also includes:

- **Data freshness**: timestamps of latest updates for prices, corporate actions, borrow data, and features.
- **Sanity checks on inputs**:
  - Proportion of missing or null values in key features.
  - Distribution summaries (e.g., min/max, quantiles) compared to historical norms.

- **Model service status**:
  - Uptime and latency for prediction APIs.
  - Error rates in scoring requests.

Contrarian strategies are often sensitive to microstructure features or short-horizon indicators. That makes them more brittle to upstream glitches. For example, a misaligned timestamp in intraday order-book features can flip a signal's sign. Automated health checks that detect abnormal feature distributions or sudden jumps in predicted scores are therefore essential.

Drift and Decay: Monitoring the Statistical Health of the Strategy

Beyond raw performance, you must track whether the statistical relationship your models exploit is still present. This is the live complement to the regime detection and model adaptation mechanisms discussed earlier.

Feature and Prediction Drift

The first sign of trouble may be that the *inputs* to the model change character. Let X_t be the feature vector at time t, and $\hat{y}_t$ the model's prediction (e.g., expected next-period residual return). Over a rolling window (say, 6 months), compare the live distributions of features and predictions to the distributions used during training.

Practical steps:

- Compute summary statistics (means, standard deviations, quantiles) for each feature and compare to baseline (training) values.
- Use statistical distance measures (e.g., Kolmogorov–Smirnov statistics, population stability index) to quantify drift.
- For predictions, track:
  - The cross-sectional dispersion of scores.

- The fraction of assets pinned at score caps/floors.
- The stability of rankings (Kendall or Spearman rank correlations between successive days).

A sudden collapse in score dispersion, for example, might indicate that upstream signals became homogenized or that a key feature went constant due to a data vendor issue.

Performance Decomposition and Hit-Rate Monitoring

Drift in model performance should be decomposed to distinguish between:

- **Market-wide shocks**: everyone is losing money; your contrarian book might be within expected drawdown bands.
- **Idiosyncratic model decay**: your strategy is underperforming even after adjusting for market conditions.

Key diagnostics include:

- Hit rate by score bucket: bin assets by predicted alpha deciles and check realized returns by bucket over rolling windows. A healthy signal should still show monotonicity (higher predicted returns correspond to better realized performance). If the curve flattens or inverts persistently, signal decay is likely.
- Long vs. short leg performance: contrarian strategies often have asymmetric behavior. Monitor returns separately for the long leg and the short leg, and for hedges vs. alpha positions.
- Factor-adjusted performance: regress strategy returns on standard factors and look at the alpha residual over time. If residual alpha collapses while factor exposures are stable, the anomaly itself may be decaying.

These diagnostics feed into the adaptation mechanisms from the previous section (reweighting, retraining, and decay), but here the focus is on monitoring and early detection rather than immediate action.

Flags, Alerts, and Escalations

Not every blip calls for intervention, but some patterns do. You should define and parameterize alert levels, such as:

- **Warning**: metrics deviate from historical norms but remain within coarse bounds. For example, rolling 3-month alpha is in the bottom 10% of historical outcomes. Action: investigate, but no automatic de-risking.
- **Action required**: thresholds breached that suggest non-random issues. For example, prediction distributions show significant drift, or decile performance curves invert for multiple consecutive windows. Action: trigger model or feature review, possibly reduce leverage.
- **Critical**: severe anomalies, such as large discrepancies between model predictions and realized behavior, data sanity check failures, or operational outages. Action: execute pre-defined de-risking or shutdown procedures.

These alert levels and actions should be encoded in configuration, not improvised in the heat of the moment.

Compliance and Ethics for Contrarian Books

Contrarian strategies often rely on short selling, leverage, and rapid trading around corporate events—all areas under heightened regulatory scrutiny. A serious operation integrates compliance into the same technical stack that handles risk and monitoring.

Short-Selling Constraints and Borrow Management

Short positions introduce specific compliance and operational requirements:

- **Locate and borrow**: Before shorting, you must ensure borrow availability and adhere to local short-selling regulations. This requires:

  - Daily feeds of borrow availability and costs from prime brokers.
  - Integration with portfolio construction so that names with insufficient borrow are not shorted or are capped.

- **Hard-to-borrow limits**: For expensive or scarce borrows, you may:
  - Embed borrow cost into your alpha or cost models.
  - Impose maximum short size or completely exclude certain names.

- **Regulatory bans or uptick rules**: Some jurisdictions impose temporary bans on shorting specific stocks or require upticks. Your trading system must ingest and implement such rules on the fly, preventing disallowed orders from leaving the firm.

These checks are not optional overlays; they must be baked into both the order-generation layer and the pre-trade compliance engine.

Watchlists, Restricted Lists, and MNPI Controls

Contrarian desks can be exposed to material non-public information (MNPI) or restricted securities via:

- Corporate access (meetings with management).
- Research produced by other parts of the firm.
- Insiders who trade in related securities.

Key safeguards:

- **Watchlists** and **restricted lists**: maintained by compliance, integrated into trading systems. Orders in these names are blocked or require additional approvals.
- **Information barriers**: ensuring that MNPI cannot leak into model development or signal generation. For example:

  - Quant teams may be physically and logically separated from banking or research divisions.
  - Data sources are vetted to avoid inadvertent inclusion of MNPI (e.g., not using non-public customer transaction data).

- **Event handling**: corporate events (earnings, mergers, secondary offerings) can trigger restrictions. Systems should:
  - Tag securities with upcoming events.
  - Apply event-specific rules (e.g., not trading during certain blackout periods).

For model-based strategies, one subtle but important point is documentation: you should be able to show that model inputs are derived from public, well-defined data sources and that research processes did not involve MNPI.

Best Execution and Market Abuse Prevention

Even systematic contrarian trading must comply with best execution obligations and market abuse rules. Monitoring should include:

- **Best execution**:
  - Periodic review of execution quality relative to benchmarks (e.g., VWAP, arrival price).
  - Documentation of broker and venue selection rationales.
- **Market abuse detection**:
  - Surveillance for patterns resembling spoofing, layering, or manipulation, even if unintended by algorithms.
  - Limits on order-to-trade ratios, cancellations, and quote stuffing.

Because contrarian strategies often provide liquidity in stressed conditions, they can look unusual in transaction-level data. Transparent documentation of the strategy's design and controls helps distinguish legitimate contrarian trading from prohibited behavior.

Governance: Who Decides What, When, and How

Governance is about decision rights and accountability. When something goes wrong—a large drawdown, a data issue, or a suspected regime change—who is empowered to act, and under what rules?

Roles and Responsibilities

A typical governance structure around a contrarian strategy involves:

- **Portfolio manager (PM)**: accountable for performance and risk within the mandate; proposes and prioritizes strategy changes.
- **Quant research team**: designs and maintains models, backtests, and adaptation rules; responsible for methodological integrity.
- **Risk management**: sets firm-level risk appetite, approves leverage and drawdown limits, reviews breaches, and can veto or mandate de-risking.
- **Compliance**: oversees adherence to laws and regulations, manages restricted lists, and reviews suspicious activity.
- **Technology and operations**: ensure reliable infrastructure, monitoring, and incident response.

Clear RACI (Responsible, Accountable, Consulted, Informed) mappings for key processes—such as launching a new model, changing risk limits, or triggering a strategy shutdown—reduce ambiguity and finger-pointing during stress.

Decision Logs and Model Risk Reviews

Every significant change to the strategy should be recorded in a *decision log*:

- Date and time of decision.

- People involved.
- Rationale, including quantitative evidence and backtest results.
- Expected impact on performance, risk, and capacity.

Periodic *model risk reviews*—formal meetings where independent reviewers challenge assumptions, test robustness, and review performance—provide another layer of governance. Questions to be addressed include:

- Are the model's documented assumptions still valid in the current market structure?
- Have there been any undocumented changes to code, data, or parameters?
- How have backtested expectations compared to live performance, after accounting for costs and slippage?

These reviews are especially important for contrarian books, where tail events and regime shifts can quickly invalidate backtest-era intuitions.

Escalation and Shutdown Playbooks

Finally, governance must define what happens when things go sufficiently wrong. A shutdown playbook answers:

- Under what conditions is the strategy partially or fully de-risked? (e.g., sustained underperformance relative to drawdown projections, repeated operational or compliance issues.)
- Who has authority to pull the plug, and does that require a committee vote or can risk management act unilaterally in emergencies?
- How is capital redeployed or held while the strategy is reviewed?

These rules should be specified in advance and, as with regime adaptation, backtested where possible. For example, you can simulate a policy of halving exposure after a certain live underperformance threshold and see how often it would have been triggered historically and with what outcome.

Taken together, live monitoring, compliance safeguards, and governance processes form the *operating system* of a contrarian trading business. They do not generate alpha on their own, but they allow alpha-generating models to operate at meaningful scale without exposing the firm to unacceptable financial, operational, or regulatory risk. In practice, the most durable contrarian desks are those that treat this operational layer with the same seriousness and quantitative rigor as they treat model development and backtesting.

www.ingramcontent.com/pod-product-compliance
Lightning Source LLC
LaVergne TN
LVHW010916300926
849194LV00025B/252
* 9 7 9 8 8 9 6 6 5 2 3 9 7 *